Turfgrass Water Conservation

Second Edition

Technical Editors
Stephen T. Cockerham
University of California, Riverside

Bernd Leinauer
New Mexico State University

University of California
Agriculture and Natural Resources

Publication 3523

To order or obtain ANR publications and other products, visit the ANR Communication Services online catalog at http://anrcatalog.ucdavis.edu or phone 1-800-994-8849. You can also place orders by mail or FAX, or request a printed catalog of our products from

University of California
Agriculture and Natural Resources
Communication Services
1301 S. 46th Street
Building 478 - MC 3580
Richmond, CA 94804-4600
Telephone 1-800-994-8849
510-665-2195
FAX 510-665-3427
E-mail: anrcatalog@ucdavis.edu

Publication 3523
ISBN-13: 978-1-60107-663-2
Library of Congress Control Number: 2011925453

Photo credits are given in the captions. Design by Chris O'Connor.

This publication has been anonymously peer reviewed for technical accuracy by University of California scientists and other qualified professionals. This review process was managed by the ANR Associate Editor for Environmental Horticulture.

Printed in the United States on recycled paper

2m-pr-5/11-SB/CO

Contents

Contributing Authors

James B. Beard
Turfgrass Science Emeritus, Texas A&M University

Robert N. Carrow
Crop and Soil Science, University of Georgia

Stephen T. Cockerham
Agricultural Operations, University of California, Riverside

Dale A. Devitt
Life Sciences, University of Nevada, Las Vegas

Ronny R. Duncan
Turf Ecosystems, LLC

Robert Green
Botany and Plant Sciences, University of California, Riverside

M. Ali Harivandi
Environmental Horticulture, University of California Cooperative Extension

Bingru Huang
Plant Biology and Pathology, Rutgers University

Michael P. Kenna
U.S. Golf Association

David M. Kopec
School of Plant Sciences, University of Arizona

Bernd Leinauer
Extension Plant Sciences, New Mexico State University

Robert L. Morris
Area Horticulturalist, Cooperative Extension, University of Nevada, Reno

James A. Murphy
Plant Biology and Pathology, Rutgers University

Paul E. Rieke
Plant and Soil Sciences Emeritus, Michigan State University

Rossana Sallenave
Extension Animal Sciences and Natural Resources, New Mexico State University

Robert C. Shearman
Agronomy and Horticulture Emeritus, University of Nebraska–Lincoln

Frank P. Wong
Plant Pathology, University of California, Riverside

Laosheng Wu
Environmental Sciences, University of California, Riverside

Introduction

Stephen T. Cockerham and Frank P. Wong

TURFGRASS HAS A DIRECT EFFECT ON THE AMERICAN LIFESTYLE, providing added value to the quality of life through home lawns, parks, cemeteries, sports fields, schoolyards, roadsides, and golf courses. Since turf areas must be irrigated in many parts of the world to maintain their functionality and sustainability, water use by turfgrasses must be optimized. Turfgrass scientists have long been leaders in research aimed at understanding the role of water in plants and the development of water management strategies.

THE FIRST SYMPOSIUM AND BOOK

Early research on turfgrass water use was scattered among several periodicals and publications until the early 1980s. On February 15 and 16, 1983, a landmark symposium was held with the objective of bringing much of that information to a single published reference.

The symposium was sponsored by the American Sod Producers Association (now known as Turf Producers International) and was held in San Antonio, Texas. The theme of the symposium was the science of water conservation in turfgrass. The topics were selected to bring as much of that information together as possible at the time. Speakers at the symposium were recognized as among the most highly respected experts in their fields. The presentations were published in 1985 in the first edition of *Turfgrass Water Conservation*, edited by V. A. Gibeault and S. T. Cockerham.

In addition to the book chapters, the authors were also asked to provide a practicum. An important part of each chapter, the practicum expanded the value of the information and provided an opportunity to reach a wider audience. The peer-reviewed book became a reference for landscape architects, designers, contractors, suppliers, consultants, sod growers, turf managers, educators, students, administrators, and political decision makers.

THE VICTOR A. GIBEAULT SYMPOSIUM ON TURFGRASS WATER CONSERVATION

The science and technologies of turfgrass water use advanced substantially between 1983 and 2007. On September 6, 2007, the Victor A. Gibeault Symposium on Turfgrass Water Conservation was held at the University of California, Riverside. The symposium was planned and held to update the first edition of *Turfgrass Water Conservation* and to bring attention to the area of turfgrass water conservation. This field of research has advanced significantly since the first symposium in 1983. Information provided by scientists of two generations made for an outstandingly successful meeting. The 2007 symposium was funded by generous gifts from John Foster of West Coast Turf, Inc., and the Friends of O. V. "Chip" Morgan, with support from the UC Riverside Agricultural Operations Department and the Department of Botany and Plant Sciences, chaired by Dr. Jodie Holt. In the symposium, Ronald G. Dodson, President, Audubon International, made a presentation entitled "Environmental Concerns and Approaches to Integrated Environmental Management." This presentation by Mr. Dodson proved to be the beginning of chapter 3, "Environmental Issues Surrounding Turf-Dominated Urban Landscapes" by Dr. Rossana Sallenave.

Aside from presenting new findings in the area of turfgrass water conservation, the objective of the symposium was also to celebrate and acknowledge the career of Dr. Victor A. Gibeault. The symposium was held in recognition of Dr. Gibeault's achievements and contributions with an event that would be significant to the turfgrass industry. For nearly four decades, Dr. Gibeault was the statewide Cooperative Extension Turfgrass Specialist based in the Department of Botany and Plant Sciences at the University of California, Riverside. He was recognized as a state and national leader in water issues that impacted the turfgrass industry.

TURFGRASS WATER CONSERVATION—SECOND EDITION

This revised and updated second edition is the result of the Victor A. Gibeault Symposium on Turfgrass Water Conservation and is intended to bring the current science of turfgrass management and turfgrass water conservation to researchers and end users. Turf managers, educators, and students in turf management will find useful information in each chapter.

Chapters 2 and 3 present the science of turfgrass water conservation and the impact of watering on the landscape. We begin with an overview of the research and evolution of the science, the psychological impact of turf, and the effect of turf on human health and on urban temperature modification. Potential environmental concerns associated with turfgrass use in urban areas are also covered to address a negative perception and acknowledge the benefits of turf.

Chapters 4 and 5 investigate our understanding of water use and the drought and salinity adaptation of grasses as part of physiological processes. The continued development of that understanding has been critical to further scientific exploration and effective management decision making.

Chapters 6 to 8 offer a detailed discussion of the role of water in modified root zone media and native soils as well as the use of water of good and poor quality. Water quality is a major factor in highly populated urban areas where turfgrass is a dominant part of the environment. Also, the politics of using water of various qualities are a part of irrigation decisions, especially when irrigating with reclaimed water.

Water is a particularly valuable commodity that is often perceived as being wasted on turfgrass. To address this, researchers are investigating new technologies (chemical and mechanical) to reduce water use by turfgrass, as discussed in chapter 9. Continued development of new products and their evaluation by academia and industry are needed to determine their performance characteristics and value to the industry.

Chapter 10 discusses integrating turfgrass management with other landscape uses of water for conservation. Turfgrass is usually planted in the landscape with trees, shrubs, and ground covers. Research on the use of water in the landscape has increased the understanding of the complex interaction among the various plant species used in urban environments.

Overview

Putting the chapters into a coherent context is a benefit to the reader. While each of the authors has focused on a component of the relationships between turfgrass and water, the combined overview of the chapters in chapter 11 lets the reader understand how the specifics fit into the subject of turfgrass water conservation as a whole, melding the major scientific and social issues of the book.

Practicum

To expand the value of the book, a summary of information from each chapter has been written in a chapter specifically for practical use. Professionally, researchers must present their information in a technical manner, using data to substantiate their conclusions and recommendations. It is often difficult for a less-technically-trained reader to derive and apply the information to a field situation. Although many readers will find all chapters important and valuable, the practicum is designed to present the information in an immediately useable form.

THE FUTURE

Water continues to be an important and increasingly limited resource. Turfgrass scientists must continue to provide leadership in developing water use strategies that not only apply directly to turfgrass and landscape management but also contribute to overall water conservation for human and environmental use. The collected body of knowledge in this book will help provide the most recent water conservation information and guidelines for the scientific community, the grounds manager in the field, and the general public.

2

Perspective: A Brief History of the Science of Turfgrass Water Use and Conservation

James B. Beard

THIS CHAPTER PRESENTS A HISTORICAL PERSPECTIVE OF published research, informational publications, and research funding concerning the relationships between turfgrass and water that occurred up to the mid-1980s. The research aspects focus on peer-reviewed studies concerning the morphological, physiological, environmental, and cultural dimensions of evapotranspiration (ET) and water stress on regularly mowed turfgrasses. Rooting, irrigation, and forage or pasture aspects are not addressed in this chapter.

RESEARCH SUMMARY

The 1920s

The first pioneering investigations concerning the relationships between plants and soil water were initiated in 1925 and published by Johns Hopkins University researchers. The key contributing authors were J. Dean Wilson and Burton E. Livingston. At that time the irrigation of turfgrass lawns was minimal.

J. D. Wilson studied what was then referred to as the water-supplying power of the soil during progressive water stress of cool-season turfgrasses. His extensive 55-page paper in *Plant Physiology* (1927) on a study of an entire growing season encompassed a diversity of experiments and observations during summer drought stress concerning turfgrass species, seasonal effects, slope, tree, mowing height, irrigation, and soil spatial variability effects.

During the same period, Wilson and Burton E. Livingston studied the comparative water stress responses among turfgrasses under glasshouse conditions. Seventeen turfgrasses were evaluated for proneness to wilt and leaf death and were correlated with atmospheric water loss from atmometers (Wilson and Livingston 1932). This was a pioneering experiment, as they originated the concept of using an evaporation monitoring device to schedule irrigation timing on turfgrasses. The relative lethal leaf stress rankings are shown in table 2.1.

Livingston and Ichino Ohga described in *Ecology* the summer variations in soil moisture of an unirrigated lawn in Baltimore, Maryland (Livingston and Ohga 1926). Porous porcelain soil points were successfully employed to monitor the soil water content available to turfgrass plants. The critical water supply index value for turfgrass was 0.1 gram per soil point for a 1-hour exposure. During two drought cycles a value below 0.1 for 4 to 5 days caused complete discoloration of the turfgrass.

The 1930s

During the 1930s turfgrass–water relationships were explored in more detail by a group of researchers at the Ohio Agricultural Experiment Station at Wooster, consisting of J. D. Wilson, F. A. Welton, and J. C. Carroll.

TABLE 2.1. Comparative total evaporation in cubic centimeters from a Livingston standard blackened atmometer sphere during the period up to when leaf death occurred for 17 turfgrasses

Common name	Scientific name	Evaporation (cc)
tall oatgrass	*Arrhenatherum elatius*	100
orchardgrass	*Dactylis glomerata*	107
Rhode Island bentgrass	*Agrostis capillaris*	124
velvet bentgrass	*Agrostis canina*	138
bromegrass	*Bromus inermis*	168
Washington creeping bentgrass	*Agrostis stolonifera*	178
dactylon bermudagrass*	*Cynodon dactylon* var. *dactylon*	209
timothy	*Phleum pratense*	212
Kentucky bluegrass	*Poa pratensis*	237
meadow fescue	*Festuca pratensis*	249
Chewings fescue	*Festuca rubra* ssp. *commutata*	252
redtop	*Agrostis gigantea*	275
perennial ryegrass	*Lolium perenne*	281
Canada bluegrass	*Poa compressa*	290
Vermont bentgrass	*Agrostis* spp.	300
sheep fescue	*Festuca ovina*	458+
red fescue	*Festuca rubra*	458+

Source: Wilson and Livingston 1932.
Note: *Winter glasshouse temperatures of 15° to 21°C were not favorable for this warm-season species.

A severe drought in 1930 offered good conditions for a drought stress study published in *Plant Physiology* (Welton and Wilson 1931). The dehydration tolerances of three cool-season turfgrasses were evaluated in the field when watered at 0, 1.5×, 2.0×, and 3.0× of the mean annual rainfall, as assessed by a soil water replacement apparatus. Chewings fescue required much less water than Kentucky bluegrass, while creeping bentgrass required slightly more than Kentucky bluegrass. The soil monitoring approach that was used had a negative aspect in terms of the failure to control excessive soil moisture that caused root loss and shoot thinning.

In 1934, F. A. Welton, J. C. Carroll, and J. D. Wilson published a preliminary paper in *Ecology* concerning the artificial watering of turfgrasses on lawns based on evaporative demand as monitored by Livingston-standardized, spherical, black atmometers. The initial experiments revealed that the approach was promising.

An evaporation index for use in watering lawns was introduced in 1935 by J. D. Wilson and F. A. Welton. Based on comparisons of irrigation timing over a 4-month period, it was determined that the best criterion was to irrigate with 2.5 cm of water when the black atmometer lost 320 cc of water without an intervening rain of 1.27 cm or more. This prevented the occurrence of visual water stress on Kentucky bluegrass.

Welton and Wilson compared the rates of water loss from bare soil, water, and turfgrass in 1938. They found that the rate of water loss was highest for a free water surface, followed by bare soil, and then by a turfgrass surface. Water loss from bare soil was reduced by a mulch of peat. Amending the soil with manure decreased the water loss rate, while sand additions caused an increase. Finally, a cutting height of 7.5 cm caused greater water loss from turfgrass than mowing at 2.5 cm.

In 1943, J. C. Carroll assessed a range of 12 and 16 mostly cool-season turfgrasses in two studies for what was then termed "atmospheric drought." The approach employed field-grown sods that were subjected to water stress in a glasshouse plus exposure to temperatures of 35° to 37°C for 5 hours for each of 3 successive days. The study actually assessed what should be termed "summerkill," in that both water and heat stresses were imposed. This is supported by the data wherein the two warm-season turfgrasses exhibited superior survival. In comparing nitrogen (N) treatments of 0 and 0.49 kg N/100 m^2 applied in April, July, and September, the higher nitrogen level resulted in increased summerkill of most turfgrass species. Even today some field experiments termed "drought studies" are strongly confounded with heat stress and are actually studies of summer stress and summerkill.

1920 to 1940 Summary

The research accomplished by the Ohio group in the 1930s on turfgrass soil–water relationships is impressive when one considers the equipment available compared with the devices now in use. Also, one should note that the turfgrasses studied in the 1920s and 1930s were subject to injury from disease and insect pests, as pest management by genetic and chemical means had not evolved to be a significant factor. The Ohio group mentioned sod webworm damage, and there was probably leaf thinning caused by Helminthosporium diseases. Thus, evapotranspiration rates and dehydration stresses could have affected the species rankings differently than they would under modern turfgrass culture.

The 1940s

Progress in significant, published, peer-reviewed research on turfgrass–water relationships was lacking during the 1940s due to the Second World War. Investigations published in the 1940s related primarily to the drought survival of native range grasses in the seedling stage. This emphasis was a response to the Dust Bowl period of the 1930s in the U.S. Great Plains. States in which this research took place included Arkansas (Julander 1945), Iowa (Klomp 1939; Silker 1941), Minnesota (Schultz and Hayes 1938), Nebraska (Weaver 1941; Weaver and Albertson 1943), and Utah (McAlister 1944).

The 1950s

The maximum evapotranspiration of dactylon bermudagrass was quantified from 1956 through 1958 under field conditions in Raleigh, North Carolina, using in-ground percolation-type lysimeters (van Bavel and Harris 1962). The authors found that the original Penman formula overestimated evapotranspiration of bermudagrass for a full season, while a modified Penman of 0.8 × H was a reliable predictor, with H representing the net radiation over the turfgrass.

The 1960s

The soil water extraction from a kikuyugrass (*Pennisetum clandestinum)* lawn under field conditions near Rehovot, Israel, from June to September was evaluated in 1962 (Mantell 1966). The water loss was 0.62 of the evaporation from a nearby screened Class A pan when irrigated every 21 days and fertilized monthly with 0.42 kg N/100 m^2. This represents 3.2 mm of water loss per day under very hot, arid conditions.

The 1970s

Detailed quantitative measurements of evapotranspiration rates from creeping bentgrass turfgrass were assessed as affected by major environmental and cultural factors in 1970–71 (Shearman and Beard 1972). Evapotranspiration (ET) under simulated, short-term, high atmospheric demand increased as the cutting height was raised, as mowing frequency was increased, and as the nitrogen rate was increased within the normal range. All three ET responses to these cultural practices were related to greater leaf area, but they were not correlated with stomatal density. ET also increased as the preassessment irradiance level was increased, and it was positively correlated with stomatal density. These were the first experiments in which the individual components of the ET assessment environment were specifically controlled in a simulator. This simulator approach is important because it is very difficult to distinguish between water stress and heat stress under field research conditions.

What the authors termed "water consumption" was assessed for nine C_4 (warm-season) and two C_3 (cool-season) grasses grown in containers elevated well above the ground under field conditions in Rehovot, Israel, in 1977 (Biran et al. 1981). Under these conditions, there was a substantial heat stress interaction. Biran et al. reported that the water consumption was higher for the C_3 grasses (tall fescue and perennial ryegrass) than for the C_4 grasses. Also, cultivars with a forage-type growth habit within a species had a higher water consumption than did those with a more dense turfgrass growth habit. Delaying irrigation until the onset of temporary wilting caused a significant decrease in water consumption. Water stress as indicated by visual wilting occurred much earlier for the two *Zoysia* species than for the *Cynodon, Eremochloa, Paspalum, Pennisetum,* and *Stenotaphrum* species.

Potential plant characteristics associated with the drought resistance of 25 Kentucky bluegrass cultivars were evaluated under cool, semiarid field conditions in Fort Collins, Colorado, in 1976–77 (Dernoeden and Butler 1978 and 1979). The researchers found significant variations but no correlation with the plant morphological characteristics assessed. Also, mowing at 3.8 cm resulted in increased drought resistance compared with a lower cutting height of 1.9 cm.

The only basic research to date that quantified the resistances to evapotranspiration of turfgrass was conducted in 1978–79 (Johns et al. 1981; Johns et al. 1983). A specially designed simulator was used in experiments with an adequately watered St. Augustinegrass *(Stenotaphrum secundatum)* turfgrass to quantify the internal, canopy, and aerodynamic resistances. The internal resistance was found to be only 25 to 50% of the external resistance to ET. This indicates that stomatal modifications would result in less water savings for irrigated turfgrasses than would turfgrass canopy modifications.

The 1980s

In-ground lysimeters were used to determine the amount of water replacement needed at 2-day intervals to assess the cultural and species effects on turfgrass ET rates under field conditions in a cool, semiarid climate in Fort Collins, Colorado, from 1979 through 1981 (Feldhake et al. 1983). In a 1979 study with Merion Kentucky bluegrass, the authors reported that mowing at 5 cm used 15% more water than mowing at 2 cm. Evapotranspiration from turfgrass in the 1979 study was essentially the same whether growing on a clay soil or on a sand-peat mix. When 4 kg N/100 m^2 was applied each month during the spring and summer of 1980, 13% more water was used, when compared with only one application of nitrogen in the spring. Evapotranspiration increased linearly with solar radiation when an advective or horizontal component of energy movement that accounted for 35% of ET was subtracted from all solar treatments. The cool-season turfgrasses Merion Kentucky bluegrass and Rebel tall fescue used over 20% more water than the warm-season turfgrasses Tifway hybrid bermudagrass and American buffalograss *(Buchloe dactyloides)*.

A study (Feldhake et al. 1984) investigated the effects of deficit irrigation on turfgrass quality using small lysimeters where the root systems were confined and ET was limited to the amount of irrigation. In most cases there was a sharp decrease in turfgrass quality as the ET deficit increased. Merion Kentucky bluegrass decreased about 10% in turfgrass quality under an irrigation schedule that provided up to a 27% ET deficit. Larger ET deficits resulted in greater relative decreases in turfgrass quality. They also studied allied temperature effects in which turfgrass canopy temperatures increased 1.7°C for each 10% decrease in irrigation up to a 70% decrease. This suggests that if irrigation is limited during dry summer months, the resultant heat effect on urban climates may become a concern.

In the mid-1980s, interspecies plant morphological characteristics associated with the turfgrass ET rates were successfully investigated under warm, humid field conditions in College Station, Texas (Kim and Beard 1988). The ET rates of eleven C_4 warm-season turfgrasses and one C_3 cool-season turfgrass were evaluated in 1982 and 1984 via in-ground, mini-lysimeters with fritted clay as the rooting medium and using the water balance method of replacement to field capacity in order to simulate nonlimiting root zone water conditions. Turfgrasses with comparatively lower ET rates generally were characterized by a high canopy resistance, including a high shoot density and relatively horizontal leaf orientation; and a low leaf area, including a slow vertical leaf extension rate and a narrow leaf texture. For three assessment periods over 2 years significant differences in mean ET rates were observed under nonlimiting soil water: Texas Common buffalograss, Georgia Common centipedegrass, and Arizona Common, Tifgreen, and Tifway bermudagrasses had very low (< 5.5 mmd^{-1}) ET rates; Adalayd seashore paspalum and Meyer Japanese zoysiagrass had a medium-low (5.5–6.0 mmd^{-1}) ET rate; and Texas Common St. Augustinegrass and hybrid Emerald zoysiagrass had medium (6.0–7.0 mmd^{-1}) ET rates. This evaluation under a nonlimiting soil water condition allows investigators to study the plant shoot ET potential in terms of genetic selection for lower ET rates. Normal field conditions where there is a dry-down phase between precipitation events or irrigations would result in a significantly lower mean ET rate per week. Net radiation was the most highly correlated as a predictor of ET for the 12 turfgrass species when compared to pan evaporation or temperature. This supports use of the Penman formula as the preferred predictor of irrigation needs. The use of fritted clay is critical to ensure that the same original reference water content can be repeatedly achieved by this water balance method.

The drought resistance of 55 Kentucky bluegrass, 34 perennial ryegrass, and 42 fine-leaf fescue (*Festuca* spp.) cultivars were assessed under cool, semiarid field conditions in Fort Collins, Colorado (Minner and Butler 1985). The turfgrasses were field grown on a clay loam soil, fertilized, and supplied with water to prevent visual wilt for a 3-year period. In the autumn of 1981, intensive culture of the trials was terminated and the drought study was initiated. From autumn 1981 until autumn 1983, the turfgrasses received only natural rainfall, except for one thorough irrigation in early May 1983. During September 1982 and 1983, water and fertilizer were applied as needed to support regrowth and recovery of the drought-stressed turfgrasses. Majestic, A-20, and America Kentucky bluegrass and Aristocrat, Bellatrix, Citation, and Yorktown perennial ryegrass had better drought resistance than did the other cultivars in the trial. None of the fine-leaf fescues produced suitable turfgrasses under the severe drought conditions that existed, except for the hard fescues *(Festuca trachyphylla)*. Evaluation of the five best cultivars within a species indicated that as drought conditions developed the perennial ryegrass remained green and viable longer than Kentucky bluegrass or fine-leaf fescue. When water became available in September the perennial ryegrass recovered faster than Kentucky bluegrass or fine-leaf fescue under the conditions of this study. It is possible that some confounding with heat stress occurred in this field study, especially for the fine-leaf fescues.

Note that in turfgrass water research, the water use rate and drought resistance are distinctly different, even though ET is a component of drought resistance.

1980 RESEARCH STATUS ASSESSMENTS

The status of water conservation research related to turfgrass in 1980 can be summarized by presentations in the following three papers.

In 1976, J. B. Beard conducted a study of turfgrass scientific-year-equivalents by state, climatic region, and problem area. He stated, "Perhaps one of the most striking deficiencies among the [29] turfgrass research subspecialities concerned irrigation and water use rates" (15). Irrigation and water use rates totaled 1.1 scientific-year-equivalents, or only 1.5% of the total turfgrass research in the United States, with 0.3% involving warm-season turfgrasses. Contrast this with the following scientific-year-equivalents in 1976: 18% chemical weed and disease control evaluations, 9% turfgrass cultivar evaluations, and 7% fertilizer evaluations, or 34% of the total 68.7.

In 1980, an International Turfgrass Research Conference (ITRC) keynote review paper (Funk 1981) that addressed turfgrass breeding and genetics did not mention the issue of water as a priority need. The paper did address problems such as pests, heat, shade, and wear stress.

In the same year, an ITRC keynote review paper on turfgrass physiology stated, "Considerable progress has been made in research concerning low temperature injury and hardiness. Significant progress has been made in the area of shade adaptation and wear tolerance. Unfortunately our progress to date in the areas of drought stress, minimal water use rates, salt tolerance, and heat tolerance is quite limited. These summer stress problems must receive increasing research emphasis during the 1980s" (Beard 1981, 466).

INFORMATION DISSEMINATION

Basic and applied turfgrass research are not fulfilled until the information is disseminated to practitioners. A major avenue for information distribution is technical books on turfgrasses and their culture. It was not until 35 years ago that turfgrass books started to properly address plant–water relationships, stresses, and cultural dimensions. This historical perspective is illustrated via the following technical books.

In 1969, the 715-page *Turfgrass Science* was published by the American Society of Agronomy. This book had 38 contributing authors in 28 chapters and was edited by A. A. Hanson and F. V. Juska. Only a few pages are devoted to turfgrass plant–water relationships and water stress: primarily soil water and irrigation were addressed in a chapter by A. Marsh of California, and there were scattered discussions of rooting.

In 1971, the 482-page *Principles of Turfgrass Culture* and the 474-page *Practical Turfgrass Management*, both written by J. H. Madison of the University of California, Davis, were published. Only the former book has a cursory mention of plant–water relations and evapotranspiration; the emphasis in both is placed on soil–root relationships and irrigation aspects.

In 1973, the 658-page *Turfgrass: Science and Culture* by J. B. Beard of Michigan State University was published. Included was a major focus on the turfgrass environment and associated stresses. For the first time a book was published in which the turfgrass–water relationships encompassing evapotranspiration and water stress were addressed, including the plant morphological and physiological aspects. The 51-page chapter on water was based on the scholarly research literature available at that time.

In 1985, 12 years later, *Turfgrass Water Conservation* was published by the University of California Division of Agriculture and Natural Resources and edited by V. A. Gibeault and S. T. Cockerham. This volume was based on a 2-day symposium on this topic held in 1983 in San Antonio,

Texas; funding for this project was provided by the American Sod Producers Association. This volume comprised 11 chapters by 14 authors totaling 155 pages. Each chapter included a practicum and a list of references, and the text was augmented by a glossary. The focus was on water use for irrigated turfgrasses, including plant, soil, water quality, cultural, and pest aspects.

In 1989, "Turfgrass Water Stress: Drought Resistance Components, Physiological Mechanisms, and Species-Genotype Diversity" was presented by J. B. Beard at the 6th International Turfgrass Research Conference in Tokyo, Japan. This keynote review paper discussed the avoidance and tolerance components of water stress plus interspecies variations, and it updated the terminology as it applied to turfgrass water stress, dehydration, and drought.

In 1992, *Turfgrass*, edited by D. V. Waddington, R. N. Carrow, and R. C. Shearman, was published with 22 chapters written by 43 turfgrass specialists. It included a 31-page chapter titled "Water Requirements and Irrigation," by W. R. Kneebone, D. M. Kopec, and C. F. Mancino. This chapter contains a good updated review of turfgrass plant–water relationships, encompassing water use and measurement. The book also includes the 38-page chapter "Controlled Environment Research Methods for Turfs," by J. B. Beard, which addresses the methodologies for turfgrass research involving glasshouse, growth chamber, and environmental stress simulators, including ET and water stress experiments.

Anyone conducting research on the relationship between turfgrass and water should read the latter six publications as a preparation for work in this field, and many elements of these publications should continue to be cited in future research papers.

In 2000, the 64-page *Water Right: Conserving Our Water, Preserving Our Environment* was published by the International Turf Producers. This publication is a quality overview of evolving water problems, landscape–turfgrass impacts and benefits, and water conservation approaches that are oriented to the general public. Ten specific case studies are presented.

In 2008, the 318-page *Water Quality and Quantity Issues for Turfgrasses in Urban Landscapes*, edited by J. B. Beard and M. P. Kenna, was published by the Council for Agricultural Sciences and Technologies (CAST). It contains 16 chapters by 25 authors. This book evolved from a 3-day workshop of paper presentations and active discussions involving turfgrass researchers, environmental specialists, and water industry managers. It was jointly funded by CAST, the USDA Agricultural Research Service, the United States Golf Association, the International Turfgrass Producers Foundation, Responsible Industry for a Sound Environment, and the Irrigation Association. This science-based book includes literature citations for each chapter and a 10-page executive summary directed toward water policy planners and decision makers. The focus throughout is on water conservation strategies and examples of successful applications.

WATER RESEARCH FUNDING BREAKTHROUGH

As illustrated in the previous section, very little turfgrass research was devoted to turfgrass plant–water relationships prior to the mid-1980s. Only a few turfgrass researchers were formally trained or interested in this aspect of the turfgrass environment. Perhaps most important, turfgrass research funding sources at the state, regional, and national levels showed no interest. Also, the funding levels available for any type of turfgrass research were very small.

In 1978, J. B. Beard developed a major water conservation research proposal, with funding to be at the $1 million level annually, for a 10-year research effort involving a consortium of university experiment stations. It was submitted to United States Golf Association Green Section (USGA), Professional Golfers Association of America (PGA), and PGA Tour.

That same year, USGA official Alexander Radko tabled the proposal as unrealistic from a funding standpoint. At that time the total national USGA Green Section funding for turfgrass research had dropped from $100,000 to a mere $30,000 annually.

In 1979, progress in funding the proposal was being made with a few board members of the PGA Tour. However, Commissioner Dean Beaman rejected the funding proposal. No further progress was made.

Initial discussions with the PGA were very positive. In 1980 the PGA, under the leadership of

President Joe Black, was in an advanced stage of developing funding for the proposal, involving seven institutions: The University of Georgia/USDA, New Mexico State University, Oklahoma State University, Pennsylvania State University, Rutgers University, and Texas A&M University were initially identified. One of the researchers submitted a separate, small funding request to the PGA for base funding of routine turfgrass field plot maintenance. President Black rejected both proposals.

Also in 1980, Executive Director Harry Easterly of the USGA attended a summit conference of golf organization leaders where the PGA reported their interest in funding a turfgrass water conservation research plan. Green Section National Director Al Radko then submitted the proposal to Easterly for his consideration.

In February 1981, Easterly studied the proposal and then met with Beard. After satisfying himself of the viability of the proposal, Easterly invited Beard to give an oral presentation before the USGA Board of Directors. As a result of Beard's presentation and extensive questions and answers by Board members, the USGA Board made a $1+ million annual commitment to support turfgrass water conservation research.

The USGA then initiated a research fundraising effort for the Water Conservation Research Project that involved brochures, television promos, and live presentations. The fundraising was successful.

In 1983 the USGA formally initiated funding for the project. Most of the 2-year delay since the commitment by the Board of Directors was due to contract negotiations among the USGA and Texas A&M University,. Much credit should be given to Harry Easterly for his leadership in bringing the original 1978 water conservation research proposal to fruition. This breakthrough in turfgrass research funding was achieved, even though many thought it was impossible.

TURFGRASS WATER REQUIREMENT CRITERIA

Specificity as to local climate, evaporative demand, seasonality, and turfgrass species will become increasingly important, when researching and advising on the water requirements of turfgrasses. In addition, there is a need to specify the practical use and need level. Five suggested need categories are as follows:

1. Provide for full beneficial needs—human quality of life.
2. Provide for turfgrass recuperative ability from usage—sport and recreation.
3. Provide for functional benefits—protect environment.
4. Provide for survival during droughts—minimal water usage.
5. No water supplement above rains.

REFERENCES

Beard, J. B. 1973. Turfgrass: Science and culture. Englewood Cliffs, NJ: Prentice-Hall.

———. 1976. Turfgrass research: Present & future. In Bicentennial symposium: Post-1976 turfgrass industry challenges in research, teaching and continuing education. Madison, WI: American Society of Agronomy. 11–20.

———. 1981. Turfgrass physiology research: A perspective for the 1980s. In R. W. Sheard, ed., Proceedings of the 4th International Turfgrass Research Conference, Guelph, Ontario. Guelph: International Turfgrass Society. 461–466.

———. 1989. Turfgrass water stress: Drought resistance components, physiological mechanisms, and species-genotype diversity. In H. Takatoh, ed., Proceedings of the 6th International Turfgrass Research Conference, Tokyo, Japan. Tokyo: Japanese Society of Turfgrass Science. 23–27.

———. 1992. Controlled environment research methods for turfs. In D. V. Waddington, R. N. Carrow, and R. C. Shearman, eds., Turfgrass. Madison, WI: American Society of Agronomy. 615–651.

Beard, J. B., and M. P. Kenna, eds. 2008. Water quality and quantity issues for turfgrasses in urban landscapes. Ames, IA: Council for Agricultural Science and Technology.

Biran, I., B. Bravdo, I. Buskin-Harav, and E. Rawitz. 1981. Water consumption and growth rate of 11 turfgrasses as affected by mowing height, irrigation frequency and soil moisture. Agronomy Journal 73(1): 85–90.

Carroll, J. C. 1943a. Atmospheric drought tests of some pasture and turf grasses. Journal of the American Society of Agronomy 356:77–79.

———. 1943b. Effects of drought, temperature, and nitrogen on turf grasses. Plant Physiology 18:19–36.

Dernoeden, P. H., and J. D. Butler. 1978. Drought resistance of Kentucky bluegrass cultivars. HortScience 13:667–668.

———. 1979. Relation of various plant characters to drought resistance of Kentucky bluegrass. HortScience 14(4): 511–512.

Feldhake, C. M., R. E. Danielson, and J. D. Butler. 1983. Turfgrass evapotranspiration. I: Factors influencing rate in urban environments. Agronomy Journal 75(5): 824–830.

———. 1984. Turfgrass evapotranspiration. II. Responses to deficit irrigation. Agronomy Journal 76(1): 85–89.

Fender, D., ed. 2000. Water right: Conserving our water, preserving our environment. Rolling Meadows, IL: International Turf Producers Foundation.

Funk, C. R. 1981. Perspectives in turfgrass breeding and evaluation. In R. W. Sheard, ed., Proceedings of the 4th International Turfgrass Research Conference, Guelph, Ontario. Guelph: International Turfgrass Society. 3–10.

Gibeault, V. A., and S. T. Cockerham, eds. 1985. Turfgrass water conservation. Oakland: University of California Division of Agriculture and Natural Resources Publication 21405.

Hanson, A. A., and F. V. Juska. 1969. Turfgrass science. Agronomy Monograph 14. Madison, WI: American Society of Agronomy.

Johns, D., C. H. M. van Bavel, and J. B. Beard. 1981. Determination of the resistance to sensible heat flux density from turfgrass for estimation of its evapotranspiration rate. Agricultural Meteorology 25(1): 15–25.

Johns, D., J. B. Beard, and C. H. M. van Bavel. 1983. Resistances to evapotranspiration from a St. Augustinegrass turf canopy. Agronomy Journal 75(3): 419–422.

Julander, O. 1945. Drought resistance in range and pasture grasses. Plant Physiology 20:573–599.

Kim, K. S. 1987. Comparative drought resistance mechanisms of eleven major warm-season turfgrasses. PhD diss., Soil and Crop Science Department, Texas A&M University.

Kim, K. S., and J. B. Beard. 1988. Comparative turfgrass evapotranspiration rates and associated plant morphological characteristics. Crop Science 28(2): 328–331.

Klomp, G. J. 1939. A comparison of the drought resistance of selected native and naturalized grasses. Master's thesis, Iowa State College.

Kneebone, W. R., D. M. Kopec, and C. F. Mancino. 1992. Water requirements and irrigation. In D. V. Waddington, R. N. Carrow, and R. C. Shearman, eds., Turfgrass. Madison, WI: American Society of Agronomy. 441–472.

Livingston, B. E., and I. Ohga. 1926. The summer march of soil moisture conditions as determined by porous porcelain soil points. Ecology 7:427–439.

Madison, J. H. 1971a. Practical turfgrass management. New York: Van Nostrand Reinhold.

———. 1971b. Principles of turfgrass culture. New York: Van Nostrand Reinhold.

Mantell, A. 1966. Effect of irrigation frequency and nitrogen fertilization on growth and water use of a kikuyugrass lawn (*Pennisetum clandestimum* Hochst.). Agronomy Journal 58:559–561.

McAlister, D. F. 1944. Determination of soil drought resistance in grass seedlings. Journal of the American Society of Agronomy 36:324–336.

Minner, D. D., and J. D. Butler. 1985. Drought tolerance of cool season turfgrasses. In F. Lemaire, ed., Proceedings of the 5th International Turfgrass Research Conference, Avignon, France. 199–212.

Schultz, H. K., and H. K. Hayes. 1938. Artificial drought tests of some hay and pasture grasses and legumes in sod and seedling stages of growth. Journal of the American Society of Agronomy 30:676–682.

Shearman, R. C., and J. B. Beard. 1972. Environmental and culture factors influencing the water use rate and stomatal density of *Agrostis palustris* Huds. cultivar Penncross. Crop Science 12(6): 424–427.

Silker, T. H. 1941. Effect of clipping upon the forage production, root development, establishment, and subsequent drought resistance of western and crested wheatgrass seedlings. Master's thesis, Iowa State College.

van Bavel, C. H. M., and D. G. Harris. 1962. Evapotranspiration rate from bermudagrass and corn at Raleigh, North Carolina. Agronomy Journal 54:319–322.

Waddington, D. V., R. N. Carrow, and R. C. Shearman, eds. 1992. Turfgrass. Agronomy Monograph 32. Madison, WI: American Society of Agronomy, Crop Science Society of America, and Soil Science Society of America.

Weaver, R. J. 1941. Water usage of certain native grasses in prairie and pasture. Ecology 22:175–192.

Weaver, J. E., and F. W. Albertson. 1943. Resurvey of grasses, forbs, and underground plant parts at the end of the great drought. Ecological Monographs 13:63–117.

Welton, F. A., and J. D. Wilson. 1931. Water-supplying power of the soil under different species of grass and with different rates of water application. Plant Physiology 6:485–493.

———. 1938. Comparative rates of water loss from soil, turf, and water surfaces. Bimonthly Bulletin of the Ohio Agricultural Experiment Station 23(190): 13–16.

Welton, F. A., J. C. Carroll, and J. D. Wilson. 1934. Artificial watering of lawn grass. Ecology 15:380–387.

Wilson, J. D. 1927. The measurement and interpretation of the water-supplying power of the soil with special reference to lawn grasses and some other plants. Plant Physiology 2:384–440.

Wilson, J. D., and B. E. Livingston. 1932. Wilting and withering of grasses in greenhouse cultures as related to water-supplying power of the soil. Plant Physiology 7:1–34.

Wilson, J. D., and F. A. Welton. 1935. The use of an evaporation index in watering lawns. Bimonthly Bulletin of the Ohio Agricultural Experiment Station 20(174): 112–119.

3 Environmental Issues Surrounding Turf-Dominated Urban Landscapes

Rossana Sallenave

The environmental consequences of land development and urbanization, which have resulted in the conversion of forests, croplands, and pastures into urban spaces, are being increasingly examined and evaluated. Among the many issues of growing concern are depleting water resources, exposure to anthropogenic chemicals, and the loss of wildlife habitat and biodiversity.

Turfgrass is a dominant feature in urban landscapes, including home lawns, parks, athletic fields, and golf courses. Despite the documented benefits of turfgrass, such as providing open spaces in urban environments, flood control, reducing heat islands, dust control, noise abatement, sequestering atmospheric carbon, and fire-buffering capabilities (Fender 2008; Beard 2008), critics contend that turfgrass wastes water and requires excessive use of pesticides and fertilizers. Golf courses account for only 9% of the total turfgrass usage in urban environments (Cockerham and Gibeault 1985), but they are large green spaces that are highly visible to the public, and as such, have been frequently criticized for their real or perceived adverse effects on the environment. The United States now has more than 16,000 courses (Lyman et al. 2007), and more are being built each year. Growth in golf course numbers is also being experienced in Japan, where more than 5000 ha of forest are lost annually to golf course developments, and in other Asian countries, causing increasing concern about environmental degradation and loss of habitat (Platt 1994). Consequently, the golf course industry is under increasing pressure to adopt strategies that mitigate adverse environmental effects and help ameliorate the industry's public image. Several golf organizations, such as the United States Golf Association (USGA), the Golf Course Superintendants Association of America (GCSAA), and the American Society of Golf Course Architects, have taken an active role in searching for science-based information that can help make existing and future golf courses more environmentally sound.

This chapter focuses on golf courses because of their size and visibility, and because turfgrass research has been largely conducted on golf courses. However, many of the conclusions drawn from the research and management strategies suggested may have relevance to other turf areas, such as parks and home lawns. The chapter reviews environmental issues surrounding their construction and management, as well as strategies and practices that can be implemented to address these concerns.

ENVIRONMENTAL ISSUES SURROUNDING GOLF COURSES

A number of potential environmental problems are associated with golf course construction and management, including water depletion, excessive runoff and soil erosion, contamination of surface water and groundwater with pesticides and nutrients, and loss of habitat and biodiversity (Terman 1997). This section reviews these issues and discusses research conducted on the environmental impact of golf course construction and management.

Water Depletion

One of the most important environmental issues that the golf industry is facing is the consumption of large amounts of water in the face of depleting water supplies in many parts of the country. This is especially problematic in areas where periods of drought often result in water restrictions being imposed on homeowners. In the United States, golf courses use an average of 300,000 gallons of water per day, or 684,000 gallons of water per acre per year, based on an average golf course size of 160 acres (Watson et al. 2003). Actual water use depends on climate, rainfall, type of grass, and surface area: for example, a golf course in southern California uses as much water in a month as a course in Baltimore, Maryland, would use in a year (Platt 1994).

To address golf's high water consumption, the golf industry has taken several steps to reduce water use and become less reliant on potable water for irrigation purposes. These strategies, which are discussed in greater detail in chapter 9 of this book, include the development of new grass varieties that use less water or can tolerate water of poorer quality; adopting improved, more efficient irrigation technology; using nonpotable water for irrigation purposes; and implementing best management practices (BMPs) for water conservation (Snow 2001). BMPs combine proper plant selection and cultural maintenance practices that together minimize water use while still maintaining adequate turf quality (Snow 2001). Along with selecting low-water-use turfgrasses and plants for a course, BMPs include adequate fertilization, using mulches around shrubs and other nonturf plants to reduce evaporation losses, using soil cultivation techniques to improve water infiltration, and limiting cart traffic to paths to reduce turf wear and soil compaction. Many golf courses in the United States have now adopted some or all of these strategies to achieve greater water conservation. For example, the most recent survey conducted by the GCSAA reported that 12% of golf courses in the United States are now irrigated with recycled water rather than potable water. This figure is higher in the southwestern states, where 37% of all courses irrigate with recycled water (GCSAA 2009). A 2003 assessment of golf courses in Colorado reported that in response to chronic regional drought, nearly every course surveyed had adopted at least one strategy to reduce water usage. These include the use of wetting agents by 85% of the courses, eliminating irrigation in selected areas (76%), reducing rough irrigation (74%), hand-watering tees (70%), and adjusting fertilization practices (71%) (Watson et al. 2003).

Pesticides

The game of golf has greatly evolved since its early beginnings as a populist game in fifteenth-century Scotland, where it was played on Scottish links, pastures, and commons, and players were challenged to overcome the natural lay of the land (Platt 1994). Today's game demands highly manicured swards that require fertilizer and pesticides to maintain their color, quality, and playability. These intensively maintained, close-mowed, heavily trafficked turfgrasses can be much more susceptible to disease and pest outbreaks. This has resulted in the widespread and common use of fungicides and pesticides on golf courses, making turfgrass the largest user of fungicides in the United States (Branham 2008). The U.S. EPA's most recent survey of golf course pesticide usage was conducted in 1982. It reported that the total estimated use of herbicide, fungicide, and insecticide in 1982 was 2.1, 2.1, and 1.5 million kg of active ingredient, respectively (Kriner 1985). A study conducted in 1990 by the New York State Department of Law reported that the average rate of pesticide application of 52 golf courses surveyed was 8.2 kg per treated acre per year, which was about seven times higher than amounts applied to agricultural land each year (1.2 kg) (Platt 1994). However, it should be noted that pesticides are normally applied only to a portion of a golf course's total acreage. While the golf industry and turfgrass experts generally believe that pesticides currently used on golf courses are quite safe and do not pose a real health risk when used correctly (see statements by Jeff Carlson, Greg Lyman, and James Snow in Barton 2008), there are several reasons why their widespread usage should be carefully examined and kept to a minimum. Pesticides in general often have acute and chronic effects on humans and wildlife and are used in formulations that include inert ingredients whose identity is protected by trade secrets and as such are not tested (Cox 1991; Cox and Surgan 2006). These inert ingredients can sometimes be more toxic than the active ingredient and include known carcinogens, teratogens and neurotoxins (Beyond Pesticides Factsheet 2005; Cox and Surgan 2006). Furthermore, while in many cases the toxicity of pesticide breakdown products is less than that of the parent compound, several metabolites of organophosphate and carbamate insecticides are as toxic or more toxic than the parent compounds (Day 1991). It should be pointed out that many organophosphate and carbamate insecticides have been phased out and replaced with less toxic compounds. However, the organophosphate chlorpyrifos and the carbamate carbaryl are still commonly used to control insect pests on golf courses (Armbrust 2001; Putnam et al. 2008). Another concern is that in some states golf courses are not required to notify golfers when pesticides have been applied, such as by posting signs indicating areas that have been treated. This can lead to illness (Cox 1991; Platt 1994) or even death, as illustrated in one tragic case in which a golfer died due to exposure to chlorothalonil, which had been sprayed on the golf course twice during the week the golfer played (Cox 1991). There are also numerous documented incidents of bird kills on golf courses due to pesticide applications (Cox 1991). Reports by the New York State Department of Conservation have summarized the deaths of hundreds of birds, including blue jays, robins, Brant and Canada geese, coots, widgeons, and mallards, on golf courses following exposure to the organophosphate insecticides diazinon, chlorpyrifos, and isofenphos (Cox 1991).

On the positive side, some of these pesticides, such as diazinon and chlordane, have been completely banned from use on golf courses.

Potential Groundwater Contamination from Pesticides and Fertilizers

One area of concern that has received a great deal of attention is the potential contamination of groundwater with pesticides and nutrients applied to golf courses, particularly to the greens, which sometimes consist of 70 to 90% sand rather than soil (Platt 1994). Numerous studies have been conducted to assess the fate of fertilizers and pesticides applied to golf courses.

In general, turf provides an excellent system for minimizing leaching of pesticides and nutrients due to its continuous plant cover and layer of thatch, which has a high sorptive capacity (Miltner et al. 1996; Branham 2008). Nonetheless, several factors, namely the chemical properties of the pesticide such as its partition coefficient (K_{oc}), water solubility, and half-life, as well as management practices such as application rates and irrigation regimes, can influence leaching and groundwater contamination.

The role of irrigation on pesticide leaching is illustrated by two studies that examined the downward migration of the fungicide metalaxyl in irrigated creeping bentgrass with sandy root zones. In one study that demonstrated that leaching decreased as turf density and amount of peat in sand increased (Petrovic et al. 1993), very high levels of the fungicide were recovered in leachate (16% of total metalaxyl applied) even when turf cover was 100%. Other research (Wu et al. 2002b), however, recovered only 0.7% of the total metalaxyl applied to root zones managed under putting green conditions. The difference can be explained by the irrigation regimes applied in both experiments. Another study (Petrovic et al. 1996) deliberately overwatered to increase the likelihood of leaching, whereas the California 2002 study conducted by Wu et al. irrigated only as needed to prevent drought stress. The leaching of organophosphate insecticides used on golf courses has also been extensively studied (e.g., Petrovic et al. 1993; Cisar and Snyder 1996; Wu et al. 2002a). In these studies the percentage of total organophosphate pesticide applied that was recovered in leachate ranged from as low as 0.0001% and 0.0005% for trichlorfon and chlorpyrifos, respectively (Wu et al. 2002a) to 1% and 4% of total trichlorfon applied at low and high rates of irrigation, respectively (Petrovic et al. 1993). Less than 0.1% of the organophosphate pesticides applied in the Cisar study were recovered in leachate, regardless of differences in rainfall and leaching (Cisar and Snyder 1996). All these studies indicate that turf is generally effective at minimizing pesticide leaching, even when the pesticides are potentially mobile. However, significant leaching can occur if pesticide applications are followed by large leaching events such as overwatering or heavy precipitation.

The potential movement of nutrients from fertilizers into groundwater has also been extensively studied (e.g., Miltner et al. 1996; Morton et al. 1988; Starr and DeRoo 1981). A major concern with nitrogen fertilization is the potential leaching of nitrate, which is a regulated groundwater contaminant (EPA 2009). The results of these studies suggest that nitrate leaching from well-maintained, healthy, fertilized turf was a minor occurrence, with only trace amounts of applied nitrogen detected in leachate. While some studies have indicated that late-fall fertilization with water-soluble nitrogen sources can lead to increased nitrate leaching (e.g., Mangiafico and Guillard 2006), Branham's 2008 study pointed out that the annual rate of nitrogen fertilization will ultimately have the greatest impact on nitrate leaching.

How do these results, which were conducted on smaller areas such as plots and individual greens or fairways, compare with groundwater monitoring results from actual golf courses around the United States? Three years of groundwater monitoring for 17 pesticides and nitrate-nitrogen was conducted at 19 test wells on four golf courses in Cape Cod, Massachusetts (Cohen et al. 1990). Of the 10 out of 17 pesticides that were detected, most were present in low concentrations (less than 5 $\mu g\ l^{-1}$), and were associated with greens and tees. The most frequently detected chemical was 2-4-dichlorobenzoic acid (DCBA), an impurity in herbicide formulations. Chlordane was detected in several wells at concentrations exceeding health advisory levels, despite its ban from use since 1978. Except for chlordane, no pesticides detected exceeded health guidance levels. Nitrate-nitrogen concentrations occasionally exceeded the 10 mg l^{-1} federal maximum contaminant level (MCL), but it averaged 1 to 6 mg l^{-1}. The study concluded that there was no cause for concern regarding pesticide use on the golf courses and that nitrate-nitrogen levels decreased with lower application rates and the use of slow-release fertilizers.

Another study (Cohen et al. 1999) reviewed surface water and groundwater quality monitoring results from golf courses around the United States. The authors concluded that widespread water quality impacts by golf courses were not occurring. Furthermore, they found that none of the authors of the individual studies reviewed observed significant toxicological effects despite health advisory levels (HALs) and MCLs being occasionally exceeded. However, these conclusions appear to be based on risk assessments rather than toxicity testing. Only nine detections, which constituted 0.07% of the groundwater database entries, exceeded an MCL or HAL, and most were in Florida. The golf courses that participated in the study were largely concentrated on the east and west coasts, with one site in Michigan and four in Minnesota. Based on the limited geographic and climatic distribution of the golf courses in the study, the authors cautioned that conclusions could not be drawn on national estimates for golf course impacts on water quality.

Impact of Golf Courses on Receiving Surface Waters

Golf courses can have potentially adverse impacts on streams and other surface waters in a number of ways. With the increasing popularity of golf, new courses are being continually built, and their construction can be potentially harmful to aquatic environments. Poorly designed golf courses can disturb and degrade wetlands, floodplains, riparian zones, and forests that contribute to maintaining stream quality (Schueler 2000).

Another risk involves the large inputs of fertilizers and pesticides to golf courses that can potentially move off the turf areas and contaminate receiving surface waters. Flowing waters that run through golf courses are highly sensitive aquatic systems that can range in quality from trout streams to drainage ditches (Lyman 2001). Runoff occurs when the rate of precipitation exceeds that of infiltration of the soil, and the volume of runoff is directly related to the duration and intensity of the rainfall (King and Balogh 2008). The highest concentrations of the herbicides 2,4-dichlorophenoxy acid (2,4-D), dicamba, and mecoprop in surface runoff from simulated bermudagrass fairways occurred during the first simulated rainfall event that followed application, at 24 hours after treatment (Smith and Bridges 1996). The percentages of the three herbicides applied that were recovered in the runoff water ranged from 8.9 to 14. The authors concluded that, given the likelihood of intense rain events following pesticide applications to golf courses in the southeastern United States, precautions should be taken when applying pesticides to fairways having a 5% slope or more in these regions. A long-term watershed-scale study was conducted in Duluth, Minnesota, to assess the quality of water exiting a golf course (King and Balogh 2008). The authors reported significantly greater median outlet concentrations of chlorothalonil and 2,4-D than inlet concentrations, but pesticide losses were comparatively small (0.9% and 0.5% of applied 2,4-D and chlorothalonil, respectively) and were similar to losses from simulated greens reported earlier (Smith and Bridges 1996). Golf course surface runoff data indicated that only 31 of the 90 chemicals tested were detected, and of those only 8 of the 2,731 samples exceeded health standards (Cohen et al. 1999). The authors concluded that based on the data, the risk to receiving surface water bodies posed by pesticides applied to healthy turfgrass on golf courses was minimal.

Other factors that affect the amount of fertilizers and pesticides in runoff, in addition to timing of rainfall events, include rate of application, chemical properties of the pesticide, and formulation (King and Balogh 2008), as well as soil properties and vegetation type or density (Walker and Branham 1992; Balogh and Anderson 1992).

Results of a long-term study that examined surface water quality (nitrogen and phosphorus sediments) in a watershed in which a Kansas golf course was built indicated that the construction phase greatly deteriorated surface water quality by tripling mass transport rates of nitrogen and phosphorus and increasing the mass transport of total suspended solids (TSS) by a factor of 10, compared with preconstruction levels (Starett et al. 2006). The authors found that once the golf course was in the early stages of operation, surface water quality greatly improved, and fractions of total nutrients applied recovered in surface runoff were less than 5%. They noted that nutrient levels in streams within the watershed remained high compared to preconstruction levels. Furthermore, losses from individual runoff events were occasionally very high when fertilizer was applied shortly before significant precipitation events. Nitrogen losses on the Minnesota golf course, while statistically significant, were too low to negatively impact the environment (King and Balogh 2008). However, the authors noted that phosphorus losses exceeded concentrations that could lead to eutrophication, despite being low in magnitude. Similarly, results from the study in which surface runoff data were compiled from 36 golf courses (Cohen et al. 1999) indicated that there were no instances of nitrate nitrogen exceeding the MCL standard of 10 mg l^{-1}.

A common and effective way to reduce or eliminate surface runoff from entering receiving waters is to maintain buffer strips around the aquatic resources (Castelle et al. 1994; Cole et al. 1997). Buffers are defined as vegetated zones between natural areas (e.g., streams or wetlands) and adjacent areas that have been modified by human activities (fig. 3.1) (Castelle et al. 1994). Buffers help reduce surface runoff in a number of ways. They dilute the chemicals applied to the treated areas, reduce surface flow velocity, act

FIGURE 3.1. Naturalized shorelines create wildlife habitat and protect water quality by providing buffer zones that reduce surface runoff. *Photo:* David Phipps, Superintendent, Stone Creek Golf Club, Oregon.

as physical filters for sediment or chemicals in solution, and increase potential for infiltration (Cole et al. 1997). Buffer strips can also be effectively used to control urban runoff from paved surfaces during nonfrozen conditions (Steinke et al. 2007). The four criteria identified that determine adequate buffer sizes are resource functional value, intensity of adjacent land use, buffer characteristics, and specific buffer functions required (Castelle et al. 1994). Several factors must be considered when determining the appropriate size of buffers. As a general rule, buffer size can be smaller when the buffer is in good condition (dense vegetation, undisturbed soils), the wetland is of comparatively low functional value, and the adjacent land has a low potential for negative impact. Buffer size must be larger when buffers are in poor condition, the wetlands are of higher value, or the adjacent land has a high potential for impact (Castelle et al. 1994). Detailed steps in establishing buffer zones on golf courses point out the importance of education and outreach to ensure both acceptance of the role of buffers and successful implementation of the necessary management steps (Lyman 2001).

Golf Courses and Wildlife Habitat

In addition to potential impacts on surface water and groundwater quality, golf course development and management activities can have adverse effects on wildlife and aquatic species' habitat. Obvious potential problems associated with golf course construction in undisturbed natural areas include loss of habitat (such as wetlands) and wild species. Changes in aquatic nutrient levels along with changes in stream habitat can negatively affect fish species. Avian habitat can also be affected, depending on how nonplaying areas are designed and managed (Mankin 2000). Although golf advocates may argue that the green spaces provided by a golf course are far more wildlife friendly than a parking lot or a strip mall, this is not a fair comparison, and much can be done to improve biodiversity and make conventional golf courses more environmentally compatible. With 70% of the total area of an average golf course considered to be rough or out-of-play (Santiago and Rodewald 2004), courses have the potential for incorporating substantial wildlife habitat into these areas.

FIGURE 3.2. ■ The Oregon Golf Club is helping the western bluebird population in the North Willamette Valley by hanging bluebird houses at several locations throughout the course. *Photo:* David Phipps, Superintendent, Stone Creek Golf Course, Oregon.

Fortunately, a growing environmental awareness by the golfing community has led a number of old and new golf courses to create more naturalistic landscapes (Terman 1997). "Naturalistic" is a term used to describe golf courses that retain the native vegetation, landforms, soils, and typical habitat of a region (Terman 1997). In addition to benefiting wildlife, naturalistic courses are often more cost effective in the long run because once they are established, they require less maintenance than conventional golf courses, resulting in lower inputs of pesticides and less water (Santiago and Rodewald 2004). Environmental organizations such as Audubon International (not affiliated with the National Audubon Society) are collaborating with golf courses by providing education and assistance to promote environmental stewardship, conservation of biological diversity, and sustainable resource management (Dodson 2004; Stangel and Distler 2002).

Numerous examples exist of golf courses that have provided habitat for, and in some cases played a role in, the conservation of, wildlife species. The Oregon Golf Club in West Linn has helped revive the western bluebird population in the North Willamette Valley by hanging bluebird houses at several locations throughout the course (fig. 3.2) (Aylward 2008). The golf course has also left a number of dead trees and snags standing to provide nesting areas for bluebirds, which are natural cavity dwellers. In a study funded by the Wildlife Links Program, a joint venture of the USGA and the National Fish and Wildlife Foundation (NFWF), research was conducted at eight golf courses in south-central Washington to determine if artificial burrows installed at the courses could help restore local burrowing owl populations (fig. 3.3), which are declining in North America (Smith et al. 2005). While four of the artificial burrows successfully fledged young, the annual fecundity of owls nesting on golf courses was lower than that for owls nesting off courses. The study concluded that if courses had large enough non-maintained areas and nesting owls were nearby, they could potentially help restore populations if nesting burrows were installed along the periphery of the courses.

In another study funded by the Wildlife Links Program, avian communities on five golf courses (four traditional and one naturalistic) in the Albuquerque, New Mexico, area were compared to communities in five paired natural areas to determine whether golf courses could serve as surrogate riparian habitats for southwestern birds (Merola-Zwartjes and DeLong 2005). The authors found that total species richness and species diversity were higher on the golf courses in three out of five cases, and indigenous species

FIGURE 3.3. Research was conducted on golf courses in south-central Washington to determine whether artificial burrows could help restore local burrowing owl populations. *Photo:* Martha Desmond, PhD, New Mexico State University

richness was higher on all five of the golf courses. In addition, the sole naturalistic golf course had greater indigenous bird species richness, diversity, and abundance than its reference site and all of the other courses, underscoring how the conservation potential of golf courses can be enhanced by increasing habitat complexity through the use of more native vegetation. In a study of Prairie Dunes Country Club, a naturalized, links-style course in Kansas, bird species richness and abundance on the course were compared with those of Sands Hill State Park, a nearby natural area (Terman 1997). The author found that total bird species richness on the golf course equaled that of the natural area, while the relative abundance of specific kinds of birds was lower. The author concluded that while naturalistic golf courses are not natural areas, courses with wildlife habitat can complement other green spaces such as biological reserves, parks, farms, and backyards, which can increase the chance of survival for many plants and animals. By involving ecologists, the growing interest in natural habitats on golf courses could significantly increase the amount of wildlife habitat. This would be especially true if naturalistic courses were built in urban areas and on disturbed or degraded wildlife-poor landscapes such as landfills, quarries, and old mines.

Although as a general rule habitat patches such as wetlands, marshes, wooded areas, and grasslands should be as large as possible, sometimes even smaller areas can be valuable if they can be connected to other natural areas with corridors of native vegetation (Terman 1997). This is illustrated by one of the most successful and highly publicized projects centered on the restoration of declining numbers of the Schaus swallowtail (fig. 3.4), the only endangered swallowtail butterfly in the United States (Daniels and Emmel 2005). Once abundant throughout southern Florida, this species was on the verge of extinction, largely due to loss of habitat and mosquito control adulticide spraying. The objective of the study initiated by the research team from the University of Florida (with funding from the Wildlife Links program and the NFWF) was to establish native larval host plants and adult nectar sources for the Schaus swallowtail on the grounds of golf courses in the Florida Keys. Creating natural habitat on golf courses where none existed previously will provide a clear corridor for adult movement and gene flow between existing colonies and allow the natural establishment of new breeding colonies within the Florida Keys (Daniels and Emmel 2005). These are just a few examples of courses around the country that can be classified as naturalistic to varying degrees. Over 2,000 courses are participating in Audubon International's Cooperative Sanctuary Program (Dodson 2004). Designing existing and new golf courses in naturalistic ways may enhance the survival of wildlife metapopulations and the ecosystems on which they depend (Terman 1997).

FIGURE 3.4. ■ Native larval host plants and adult nectar sources have been planted on golf courses in southern Florida in an effort to improve and expand suitable habitat for the endangered Schaus swallowtail *(Heraclides aristodemus ponceanus). Photo:* Jaret Daniels, PhD.

RECOMMENDATIONS AND MANAGEMENT STRATEGIES TO PROMOTE ENVIRONMENTAL STEWARDSHIP

Environmental stewardship has become an increasingly important issue on golf courses throughout the United States. This is evidenced by the number of studies that have contributed greater understanding of the influence of construction, design, and management practices of golf courses on water resources and ecosystems, as well as by the numerous publications and resources that outline integrated environmental management strategies for golf courses (e.g., Carrow and Duncan 2008; Dodson 2005; the Environmental

Institute for Golf Web site; McCarty 2005; Powell and Jollie 1993; Stangel 2006). From a purely environmental standpoint, golf courses should not be built on undisturbed, natural areas with pristine water resources and rare flora and fauna (Barton 2008). Golf courses should be organic (defined by Jeff Carlson in Barton 2008 as using no pesticides or fertilizers whose active ingredients are synthetically produced), maintenance equipment should be powered by solar energy, recycled water should be used for irrigation, and courses should all have a variety of wildlife habitats. While these conditions may not all be feasible on most courses, strides have been taken to mitigate many potential environmental problems associated with golf course maintenance, and many courses have implemented environmental improvements. A recent survey of 16,009 golf courses throughout the United States indicated that approximately 44% of golf courses have increased their nonturfgrass areas by almost 4 ha over the past 10 years, and an average of five environmental improvements have been made on 18-hole golf courses in the same time period (Lyman et al. 2007). Several examples of environmentally friendly golf courses have been described in previous sections of this chapter. The following is a summary of management strategies intended to address the major environmental issues concerning golf courses that were previously discussed. It is not intended to be an exhaustive coverage of management practices, as excellent references on the subject exist, but rather a series of general guidelines and recommendations.

Avoiding Environmental Damage during Design and Construction of New Courses

From an ecological standpoint, choosing a location for a new golf course is one of the most important decisions that will be made (Terman 1997). Unique natural ecosystems should be preserved and may be unsuitable sites for golf courses. Organizations involved with the preservation of natural communities such as the Nature Conservancy should be consulted to better assess the ecological characteristics and uniqueness of the site. If it is not possible to preserve a site, an ecologically designed naturalistic course may provide an acceptable option that would allow some of the environmental integrity of the site to be saved (Terman 1997). Other steps (see McCarthy 2005) include:

- Avoid disturbing or damaging sensitive wildlife areas and wetlands during initial design and construction.
- Select plant species that are adapted to local conditions and require minimum inputs of fertilizers and pesticides.
- Take all necessary steps during the construction phase to prevent soil erosion and manage storm water runoff on disturbed areas.

Finally, when developing a golf course on reclaimed land, golf course developers should use the natural (predevelopment) environment of a region as a template. This would encourage the reestablishment of native species that may have been extirpated from the area due to spreading urbanization.

Reducing Pesticide and Nutrient Runoff Losses from Turf

Best management practices (BMPs)—science-based, holistic environmental management approaches—can be aimed at alleviating environmental problems such as concerns about pesticides, nutrients, and sediments as they relate to water quality protection (Carrow and Duncan 2008). BMPs that can reduce the possibility of these chemicals and sediments moving off treated areas into receiving waters bodies include the following (see McCarty 2005):

- Grow a solid turf stand that reduces off-site transport of sediments and applied chemicals.
- Control the rate, method, timing, and type of chemicals being applied.
- Establish and maintain buffer strips between treated areas and receiving surface waters.
- Avoid applying pesticides and fertilizers when soil moisture conditions are high.
- Develop management programs that use pesticide and fertilizer formulations that have low runoff potential. These can include slow-release nitrogen fertilizers, liquid applications rather than granular formulations of pesticides, water-soluble fertilizers applied frequently at low amounts ("spoon feeding"), and pesticides with lower water solubilities and stronger adsorption.

- Adopt an integrated pest management (IPM) approach to use the least amount and least toxic pesticides possible to achieve acceptable pest control.
- Avoid excessive application rates of nutrients, particularly nitrogen and phosphorus.
- Follow federal and state regulations to locate mixing, loading, and equipment rinsing sites the minimum required distance from surface waters or wells with links to groundwater.

Increasing Wildlife Habitat and Maintaining a Healthy Environment

In designing naturalistic golf courses, the goal should be to find a balance between the needs of golfers and those of other living organisms sharing the course. This goal underscores the need for cooperation between golf course architects and ecologists familiar not only with ecosystems but with the game of golf (Terman 1997). From an ecological viewpoint, golf holes should be designed to preserve as much natural habitat as possible. Several strategies can be adopted to achieve this goal. For example, tee areas can be elevated so golfers hit shots over areas of natural habitat, such as wetlands and prairies, and onto target areas of managed turf (Terman 1997). Another strategy is to build raised walkways and cart paths so golfers do not disturb wetlands and other sensitive habitat. This strategy was used at Maryland's Queenstown Harbor Golf Links on Chesapeake Bay, where a boardwalk was built over sensitive wetlands and marshes to preserve the local flora and fauna (Platt 1994).

From an economic perspective, golf courses are expensive to build and maintain, placing them financially out of reach for many potential players. Naturalistic courses move less soil at construction and contain fewer areas of managed turf; they therefore require less irrigation, fertilizing, pesticide use, and maintenance, and thus have lower costs, making them more affordable for many potential players (Terman 1997).

Steps to increase wildlife habitat include the following (Santiago and Rodewald 2004):

- Retain dead limbs and snags to create cover and increase habitat diversity.
- Establish food and water sources.
- Provide nesting boxes (fig. 3.5).
- Maintain natural areas by limiting human contact.
- Plant native species that offer berries, seeds, and nuts.
- Create vegetation corridors to link isolated habitats throughout the course.
- Avoid spreading fertilizers and pesticides on paved surfaces.
- Leave buffer strips of vegetation along streams and receiving waters not only to reduce surface runoff of chemicals and sediments but also to increase habitat diversity and wildlife species distribution.
- Conserve water by recapturing and reusing water.
- Compost organic debris such as turf clippings, tree branches, etc.
- Consult a wildlife biologist during planning and construction.

Natural methods of pest control should be also considered. Providing habitat for a number of insectivores could reduce the need for pesticide applications. For example, bat boxes can be hung to encourage bats to live on the golf course. Bats consume up to 3,000 insects per night (Santiago and Rodewald 2004), including leafhoppers and mosquitoes. Another example would be to create a wetland rather than a pond, because wetlands support more dragonflies and damselflies, which feed on mosquitoes.

Finally, although most wildlife is welcomed on golf courses, superintendents are faced with special problems associated with certain species, such as some gnawing and burrowing rodents, large herbivores, and geese. By far, the animals that present the greatest challenge to many superintendents are Canada geese. Again, naturalistic courses may have an advantage over traditional courses when it comes to these species. If the natural habitat areas are of sufficient size, they will attract most of the wildlife, confining their movements to the native vegetation (Terman 1997). Even Canada geese, which are attracted to mowed areas, may be discouraged from using these areas by planting tall vegetation along fairways and bodies of water, which prevents the

FIGURE 3.5. Bird boxes provide homes for nesting birds such as swallows, nuthatches, and western bluebirds. *Photo:* Alan Nielsen, Superintendent, Royal Oaks Country Club, Vancouver, WA.

geese from seeing potential predators. While Canada geese were frequent visitors on traditional courses in the area, they were rarely seen on the fairways or greens at Prairie Dunes Country Club (Terman 1997). Indeed, habitat-modification strategies, in combination with repellents, fencing, egg addling, harassment with trained dog teams, and public education programs that discourage people from feeding the birds have proven to be effective means to deal with Canada geese without the need for controlled hunts and roundups, methods that in most cases do nothing to solve the problem (Shackelford 2006).

CONCLUSION

There are currently over 16,000 golf courses in the United States, and many more are being built every year to meet the growing popularity of the game. The construction of golf courses has the potential to create adverse impacts on the aquatic environment by disrupting and degrading wetlands, floodplains, riparian zones and forests that contribute to water quality. This can also lead to loss of wildlife habitat and species diversity. Fertilizers and pesticides may also degrade water and habitat quality. As a result of growing public environmental awareness, a philosophy of environmental stewardship and best management practices is being increasingly adopted by the turfgrass industry. Greater commitment to ecosystem management and promotion of these strategies will be needed to overcome the negative image of golf courses in a world of increasing urban growth and diminishing natural resources.

REFERENCES

Armbrust, K. L. 2001. Chlorothalonil and chlorpyrifos degradation products in golf course leachate. Pest Management Science 57:797–802.

Aylward, L. 2008. On the Oregon trail: Golf and the environment meet up in the Great Northwest. Golfdom (Feb. 1).

Balogh, J. C., and J. L. Anderson. 1992. Environmental impacts of turfgrass pesticides. In J. C. Balogh and W. J. Walker, eds., Golf course management and construction: Environmental issues. Chelsea, MI: Lewis Publishers. 221–353.

Barton, J. 2008. How green is golf? Golf Digest 59(6): 1–27.

Beard, J. B. 2008. Integrated multiple factor considerations in low-precipitation landscape approaches. In Beard and Kenna 2008. 33–40.

Beard, J. B., and M. P. Kenna, eds. 2008. Water quality and quantity issues for turfgrasses in urban landscapes. Ames, IA: Council for Agricultural Science and Technology.

Beyond Pesticides. 2005. Lawn pesticide facts and figures. Beyond Pesticides Web site, http://www.beyondpesticides.org/lawn/factsheets/LAWNFACTS&FIGURES_8_05.pdf.

Branham, B. 2008. Leaching of pesticides and nitrate in turfgrasses. In Beard and Kenna 2008. 107–120.

Carrow, R. N., and R. R. Duncan. 2008. Best management practices for turfgrass water resources: Holistic-systems approach. In Beard and Kenna 2008. 273–294.

Castelle, A. J., A. W. Johnson, and C. Connolly. 1994. Wetland and stream buffer size requirements: A review. Journal of Environmental Quality 23:878–882.

Cisar, J. L., and G. H. Snyder. 1996. Mobility and persistence of pesticides applied to a USGA Green. III: Organophosphate recovery in clippings, thatch, soil, and percolate. Crop Science 36:1433–1438.

Cockerham, S. T., and V. A. Gibeault. 1985. The size, scope, and importance of the turfgrass industry. In V. A. Gibeault and S. T. Cockerham, eds., Turfgrass water conservation. Oakland: University of California Division of Agriculture and Natural Resources Publication 21405. 7–12.

Cohen, S., S. Nickerson, R. Maxey, A. Dupuy Jr., and J. A. Senita. 1990. A ground water monitoring study for pesticides and nitrates associated with golf courses on Cape Cod. Ground Water Monitoring Review 10(1): 160–173.

Cohen, S., A. Svrjcek, T. Durborow, and N. LaJan Barnes. 1999. Water quality impacts by golf courses. Journal of Environmental Quality 28:798–809.

Cole, J. T., J. H. Baird, N. T. Basta, R. L. Huhnke, D. E. Storm, G. V. Johnson, M. E. Payton, M. D. Smolen, D. L. Martin, and J. C. Cole. 1997. Influence of buffers on pesticide and nutrient runoff from bermudagrass turf. Journal of Environmental Quality 26:1589–1598.

Cox, C. 1991. Pesticides on golf courses: Mixing toxins with play? Journal of Pesticide Reform 11(3): 2–7.

Cox, C., and M. Surgan. 2006. Unidentified inert ingredients in pesticides: Implications for human and environmental health. Environmental Health Perspectives 114(12): 1803–1806.

Daniels, J. C., and T. C. Emmel. 2005. Florida golf courses help an endangered butterfly. USGA Green Section Record 43(1): 22–25.

Day, K. E. 1991. Pesticide transformation products in surface waters: effects on aquatic biota. In L. Somasundaram and J. R. Coats, eds., Pesticide transformation products: Fate and significance in the environment. ACS Symposium Series 459. Washington, DC: American Chemical Society. 217–241.

Dodson, R. G. 2004. The Audubon Cooperative Sanctuary Program for golf courses. USGA Turfgrass Environmental Research Summary. Far Hills, NJ: USGA. 43–44.

———. 2005. Sustainable golf courses: A guide to environmental stewardship. Hoboken, NJ: Wiley.

Environmental Institute for Golf (EIFG). EIFG Web site, http://www.eifg.org.

EPA (U.S. Environmental Protection Agency). 2009. Basic information on drinking water contaminants. EPA Web site, http://www.epa.gov/safewater/contaminants/basicinformation.html.

Fender, D. H. 2008. Urban turfgrasses in times of a water crisis: Benefits and concerns. In Beard and Kenna 2008. 11–31.

GCSAA (Golf Course Superintendents Association of America). 2009. Golf course environmental profile. 2: Water use and conservation practices on U.S. golf courses. Lawrence, KS: GCSAA.

King, K. W., and J. C. Balogh. 2008. Nutrient and pesticide transport in surface runoff from perennial grasses in the urban landscapes. In Beard and Kenna 2008. 121–152.

Kriner, R. 1985. Final report on the results of a national survey of pesticide usage on golf courses in the U.S. conducted in July–September 1982. Washington, DC: U.S. Environmental Protection Agency.

Lyman, G. T. 2001. Alternative strategies for turfgrass management near water. In Proceedings of the [71st] Michigan Turfgrass Conference. Vol. 30. 150–151.

Lyman, G. T., C. S. Throssell, M. E. Johnson, and G. A. Stacey. 2007. Golf course profile describes turfgrass, landscape, and environmental stewardship features. Applied Turfgrass Science, http://www.plantmanagementnetwork.org/ats/, doi 10.1094/ATS-2007-1107-01-RS.

Mangiafico, S. S., and K. Guillard. 2006. Fall fertilization timing effects on nitrate leaching and turfgrass color and growth. Journal of Environmental Quality 35:163–171.

Mankin, K. R. 2000. An integrated approach for modelling and managing golf course water quality and ecosystem diversity. Ecological Modelling 133:259–267.

McCarty, L. B. 2005. Best golf course management practices. 2nd ed. Upper Saddle River, NJ: Prentice Hall.

Merola-Zwartjes, M., and J. P. DeLong. 2005. Avian species assemblages on New Mexico golf courses: Surrogate riparian habitat for birds? Wildlife Society Bulletin 33(2): 435–447.

Miltner, E. D., B. E. Branham, E. A. Paul, and P. E. Rieke. 1996. Leaching and mass balance of 15N-labeled urea applied to a Kentucky bluegrass turf. Crop Science 36(6): 1427–1433.

Morton, T. G., A. J. Gold, and W. M. Sullivan. 1988. Influence of overwatering and fertilization on nitrogen losses from home lawns. Journal of Environmental Quality 17:124–130.

Petrovic, A. M., R. G. Young, C. A. Sanchirico, and D. J. Lisk. 1993. Downward migration of trichlorfon insecticide in turfgrass soils. Chemosphere 27:1273–1277.

Petrovic, A. M., W. C. Barrett, I. Larsson-Dovach, C. M. Reid, and D. J. Lisk. 1996. The influence of a peat amendment and turf density on downward migration of metalaxyl fungicide in creeping bentgrass sand lysimeters. Chemosphere 33:2335–2340.

Platt, A. E. 1994. Toxic green: The trouble with golf. World Watch 7(3): 27–32.

Powell, R. O., and J. B. Jollie. 1993. Environmental guidelines for the design and maintenance of golf courses. Baltimore County, MD: Department of Environmental Protection and Resources Management.

Putnam, R. A., J. J. Doherty, and J. M. Clark. 2008. Golfer exposure to chlorpyrifos and carbaryl following applications to turfgrass. Journal of Agricultural and Food Chemistry 56(15): 6616–6622.

Santiago, M. J., and A. D. Rodewald. 2004. Considering wildlife in golf course management. Ohio State University Extension Fact Sheet, http://ohioonline.osu.edu/w-fact/0015.html.

Schueler, T. R. 2000. Minimizing the impact of golf courses on streams. In T. S. and H. Holland, eds., The practice of watershed protection. Ellicott City, MD: Center for Watershed Protection. 73–74.

Shackelford, G. 2006. PETA leader speaks out. Golfdom (Feb. 1).

Smith, A. E., and D. C. Bridges. 1996. Movement of certain herbicides following application to simulated golf course greens and fairways. Crop Science 36:1439–1445.

Smith, M. D., C. J. Conway, and L. A. Ellis. 2005. Burrowing owl nesting productivity: A comparison between artificial and natural burrows on and off golf courses. Wildlife Society Bulletin 33(2): 454–462.

Snow, J. T. 2001. Water conservation on golf courses. In D. Fender, ed., Water right: Conserving our water, preserving our future. Rolling Meadows, IL: International Turf Producers Foundation.

Stangel, P. 2006. Wildlife links: Improving golf's environmental game. Far Hills, NJ: USGA Green Section.

Stangel, P., and K. Distler. 2002. Golf courses for wildlife: Looking beyond the turf. USGA Turfgrass and Environmental Research Online 1(2): 1–8.

Starr, J. L., and H. C. DeRoo. 1981. The fate of nitrogen fertilizer applied to turfgrass. Crop Science 212:531–536.

Starrett, S., Y. Su, T. Heier, J. Klein, and J. Holste. 2006. Nutrient runoff from three phases of a golf course project. USGA Turfgrass Environmental Research Online 5(8): 1–8.

Steinke, K., J. C. Stier, W. R. Kussow, and A. Thompson. 2007. Prairie and turf buffer strips for controlling runoff from paved surfaces. Journal of Environmental Quality 36:426–439.

Terman, M. R. 1997. Natural links: Naturalistic golf courses as wildlife habitat. Landscape Urban Planning 38:183–197.

Walker, W. J., and B. Branham. 1992. Environmental impacts of turfgrass fertilization. In J. C. Balogh and W. J. Walker, eds., Golf course management and construction: Environmental issues. Chelsea, MI: Lewis Publishers. 105–219.

Watson, P., S. Davies, and D. Thilmany. 2003. The economic contributions of Colorado's golf industry: Environmental aspects of golf in Colorado. Colorado State University Department of Agricultural and Resource Economics Web site, http://dare.agsci.colostate.edu/thilmany/golfresource.pdf.

Wu, L., G. Liu, M. V. Yates, R. L. Green, P. Pacheco, J. Gan, and S. R. Yates. 2002a. Environmental fate of metalaxyl and chlorothalonil applied to a bentgrass putting green under southern California conditions. Pest Management Science 58:335–342.

———. 2002b. Partitioning and persistence of trichlorfon and chlorpyrifos in a creeping bentgrass putting green. Journal of Environmental Quality 31:889–895.

4

Developing Turfgrasses with Drought Resistance and Heat and Salinity Stress Tolerance

Robert C. Shearman and Michael P. Kenna

Breeding and improving turfgrasses is a long-term program that can often take 15 to 20 years to produce a new cultivar. With this in mind, the challenge for turfgrass breeders is to be constantly looking forward and attempting to anticipate future trends for the industry. This sort of speculation is not always an easy task and can be risky to say the least. A considerable commitment of time, labor, and other resources is required by the breeding program to accomplish the goal of releasing a new cultivar to the industry.

Currently, the turfgrass industry faces concerns over water quality and quantity, reduced inputs, and energy conservation. It is likely that these issues will continue to intensify as concerns for turfgrass managers in the future, and they are clearly trends that turfgrass plant breeders are attempting to address (Watson 1994; Shearman 2006).

Certainly, conventional turfgrass breeding programs have made considerable progress in improving turfgrass performance and adaptation in the past few decades (Shearman 2006). Improved drought-resistant and heat-tolerant turfgrasses will ultimately be needed to reduce irrigation requirements and conserve water, and grasses with enhanced salinity stress tolerance will allow the industry to increase its use of effluent and other nonpotable water sources in the future. In the early 1980s, a considerable research effort on turfgrass water use and drought resistance was initiated, and several reviews have been published regarding the progress of these research efforts (Gibeault and Cockerham 1985; Beard 1989; Carrow et al. 1990).

Conventional breeding methods continue to be important in improving turfgrasses, but even more directed approaches are needed to address the development of improved drought, heat, and salinity stress tolerant cultivars that will be required by the industry in the future. Technologies such as molecular markers, marker-assisted selection, transgenic techniques, and interspecific hybridization are likely to play an ever increasing role in future turfgrass improvements (Casler and Duncan 2003). This chapter covers the current state of plant breeding and genetic efforts to improve turfgrass drought, heat, and salinity stress tolerance, and identifies potential opportunities for future improvements as well.

TRADITIONAL APPROACHES TO TURFGRASS IMPROVEMENT

Natural selection pressure has created opportunities for relatively rapid genetic shifts in perennial grass populations. Thus, grasses have evolved defense mechanisms for biotic and abiotic stress that have enhanced their adaptation and potential benefits to mankind. It is this inherent diversity that has led to the widespread dispersion of grasses on a global basis (Gould 1968). Grasses evolved interspecific, intraspecific, and ecotypic variation that make them attractive as diverse germplasm for manipulation and use as turfgrass species (fig. 4.1).

Much of the early improvements with turfgrasses took advantage of the natural selection process, and many of our existing cultivars are the result of natural selection. Selections were made from naturally occurring populations using plants that expressed desirable turfgrass characteristics, such as a reduced vertical growth rate, rapid lateral spread, dark green color, and tolerance to biotic and abiotic stresses. Under naturally evolving conditions, perennial grass populations are generally highly heterogeneous, and with each flowering cycle, they generate considerable genotypic variation. An exception to this population diversity might occur with species such as Kentucky bluegrass (*Poa pratensis* L.) due to its apomixis.

Breeding and improving perennial grasses is not an easy task. Perennial grasses are highly heterozygous, express cross-species compatibility, often form ploidy series, and are mostly self-incompatible. Each of these characteristics serves as a benefit to grass species evolution and adaptation due to similarity in genomic structures, free exchange of genes with related species, and the potential to form mutations, but these characteristics, while being potentially beneficial to diversity of germplasm, also establish potential barriers for turfgrass plant breeders, limiting their opportunities to manipulate and improve various species.

Turfgrass breeders interested in developing grasses with improved drought resistance, heat tolerance, and salinity tolerance generally develop germplasm with these characteristics by selecting genotypes from naturally occurring populations that evolved under these abiotic stresses (Casler and Duncan 2003). Turfgrass breeders use phenotypic and genotypic recurrent selection to further delineate cultivars with improved stress performance. Using this approach, plant breeders select plants from the original population and develop crosses among the individuals expressing the desired traits (Brilman 2005). Selections in the cycle I population can be exposed to drought, heat, and salinity

FIGURE 4.1. ■ Turfgrass breeding programs designed to develop culitvars with improved drought resistance and heat and salinity tolerance require an extensive, diverse germplasm. *Photo:* University of Nebraska-Lincoln.

stresses to further delineate expressing and developing the desired traits. Seed collected from these crosses are planted and evaluated in turfgrass trials, and plants are further screened through exposure to drought, heat, or salinity stress under controlled environment and field conditions. Repetition of the recurrent selection process is used to develop cultivars (fig. 4.2). This approach has proven to be quite successful when making improvements in highly heterogeneous species, like most turfgrasses, and is often called the conventional or traditional breeding method by plant breeders in the turfgrass industry.

IMPROVING TURFGRASS DROUGHT RESISTANCE

Identifying drought-resistant germplasm is an integral part of a breeding program designed to develop cultivars with improved turfgrass performance under drought stress conditions. Drought resistance describes a range of mechanisms that plants use to withstand periods of below-normal soil moisture conditions. Drought resistance is comprised of several mechanisms, including tolerance, avoidance, and escape (Levitt 1980; Beard 1989). The drought escape mechanism involves a plant completing its life cycle prior to the onset of drought and regenerating growth, usually from seed germination, when sufficient moisture becomes available again for adequate plant growth and development. The escape mechanism is of limited or little interest to turfgrass breeders, since plants expressing the escape mechanism complete their life cycle prior to the onset of drought stress and generally start a new cycle from seed sources with the onset of favorable growing conditions.

Drought-avoidant and -tolerant grasses, on the other hand, are of considerable interest. Drought-

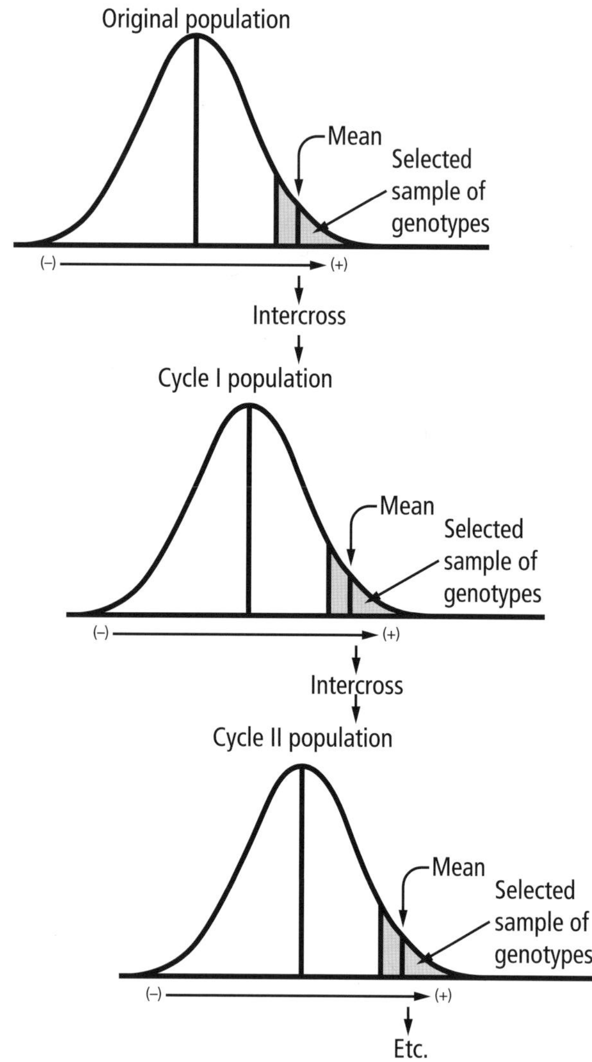

FIGURE 4.2. Expected results from recurrent selection method of plant breeding. *Source:* Redrawn from Frey 1981.

avoidant grasses maintain high internal water potential, show no signs of wilt, and continue to grow and develop when exposed to drought stress conditions (Thomas 1987; Beard 1989; White et al. 2001). Drought-tolerant genotypes withstand low internal water potential and tissue dehydration and have the ability to recover growth after exposure to long periods of drought stress when moisture stress is no longer a limiting factor. Buffalograss (*Buchloe dactyloides* (Nutt.) Engelm.) is an excellent example of a drought-tolerant turfgrass species that also has drought-avoidant attributes (Beard 1989; Shearman et al. 2004), while tall fescue (*Festuca arundinacea* Schreb.) exhibits excellent drought-avoidance characteristics (Beard 1973).

A number of studies have reported turfgrass drought-avoidant characteristics, such as reduced evapotranspiration (ET) rates, deep and extensive root system, root plasticity, high root-to-shoot ratios, reduced radiation absorption, and xeromorphic characteristics, on an interspecific and intraspecific basis among cool-season (C_3) and warm-season (C_4) grasses (Shearman 1986; Kopec et al. 1988; Beard 1989; Salaiz et al. 1995; Carrow 1996; White et al. 1992; Qian et al. 1997; Ebdon et al. 1998; Huang et al. 1998; Carrow and Duncan 2003; Ebdon and Kopp 2004). Researchers have also demonstrated that water uptake is an important trait for improved drought resistance and have reported that water uptake depends on the depth and extent of turfgrass rooting, root plasticity, and root health (Hays et al. 1991; White et al. 1992; Marcum et al. 1995; Carrow 1996; Qian et al. 1997; Huang and Gao 1999). A number of these and other criteria have been suggested as potential screening tools for selecting drought-resistant turfgrass genotypes (fig. 4.3). Some of the mechanisms suggested by researchers include canopy resistance mechanisms (Shearman 1986; Beard 1989); leaf firing (Carrow and Duncan 2003); root extension and root length (Lehman and Engelke

FIGURE 4.3. A drought-resistant buffalograss line growing in Nebraska mowed at 0.625 inch *(foreground)* and 2.0 inches *(background)*, and irrigated with 1.0 inch of water per month. *Photo:* University of Nebraska-Lincoln.

1991; Bonos et al. 2004); root thickness, root length density, and root pulling force (Nguyen et al. 1997); leaf water potential (Lehman et al. 1993; Huang et al. 1998; White et al. 2001); leaf canopy temperature (Zhoa et al. 1994; Bonos and Murphy 1999); relative water content (Huang and Gao 1999); leaf conductance and y activity (Huang and Gao 1999); and ^{13}C discrimination and water use efficiency (Ebdon and Kopp 2004). Another study (Yang et al. 1991) reported that excised-leaf water loss, glaucousness, plant height, chlorotic leaf spots, days to flowering, and days to maturity could be used as selection criteria to improve durum wheat (*Triticum turgidum* L. var. *durum*).

These mechanisms were all reported to have merit as potential selection tools for drought-resistant genotypes. Although these tools show promise, most are not suited for widespread use in turfgrass breeding programs due to the sheer numbers of genotypes involved: they are too time consuming and labor intensive to be readily applied in most turfgrass breeding programs. Therefore, most turfgrass breeding programs still rely on selection from naturally occurring populations that are regularly exposed to drought stress. Such efforts are typically slow to show improvement because of the potentially low heritability of drought stress mechanisms, spatial variation in field studies, and the limitation of cycles that can be obtained in a growing season with perennial grasses. These improvement efforts depend on reliable, rapid screening techniques that can handle large numbers of potential drought resistance genotypes, and there must be adequate genetic diversity in the germplasm being screened to respond to the drought stress selection criteria.

IMPROVING TURFGRASS HEAT TOLERANCE

Cool-season turfgrasses are often exposed to heat and drought stress simultaneously, making it important to screen for heat tolerance as well as drought resistance when breeding grasses for improved drought avoidance and tolerance. High-temperature stress limits growth and development of turfgrasses whenever temperatures exceed the optimum for the species. Therefore, high temperature stress can occur with warm-season as well as cool-season species. Most breeding efforts to improve high-temperature tolerance and performance have occurred in cool-season species.

The top and root growth of cool-season turfgrass decline as soil temperatures rise above the optimum for the species (Beard 1973). Since rooting depth, plasticity, and health are so important to turfgrass drought resistance, any decline in root production associated with heat stress could be used as selection criteria to eliminate genotypes that lack heat and drought tolerance traits. Researchers in Texas screened seedling plants of creeping bentgrasses (*Agrostis stolonifera* L.) using a heat bench designed to elevate soil temperatures (Engelke 1993; Lehman et al. 1998). They used the surviving plants to develop germplasm expressing superior heat tolerance. The impacts of soil and air temperatures on creeping bentgrass physiological responses have been investigated (Xu and Huang 2000). The authors exposed shoots and roots to high-temperature stress. They reported soil and air temperatures of 35/35°C reduced turfgrass quality, root numbers, canopy photosynthetic rate, and photochemical efficiency. In an additional study, the authors reported that leaf width, plant size, shoot density, and root-to-shoot ratio could be used to screen grasses for improved heat stress tolerance (Xu and Huang 2001).

Photochemical efficiency and chlorophyll content can be used as physiological criteria for selecting heat-tolerant germplasm in Kentucky bluegrasses (Huang and Wang 2005). Also, protein changes can be associated with heat tolerance in Kentucky bluegrass cultivars (Yali and Huang 2007). In cultivars susceptible to high-temperature stress, cytoplasmic and membrane proteins declined during heat stress to a larger extent than in the heat-tolerant cultivars. Heat-stress-induced expression of several heat shock proteins in the cytoplasm and membranes occurred earlier in the heat-tolerant cultivars than in the susceptible ones. These results suggested that better heat tolerance in Kentucky bluegrasses was associated with induction of heat shock proteins during the early phases of heat stress expression, and maintenance of higher protein levels and reduced protein degradation rates during periods of prolonged heat stress.

Marker-assisted selection for heat stress

tolerance in creeping bentgrass was also proposed (Huang et al. 2006). The authors used *Agrostis scabra*, which was identified as a heat-tolerant species growing in geothermal areas in Yellowstone National Park (Stout and Al-Niemi 2002), taking a heat-induced gene from the plant as a potential marker for selecting creeping bentgrass cultivars with improved high-temperature tolerance. The gene identified had a strong identity with the expansin gene in *Schedonorus pratensis*, and was highly related to the *Festuca pratensis* expansin exp2 gene. Genes encoding the expansin proteins are important for regulating stress tolerance. The authors found the expansin gene fragment was highly up regulated during heat stress tolerance in *A. scabra*, and it was expressed strongest in creeping bentgrass cultivars with demonstrated summer stress tolerance and when cytoplasmic- and membrane-related protein concentrations declined.

That same study (Huang et al. 2006) evaluated the decline in creeping bentgrass performance induced by heat stress. Their results indicated that increased endogenous cytokinin levels or suppressed ethylene production could be used to identify improved heat tolerance and delayed foliar senescence in cool-season grasses such as creeping bentgrass. The authors suggested that endogenous cytokinin levels might be enhanced by transgenic approaches. In another part of this study, they transformed creeping bentgrass plants with a gene controlling cytokinin synthesis and found that transgenic plants exhibited improved heat tolerance compared to non-transgenic plants. They concluded that heat tolerance in creeping bentgrass was associated with the maintenance of cytokinin production and leaf chlorophyll content during heat stress.

Clearly, there are opportunities to use selection criteria to identify germplasm in cool-season species with improved heat tolerance characteristics. Research in Texas with creeping bentgrass is a good example of an effort for improving the high-temperature performance of a species (Engelke 1993). Turfgrass breeding programs may use these criteria for selection and for identification of plant materials for establishing marker-assisted selection in their breeding approaches.

IMPROVING TURFGRASS SALINITY TOLERANCE

Water conservation strategies include increased use of nonpotable water sources and sources that are increasingly marginal in quality based on salinity hazards. These trends are expected to continue in the future. Therefore, improving salinity stress tolerance is also important in meeting the future needs of the turfgrass industry. Water conservation and potential drought stress go hand-in-hand with the need to develop improved drought resistance in turfgrass species.

Identifying genetic variation for salinity tolerance is a key step in improving salt tolerance in a species. Much of the current improvement in turfgrass salinity tolerance has been achieved through selection of salt-tolerant genotypes based on their growth and turfgrass performance from naturally occurring populations exposed to salt stress. The selection criteria used for salinity tolerance assessment in agronomic and horticultural crops, such as biomass production and crop yield reduction, were also described (Maas and Hoffman 1977; Maas 1986, 1994). Turfgrasses require different considerations, such as salinity impacts on shoot and root growth, turfgrass color and quality, and overall stress tolerance.

Breeding efforts are currently under way to develop improved salinity tolerance and to introduce new potential turfgrasses that will perform more successfully where salt stress conditions are an issue (Duncan 2003; Hughes 2002; Bonos et al. 2007; Raymer et al. 2008). Improvements in seashore paspalum (*Paspalum vaginatum* Sw.) by the turfgrass breeding program at the University of Georgia resulted in recent releases of new cultivars with improved salt stress tolerance for greens, tees, fairways, and roughs on golf courses (Duncan 2003). A joint research effort between the University of Arizona and Colorado State University is under way to develop inland saltgrass (*Distichlis spicata* (L.) Greene) cultivars for use in salt-stressed conditions (Kopec and Marcum 2001; Hughes 2002). This program collected numerous inland saltgrass selections and exposed them to evaluation in turfgrass plots. Their research has identified lines with superior turfgrass quality and salinity tolerance (Pessarakli and Kopec 2005).

Other research efforts are under way to improve more traditional turfgrass species, such as Kentucky bluegrass and perennial ryegrass (*Lolium perenne* L.) (Bonos et al. 2007).

A study (Marcum and Pessarakli 2006) reported on salt tolerance in commercially available cultivars of bermudagrass. The authors found that salinity tolerance was negatively correlated with leaf tissue sodium (Na^+) concentration and positively correlated with leaf salt gland sodium excretion rate. They felt that salt tolerance in bermudagrass was associated with shoot saline ion exclusion and leaf salt gland excretion efficiency. Another study (Bonos et al. 2007) screened perennial ryegrass and Kentucky bluegrass for salt tolerance and found cultivar differences. It used field and greenhouse trials to screen numerous plants for root lengths, root and shoot weights, and percentage of green ratings when exposed to salt stress.

Screening methods for turfgrass salt tolerance are often expensive and time consuming. Techniques such as salt gland density may be useful to breeders, since it can be relatively simple screening tool (Marcum et al. 2003). Salinity tolerance was reported to be complicated by attempting to develop screening criteria for more salt-tolerant ecotypes, since more-traditional approaches are less reliable for these halophytic selections (Lee et al. 2005). The authors also concluded that comprehensive assessments, using evaluations at low and high salinity levels, would be more effective in identifying salt-tolerant nonhalophytic genotypes.

More efforts are needed to identify potential salt stress tolerance in traditional cool-season (C_3) and warm-season (C_4) turfgrass species. Other opportunities may come as more in-depth molecular approaches are used to identify genomic salt tolerance contributions within these species.

BIOTECHNOLOGY AND MOLECULAR APPROACHES

Plant biotechnology and molecular approaches have been used in turfgrass improvement during the last 15 to 20 years. Plant biotechnology, which uses cellular and molecular levels of plant biology to better understand turfgrass genetics, is a useful tool in supplementing traditional plant breeding efforts through the improved understanding of genome relationships, use of molecular markers, marker-assisted selection, gene transfer, and similar approaches to speed up breeding and genetic improvements (fig. 4.4).

An excellent overview of biotechnology and its uses in supplementing conventional plant breeding approaches (Jauhar 2006) pointed out that traditional plant breeding and wide hybridization coupled with manipulation of chromosome pairing were important in producing superior cultivars of many crops, especially cereals such as wheat (*Triticum aestivum* L.). Wide hybridization is an effective approach for introducing alien genes into plant species. Examples of wide hybridization in improving turfgrass performance include Kentucky bluegrass and Texas bluegrass (*Poa arachnifera* Torr.) (Read et al. 1994, 1999); perennial ryegrass and tall fescue (*Festuca arundinacea* Schreb.) (Jones and Humphreys 1993; Brilman 2001); perennial ryegrass and annual ryegrass (*Lolium multiflorum* Lam.) (Brilman 2001); creeping bentgrass and colonial bentgrass (*Agrostis capillaris* L.) (Brilman 2001; Belanger et al. 2003); and hybrid bermudagrasses (*Cynodon dactylon* (L.) × *C. transvaalensis* Burtt-Davy) (Burton 1991). Bluegrass hybrids (*Poa pratensis* × *P. arachnifera*) have demonstrated improved heat and drought stress tolerance when compared to Kentucky bluegrass cultivars and improved turfgrass quality when compared to Texas bluegrass (Read et al. 1999; Abraham et al. 2004; Bremer et al. 2006), while interspecific hybrids among *Cynodon* species have demonstrated potential for improved salinity tolerance (Marcum 1998). It is apparent from these interspecific hybridization efforts that opportunities exist for improved turfgrass performance through interspecific hybridization. These opportunities facilitate expansion of the gene base and enhance development of more stress-tolerant cultivars.

Crops such as soybeans (*Glycine max* (L.) Merr.), wheat, and rice (*Oryza sativa* L.), have considerable resources in terms of plant-breeding efforts and financial support available for their improvement. As a result, molecular approaches, such as marker-assisted selection and breeding and gene transfer, have been a successful part of efforts to improve these crops for biotic and abiotic stresses (Zang et al. 2006). However, the use of molecular

FIGURE 4.4. Plant biotechnology is a useful tool for supplementing traditional turfgrass breeding programs through the improved understanding of genome relationships, use of molecular markers, marker-assisted selection, and gene transfer to decrease the time required to develop a new cultivar *Photo:* University of Nebraska-Lincoln.

approaches to improve stress tolerances in turfgrass is not as readily apparent (Kenna et al. 2004). In this regard, the lack of success is partially due to the complexity of perennial turfgrass systems, as well as the differences in resources being committed to the improvement of turfgrasses compared with other crops. The complexities of breeding and improvement in perennial grasses have been pointed out: self-incompatibility, polyploidy, quantitative traits, and lack of well-defined germplasm are among many issues that impede progress (Zang et al. 2006; Brilman 2005). Still, progress has been made in the past few years using various molecular and cellular approaches for turfgrass improvement.

An excellent review (Chai and Stricklen 1998) provided biotechnology applications for the improvement of turfgrasses. They concluded that biotechnology provides feasible opportunities to develop improved turfgrass cultivars with enhanced drought resistance and heat and salt tolerance. They also indicated that turfgrass improvements will benefit from work done with other grasses, such as wheat and rice, where somaclonal variants that tolerate salt and drought stress have already been identified. Other opportunities exist to identify genes from plants that might be transferred to turfgrasses or used for marker-assisted selection. The expansin gene fragment identified in *A. scabra* was used as a potential marker to identify creeping bentgrasses with improved summer stress tolerance and cytoplasmic- and membrane-related protein concentrations during heat stress (Huang et al. 2006).

CONCLUSION

It is apparent that drought resistance and the associated heat and salinity tolerance will continue to play an increasingly important role in turfgrass breeding programs of the future. Certainly, progress in addressing these abiotic stresses has been made by turfgrass breeders. This is evidenced by the improved performance and enhanced biotic and abiotic stress tolerance of many current cultivar releases. It is also evident from the recent improvements in water-conserving species such as buffalograss, in heat-tolerant releases of creeping bentgrass, and in salt-tolerant species such as seashore paspalum that new turfgrass sources offer improved opportunities as well.

Researchers continue to identify physiological and morphological criteria that are applicable for screening and selecting genotypes with improved drought, heat, and saline stress tolerance. These criteria will continue to help turfgrass breeders focus on improvements in these important areas. Using interspecific hybridization to introduce alien genes with desired stress tolerance characteristics, such as those obtained with Kentucky bluegrass × Texas bluegrass hybrids, also shows strong potential for improving turfgrass cultivars in the future.

The use of molecular and genomic tools, such as molecular markers, marker-assisted selection, genetic linkage maps for quantitative traits, and genetic transformation, will receive even greater emphasis for turfgrass improvement in the future. More turfgrass research is needed to improve our understanding of biotic and abiotic stress mechanisms at the molecular and cellular levels. Ongoing research in the molecular aspect of stress tolerance in cereal crops such as wheat and rice will continue to play a beneficial role for turfgrass improvement due to synteny and gene conservation among members of the grass family. Certainly, researchers will continue to develop, improve, and better understand these molecular tools and cellular approaches. These improved understandings will be important to turfgrass breeders and geneticists as they continue to seek improvement of turfgrass drought, heat, and salinity stress tolerance.

These are exciting and challenging times for the turfgrass industry and plant breeding in general. Turfgrass plant breeders will certainly be assisted by the increased emphasis by researchers in developing improved screening and selection criteria for stress tolerance and more in-depth cellular and molecular approaches, but breeders will be challenged as they continue to speculate on the future needs of the industry in an effort to keep pace with changing issues and concerns. It will be critically important that we have drought-resistant and heat- and salt-tolerant turfgrass cultivars in the pipeline to meet the future needs of our industry.

REFERENCES

Abraham, E. M., B. Huang, S. A. Bonos, and W. A. Meyer. 2004. Evaluation of drought resistance for Texas bluegrass, Kentucky bluegrass, and their hybrids. Crop Science 44:1746–1753.

Beard, J. B. 1973. Turfgrass: Science and culture. Englewood Cliffs, NJ: Prentice-Hall.

———. 1989. Turfgrass water stress: Drought resistance components, physiological mechanisms, and species-genotype diversity. In H. Takatoh, ed., Proceedings of the 6th International Turfgrass Research Conference, Tokyo, Japan. Tokyo: Japanese Society of Turfgrass Science. 23–27.

Belanger, F. C., K. A. Plumley, P. R. Day, and W. A. Meyer. 2003. Interspecific hybridization as a potential method for improvement of *Agrostis* species. Crop Science 43(6): 2172–2176.

Bonos, S. A., and J. A. Murphy. 1999. Growth responses and performance of Kentucky bluegrass under summer stress. Crop Science 39:770–774.

Bonos, S. A., D. Ruch, K. Hignight, and W. A. Meyer. 2004. Selection for deep root production in tall fescue and perennial ryegrass. Crop Science 44:1770–1775.

Bonos, S. A., M. Koch, and E. N. Weibel. 2007. Breeding for salt tolerance in cool-season turfgrasses. In Proceedings of the 16th Annual Rutgers Turfgrass Symposium. 22–23.

Bremer, D. J., K. Su, S. J. Keeley, and J. D. Fry. 2006. Performance in the transition zone of two hybrid bluegrasses compared with Kentucky bluegrass and tall fescue. Applied Turfgrass Science Online, http://www.plantmanagementnetwork.org/ats/, doi:10.1094/ATS-20060808-02-RS.

Brilman, L. A. 2001. Utilization of interspecific crosses for turfgrass improvement. International Turfgrass Society Research Journal 9:157–161.

———. 2005. Turfgrass breeding in the United States: Public and private, cool and warm season. International Turfgrass Society Research Journal 10:508–514.

Burton, G. W. 1991. A history of turf research at Tifton. USGA Green Section Record 29(3): 12–14.

Carrow, R. N. 1996. Drought avoidance characteristics of diverse tall fescue cultivars. Crop Science 36:371–377.

Carrow, R. N. and R. R. Duncan. 1998. Salt-affected turfgrass sites: Assessment and management. Chelsea, MI: Ann Arbor Press.

———. 2003. Improving drought resistance and persistence in turf-type tall fescue. Crop Science 43:978–984.

Carrow, R. N., R. C. Shearman, and J. R. Watson. 1990. Turfgrass. In B. A. Stewart and D. R. Nielson, eds., Irrigation of agricultural crops. Agronomy Monograph 30. Madison, WI: American Society of Agronomy. 889–919.

Casler, M. D., and R. R. Duncan. 2003. Origins of the turfgrasses. In M. D. Casler and R. R. Duncan, eds., Turfgrass biology, genetics, and breeding. Hoboken, NJ: Wiley.

Chai, B., and M. B. Sticklen. 1998. Applications of biotechnology in turfgrass genetic improvement. Crop Science 38:1320–1338.

Christensen, D., and Y. Qian. 2004. Development of stress-tolerant, turf-type saltgrass varieties. Turfgrass Environmental Research Summary. Far Hills, NJ: USGA.

Duncan, R. R. 2003. Seashore paspalum (*Paspalum vaginatum* Swartz). In M. D. Casler and R. R. Duncan, eds., Turfgrass biology, genetics, and breeding. Hoboken, NJ: Wiley. 295–307.

Ebdon, J. S., and K. L. Kopp. 2004. Relationships between water use efficiency, carbon isotope discrimination, and turf performance in genotypes of Kentucky bluegrass during drought. Crop Science 44:1754–1762.

Ebdon, J. S., A. M. Petrovic, and T. E. Dawson. 1998. Relationship between carbon isotope discrimination, water use efficiency, and evapotranspiration in Kentucky bluegrass. Crop Science 38:157–162.

Engelke, M. 1993. Bentgrass breeding Texas style. USGA Green Section Record 31(6): 16–18.

Frey, K. J. 1981. Capabilities and limitations of conventional plant breeding. In K. O. Rachie and J. M. Lyman, eds., Genetic engineering for crop improvement: A Rockefeller Foundation conference. New York: Rockefeller Foundation.

Gibeault, V. A., and S. T. Cockerham, eds. 1985. Turfgrass water conservation. Oakland: University of California Division of Agriculture and Natural Resources Publication 21405.

Gould, F. W. 1968. Grass systematics. New York: McGraw-Hill.

Hays, K. L., J. F. Barber, M. P. Kenna, and T. G. McCollum. 1991. Drought avoidance mechanisms of selected bermudagrass genotypes. HortScience 26:180–182.

Huang, B., and H. Gao. 1999. Physiological responses of diverse tall fescue cultivars to drought stress. HortScience 34:897–901.

Huang, B., and Z. Wang. 2005. Cultivar variation and physiological factors associated with heat tolerance for Kentucky bluegrass. International Turfgrass Society Research Journal 10:559–564.

Huang, B., and Y. Xu. 2007. Mechanisms controlling heat-induced leaf senescence and heat tolerance in bentgrass. USGA Turfgrass and Environmental Research Online 6(15): 1–6.

Huang, B., J. Fry, and B. Wang. 1998. Water relations and canopy characteristics of tall fescue cultivars during and after drought stress. HortScience 33:837–840.

Huang, B., J. Xu, and F. Belanger. 2006. Heat-inducible gene expression associated with stress tolerance in *Agrostis* species. In Abstracts: 2006 International Annual Meetings [ASA/CSSA/SSSA]. 2.

Hughes, H. 2002. Selection of turf type and seed production on inland saltgrass. Turfgrass Environmental Research Summary. 23.

Jauhar, P. P. 2006. Modern biotechnology as an integral supplement to conventional plant breeding: The prospects and challenges. Crop Science 46:1841–1859.

Jones, M. I., and M. W. Humphreys. 1993. Progress in breeding interspecific hybrid ryegrass. Grass Forage Science 48:18–25.

Kenna, M., W. K. Hallman, C. A. Auer, M. D. Casler, A. Hopkins, K. J. Karnok, C. M. Mallory-Smith, R. C. Shearman, J. C. Stier, C. M. Taliaferro, and F. Yelverton. 2004. Biotechnology-derived perennial turf and forage grasses: Criteria for evaluation. Ames, IA: Council for Agricultural Science and Technology.

Kopec, D. M., and K. Marcum. 2001. Desert saltgrass: A potential new turfgrass species. USGA Green Section Record 39(1): 6–8.

Kopec, D. M., R. C. Shearman, and T. P. Riordan. 1988. Evapotranspiration of tall fescue turf. HortScience 23:300–301.

Lee, G., R. N. Carrow, and R. R. Duncan. 2005. Criteria for assessing salinity tolerance of the halophytic turfgrass seashore paspalum. Crop Science 45:251–258.

Lehman, V. G., and M. C. Engelke. 1991. Heritability estimates of creeping bentgrass root systems grown in flexible tubes. Crop Science 31:1680–1684.

———. 1993. Heritability of creeping bentgrass shoot water content under soil dehydration and elevated temperatures. Crop Science 33:1061–1066.

Lehman, V. G., M. C. Engelke, and R. H. White. 1993. Leaf water potential and relative water content variation in creeping bentgrass clones. Crop Science 33:1350–1353.

Lehman, V. G., M. C. Engelke, K. B. Marcum, P. F. Colbaugh, J. A. Reinert, B. A. Ruemmele, and R. H. White. 1998. Registration of 'Mariner' creeping bentgrass. Crop Science 38:537.

Levitt, J. 1980. Responses of plants to environmental stresses. New York: Academic Press.

Marcum, K. B. 1998. Relative salinity tolerance of bermudagrass species. Annual Meeting Abstracts, American Society of Agronomy. 128.

Marcum, K. B., and M. Pessarakli. 2006. Salinity tolerance and salt gland excretion efficiency of bermudagrass turf cultivars. Crop Science 46:2571–2574.

Marcum, K. B., M. C. Engelke, S. J. Morton, and R. H. White. 1995. Rooting characteristics and associated drought resistance of Zoysiagrasses. Agronomy Journal 87:534–538.

Marcum, K. B., G. Wess, D. T. Ray, and M. C. Engelke. 2003. Zoysiagrass, salt glands, and salt tolerance. USGA Green Section Record 41(6): 20–21.

Mass, E. V. 1986. Salt tolerance of plants. Applied Agricultural Research 1:12–26.

———. 1994. Testing crops for salinity tolerance. In J. W. Maranville, et al., eds., Proceedings of the Workshop on Adaptation of Plants to Soil Stresses. INTSORMIL Pub. No. 94-2. Lincoln: University of Nebraska Cooperative Extension. 234–247.

Mass, E. V., and G. J. Hoffman. 1977. Crop salt tolerance: Current assessment. American Society of Civil Engineers Journal of Irrigation and Drainage 103:115–134.

Nguyen, H. T., R. C. Babu, and A. Blum. 1997. Breeding for drought resistance in rice: Physiology and moleculare genetics considerations. Crop Science 37:1426–1434.

Pessarakli, M., and D. M. Kopec. 2005. Responses of twelve inland saltgrass accessions to salt stress. USGA Turfgrass Environmental Research Online 4(20): 1–5.

Qian, Y. L., J. D. Fry, and W. W. Upham. 1997. Rooting and drought avoidance of warm-season turfgrasses and tall fescue in Kansas. Crop Science 37:905–910.

Raymer, P. L., S. K. Braman, L. L. Burpee, R. N. Carrow, Z. Chen, and T. R. Murphy. 2008. Seashore paspalum: Breeding a turfgrass for the future. USGA Green Section Record 46(1): 22–26.

Read, J. C., D. Walker, and B. W. Hipp. 1994. Potential of Texas bluegrass × Kentucky hybrids for turfgrass. Agronomy Abstracts. 183.

Read, J. C., J. A. Reinert, P. F. Colbaugh, and W. W. Knoop. 1999. Registration of 'Reveille' hybrid bluegrass. Crop Science 39:590.

Salaiz, T. A., G. L. Horst, and R. C. Shearman. 1995. Mowing height and vertical mowing frequency effects on putting green quality. Crop Science 35:1422–1425.

Shearman, R. C. 1986. Kentucky bluegrass cultivar evapotranspiration rates. HortScience 21:455–457.

———. 2006. Fifty years of splendor in the grass! Crop Science 46:2218–2229.

Shearman, R. C., T. P. Riordan, and P. G. Johnson. 2004. Buffalograss. In L. Moser, ed., Warm season grasses. Agronomy Monograph 45. Madison, WI: American Society of Agronomy. 1003–1026.

Stout, R. G., and T. S. Al-Niemi. 2002. Heat-tolerant flowering plants of active geothermal areas in Yellowstone National Park. Annals of Botany 90:259–267.

Thomas, H. 1987. Physiological responses to drought of *Lolium perenne* L.: Measurement of, and genetic variation in, water potential, solute potential, elasticity and cell hydration. Journal of Experimental Botany 38:115–125.

Watson, J. R. 1994. Water: where will it come from? In J. T. Snow, et al., eds., Wastewater reuse for golf course irrigation. Ann Arbor, MI: Lewis Publishers. 2–23.

White, R. H., M. C. Engelke, S. J. Morton, and B. A. Ruemmele. 1992. Competitive turgor maintenance in tall fescue. Crop Science 32:251–256.

White, R. H., M. C. Engelke, S. J. Anderson, B. A. Ruemmele, K. B. Marcum, and G. R. Taylor II. 2001. Zoysiagrass water relations. Crop Science 41:133–138.

Xu, Q., and B. Huang. 2000. Growth and physiological responses of creeping bentgrass to changes in air and soil temperatures. Crop Science 40:1363–1368.

———. 2001. Morphological and physiological characteristics associated with heat tolerance in creeping bentgrass. Crop Science 41:127–133.

Yali, H., and B. Huang. 2007. Protein changes during heat stress in three Kentucky bluegrass cultivars differing in heat tolerance. Crop Science 47:2513–2520.

Yang, R. C., S. Jana, and J. M. Clarke. 1991. Phenotypic diversity and associations of some potentially drought-responsive characters of durum wheat. Crop Science 31:1484–1491.

Zang, Y., A. R. Mian, and J. H. Bouton. 2006. Recent molecular and genomic studies on stress tolerance of forage and turfgrasses. Crop Science 46:497–511.

Zhoa, Y., G. C. J. Fernandez, D. C. Bowman, and R. S. Nowak. 1994. Selection criteria for drought-resistance breeding in turfgrass. HortScience 119:1317–1324.

Water Use Physiology of Turfgrasses

Bingru Huang

INADEQUATE WATER SUPPLY DUE TO LIMITED RAINFALL IS ONE of the most detrimental environmental factors causing loss of turf ground cover, which can have significant negative impacts on the aesthetics and functionality of turfgrasses. As water availability is becoming increasingly limited and more costly, developing efficient irrigation management programs and improving drought tolerance of turfgrasses through breeding or genetic engineering have become extremely important in order to maintain functional turfgrass with limited water resources. The design of effective management programs and the development of drought-resistant turfgrass require a thorough understanding of the processes of water uptake and water use in turfgrass plants and the physiological factors controlling water uptake and use.

Plant water status is controlled by the amount of water uptake through root systems, translocation throughout the plant, and the amount of water loss through transpiration from the turfgrass canopy. Water uptake and use are genetically controlled and physiologically regulated, but they can be affected by external factors such as climatic conditions and cultural practices. Comprehensive reviews of the impact of environmental factors and cultural practices on water use have been presented in a recent book on water quantity and water quality (Huang 2008; Shearman 2008) and in a review of literatures on physiology of water use in turfgrass up to 1985 (Youngner 1985). This chapter reviews current literature on physiological processes controlling water absorption and water use and introduces research methods and techniques for the evaluation of water uptake, water use rate, and plant water status for turfgrasses.

WATER UPTAKE AND ROOTING CHARACTERISTICS

Water uptake from the soil is a crucial function of a root system and largely determines the water status of the plant. Water uptake capacity depends on root morphological characteristics (e.g., size of a root system, root length density, and root distribution) and physiological properties (e.g., viability and hydraulic conductivity).

The water uptake rate of a root system generally is considered to be proportional to the extensiveness of the root system, which is often measured by total root length or root length density (defined as root length per unit volume of soil). However, this relationship of total root length to water uptake may not hold in some cases, depending largely on plant species, soil water availability, and soil depths. The water uptake capacity of a root system is positively correlated with total root length or density, assuming all roots are viable and functional, when water is uniformly distributed across the soil profile. Therefore, developing an extensive root system is critical for turfgrasses growing in non-water-limiting environments in order to explore a large volume of soil and efficiently use available water. However, soil water is typically unevenly distributed, and it is common that the surface soil is dry while water content is high in deeper soil layers. Roots may die when soil dries and cause a loss of water uptake capacity. Thus, even though total root length or density may be high, it may not be highly correlated to overall water absorption capacity. Extensive root mortality occurs as a result of drought, especially of fine roots (Huang et al. 1997; Huang and Fry 1998). Turfgrass water uptake was more closely related to root plasticity and root viability than to total root mass or length under drought stress (Huang et al. 1997). Therefore, developing turfgrass species or cultivars with root systems of high viability in combination with extensive root size and distribution patterns will increase water uptake capacity as well as water use efficiency.

Typically, under natural field conditions the soil surface dries out more quickly than the deeper soil profile layers. As such, deep rooting is considered an important drought resistance trait and contributes positively to increased water uptake under stress in various turfgrass species (Sheffer et al. 1987; White et al. 2001; Carrow 1996; Qian et al. 1997; Huang and Fry 1998; Bonos and Murphy 1999). It has been reported that turf performance was more consistently associated with root distribution than with total root mass in Kentucky bluegrass (*Poa pratensis* L.) (Keeley and Koski 2002). Better turf performance of Kentucky bluegrass cultivars was associated with increased water uptake activity at 15 to 30 cm, but it was not attributable to differences in root mass within these same layers (Bonos and Murphy 1999). Tall fescue (*Festuca arundinacea* Schreb.), with increased rooting deep in the soil profile, was found to have a greater capacity to exploit deep soil moisture when surface soil moisture was limited than was Kentucky bluegrass, which was reflected in fescue's significantly higher quality ratings, lower leaf-firing ratings, and lower canopy temperatures (Ervin and Koski 1998). Kentucky bluegrass cultivars or selections that were able to exploit soil moisture through increased rooting in the deeper soil profile under heat and drought conditions maintained significantly lower stomatal resistance and cooler canopy temperature (5°C cooler) than intolerant cultivars or selections (Bonos and Murphy 1999).

Deep rooting is associated with increased carbon allocation to roots (Huang and Gao 2000). Development of a deep root system could be related to a faster elongation rate of roots under drying conditions. However, when limited soil water is stored in deeper soil profiles, faster root extension into deeper soil profiles may be detrimental for plants because of rapid depletion of water. In contrast, water will be conserved if the plant has a sparse root system with high hydraulic resistance and slow growth rate with a slow rate of extension. Deep rooting must be coupled with high water use efficiency or water conservation methods for deep rooting to be effective in water savings. Deep roots not only enhance water utilization in deeper soil profiles but also appear to act as a water transport system and can deliver water absorbed from deep in the soil profile to the dry surface soil at night (hydraulic lift) in some plant species. Deep roots of buffalograss (*Buchloe dactyloides* (Nutt.) Engelm.) are capable of hydraulic lift, in which water is absorbed by roots deep in the soil and deposited near the soil surface when there is no transpiration at night (Huang 1999). Water supply from deeper soil profiles helps root survival and nutrient uptake in the surface soil.

The pathway for water movement in a single root is from bulk soil to the rhizosphere, across the rhizosphere and the soil-root interface, across the cortex and the endodermis, and then into the lumen of the xylem. Water then moves through the xylem to stems and leaves. Hydraulic conductivity is a coefficient relating the gradient of water potential to the water flow rate. Root resistance can represent a major limitation on water movement within a plant (Moreshet et al. 1995). Thus, it can have a major influence on leaf water status and, in turn, on plant growth in both moist and dry soil. Hydraulic conductivity varies with root age even within a species. It typically decreases with root age or from the root tip to the base due to the increase in the number of suberized hypodermal and endodermal cells, which have low permeability to water, especially under dry conditions. Differences in root hydraulic conductivity among species may result in differences in water transport to shoots that could influence plant growth and physiological responses during drought stress. In an environment where drought is temporary or soil water is often supplied by irrigation, high root hydraulic conductivity may be advantageous for rapid water uptake and plant growth in dry soils.

Rapid regrowth of existing roots and production of new roots are important for rapid exploitation of water following rainfall or irrigation events. This ability may be expected to confer superior turf performance under transient drought conditions typical in semiarid regions. The continued response to increased water availability is made possible by the appearance of new roots. In some species, new roots are produced within hours after rewetting. The new root growth increases the absorption rate and expands the root system, which increases contact with wet soil. New roots have higher hydraulic conductivity than older roots. Plants in regions where rainfall events are short and sporadic may favor roots that can readily proliferate near the soil surface so that water can be captured before it is evaporated. Species adapted to relatively wet sites where mineral nutrients are limiting and irregularly distributed may also tend to build fine root systems. On the other hand, areas where there are more distinct wet and dry seasons may favor root systems that promote development of a deep root architecture, which should favor substantial investment in large-diameter framework roots that can sustain growth through dry surface layers. In addition, maintaining viable roots during prolonged periods of drought is also an important factor for resumption of water uptake when soil is rewetted after irrigation or rain (Huang 2000).

WATER USE, SHOOT GROWTH, AND PHYSIOLOGICAL CHARACTERISTICS

Of the total amount of water absorbed into a plant and transported to leaves, over 90% is transpired from the leaves and only 1 to 3% of the water is actually used for metabolic processes (Beard 1973; Hopkins 1999). For a turf canopy, some water is also lost through evaporation from the soil. Therefore, turfgrass water use rates are typically quantified by evapotranspiration (ET) rate.

Genetic Variation in Water Use

Turfgrass ET rates vary among species and among cultivars within a species. Typical water use rates range from 3 to 8 mm per day for cool-season turfgrasses and 2 to 5 mm per day for warm-season grasses under nonlimiting soil moisture conditions.

Among cool-season species, tall fescue, creeping bentgrass (*Agrostis stolonifera* L.), perennial ryegrass (*Lolium perenne* L.), annual bluegrass (*Poa annua* L.), and Italian ryegrass (*Lolium multiflorum* L.) have the highest ET rates; Kentucky bluegrass and rough bluegrass (*Poa trivialis* L.) have intermediate rates; and hard fescue (*Festuca longifolia* Thuill.), Chewings fescue (*Festuca rubra* L. ssp. *commutata* Gaud.), and creeping red fescue (*Festuca rubra* L. ssp. *rubra*) have the lowest ET rates. Warm-season grasses that have relatively low ET rates include bermudagrass (*Cynodon* spp.), zoysiagrass (*Zoysia* spp.), and buffalograss. Centipedegrass (*Eremochloa ophiuroides* (Munro) Hack.), seashore paspalum (*Paspalum vaginatum* Swartz.), bahiagrass (*Paspalum notatum* Flugge), and St. Augustinegrass (*Stenotaphrum secundatum* (Walt.) Kuntze.). Cultivars within a species also vary in water use rate, and the variation can range from 20 to 60% (Kjelgren, Rupp, and Kilgren 2000).

Growth Characteristics and Physiological Factors Controlling or Regulating Water Use

Species and cultivar variations in water use rate are largely controlled by genetic variability in growth and metabolic activities. Major growth characteristics associated with water use include leaf morphological and anatomical characteristics, canopy configuration, growth rate, tiller or shoot density, and growth habit (Beard 1973; Huang and Fry 1999). Physiological activities such as hormone synthesis and osmotic adjustment also regulate water use in turfgrass.

Transpiration is the process whereby water is lost from the leaf into the atmosphere as water vapor, mainly through the leaf's surface. Transpiration is a beneficial mechanism used by plants to cool themselves; it also pulls the water stream up the plant for nutrient transport. Conversely, when transpiration occurs at a rate that exceeds the rate of water uptake (for various reasons), wilt and desiccation of the turf occur. Transpiration by individual leaves is mainly controlled by three major factors: the vapor pressure gradient between atmosphere and leaf; boundary layer resistance; and internal leaf diffusion resistance. The vapor pressure gradient is influenced by climatic factors, including temperature, solar radiation, humidity, and wind. Higher temperature, higher light intensity, lower humidity, and higher wind speed increase vapor pressure gradient, and thus enhance transpiration rate. The boundary layer is a layer of undisturbed air on the surface of the leaf that restricts water loss from the leaf. Wider leaves have a thicker boundary layer and greater resistance to water loss. Boundary layer thickness can be affected by wind or anything causing air movement around the leaf, such as mowing. Therefore, high wind and frequent mowing reduce boundary layer resistance and lead to a higher transpiration rate. Internal leaf diffusion resistance is mainly regulated by stomata, cuticle layer thickness, leaf cell density, and leaf thickness. Leaves with larger stomatal openings, thinner cuticles, loosely packed cells, and thinner blades tend to have higher transpiration rates. Stomata transpiration accounts for 90 to 95% of the water loss from a leaf. Cuticular transpiration accounts for 5 to 10% total water loss.

Morphological and growth traits associated with water use

Water loss from a dense turf canopy occurs primarily through transpiration, but the proportion of soil evaporation increases as turf density decreases. The water use by a turf canopy is mainly controlled by the growth rate of the turf, amount of leaf surface area, shoot density, and growth habits, in addition to factors controlling transpiration rate of individual leaves (Huang and Fry 1999). Environment also has significant impact on ET. Generally, turfgrasses with a rapid vertical shoot extension rate tend to have higher water use rates than slower growing or dwarf-type grasses because of increasing leaf area from which transpiration occurs (Shearman and Beard 1973; Kim and Beard 1988). Shoot vertical extension rate was positively correlated with water use rate for 20 Kentucky bluegrass cultivars with an upright growth pattern (Shearman 1986). However, no correlation was found between water use and leaf extension rate within several warm-season turfgrass species that have a prostrate growth habit, such as bermudagrass (Beard et al. 1992) and zoysiagrass (Green et al. 1991). Dense and compact turfgrass canopies have lower water loss from soil evaporation than thin, open canopies. Low ET rates in some Kentucky bluegrass cultivars under well-watered conditions have been attributed to horizontal leaf orientation, high shoot density, slow vertical leaf extension rate, and fine leaf texture (Ebdon and Petrovic 1998).

Better turfgrass performance under drought stress is also positively related to leaf thickness, epicuticular wax content, and tissue density, but it is negatively associated with stomatal density and leaf width in tall fescue cultivars (Fu and Huang 2004). These structural characteristics are major factors affecting evapotranspirational water use. Better dehydration avoidance of *Cynodon* species when compared with *Zoysia* species was attributed to a lower ET due to faster rate of wax formation over the stomata during progressive drought stress (Beard and Sifers 1997). Zoysiagrass genotypes with a high relative water content at zero turgor, high cell wall elasticity, and high apoplastic water fraction demonstrated better recovery from stress and required less supplemental irrigation, suggesting that the improvements in biophysical as well as morphological traits contribute to development of water-conserving zoysiagrass germplasm (White et al. 2001).

Stomatal regulation of water use

Stomatal closure is a key factor regulating plant water use and thus a critical factor controlling plant survival in dry environments. Excessive water loss through transpiration can result in water deficits and desiccation. Rapid stomatal closure may protect plants from being desiccated in water-limiting environments. If transpirational water loss through stomata can be controlled to any extent, it is possible to maintain plant growth with the use of much less water. Abscisic acid (ABA), a plant hormone naturally accumulating in plants experiencing water deficit, has been shown to regulate stomatal closure via its influence on guard cell turgidity (Blackman and Davies 1985). Increased levels of ABA result in loss of turgor pressure in guard cells and thus closing of stomata and water conservation. The importance of ABA as a metabolic factor in the regulation of water use has received great attention in recent years in other species; however, limited information is available on the association of ABA and water use in turfgrass species. In addition, most current research on ABA regulation of water use in turfgrass was performed in controlled environments, and little research has been done on the practical use of ABA to reduce water requirements and enhance drought tolerance in turfgrasses under natural field conditions.

Exogenous foliar application of ABA in drought-stressed turf reduced stomatal conductance, increased plant water use efficiency, and maintained more-turgid, greener leaves (Jiang and Huang 2002; Wang et al. 2003). Earlier research (Stahnke and Beard 1982) reported that ABA reduced transpiration on bentgrass by 59%. Drought-tolerant cultivars of Kentucky bluegrass exhibited higher stomatal sensitivity to changes in leaf ABA content than did drought-sensitive cultivars, which led to earlier stomatal closure, less cell membrane damage, and delay in the decline of overall turfgrass quality (Wang and Huang 2003). The authors concluded that drought tolerance of Kentucky bluegrass was associated with the sensitivity of stomata to increases in ABA production. Kentucky bluegrass cultivars tolerant of drought exhibited a slower ABA accumulation rate than drought-sensitive cultivars during short-term drought stress, suggesting that low accumulation rate of ABA in leaves would be beneficial for the maintenance of photosynthesis during short-term drought and would allow dry matter to accumulate to support plant survival during prolonged drought. These studies suggest that sensitivity of the stomatal complex to ABA accumulation is an important factor for ABA-induced stomatal closure in turfgrass.

While the effect of ABA on stomatal conductance is the most widely reported response of plants to ABA, many other processes of growth and development can also be affected by ABA in the absence of stress, including leaf area and plant height. For a plant growing in a water-limiting environment, which results in higher endogenous ABA levels, those responses to ABA, such as reduced plant size, would help to maintain plant water status by reducing the demand for water.

Osmotic regulation of plant water relations

Cellular hydration status is largely controlled by the level of osmotic adjustment (Nilsen and Orcutt 1996). Osmotic adjustment is the ability of cells to accumulate inorganic and organic solutes that lower osmotic potential when exposed to water stress (Blum 1988). Various solutes, including nonprotein amino acids (e.g., proline), ammonium compounds (e.g., glycine betaine), sugars (e.g., fructans, sucrose), polyols (e.g., mannitol), inorganic ions (e.g., potassium, calcium), organic acids (e.g., malate), and hydrophilic proteins (e.g., late embryogenesis abundant, LEA) are involved in osmotic adjustment (Chaves et al. 2003). The accumulation of inorganic ions and organic solutes such as soluble sugars and proline in leaves has been associated with osmotic adjustment and increased drought tolerance in various turfgrass species, including bentgrass (DaCosta and Huang 2006), Kentucky bluegrass (Jiang and Huang 2001), perennial ryegrass (Thomas 1990), tall fescue (Richardson et al. 1992), and zoysiagrass (Qian and Fry 1997).

Osmotic adjustment facilitates movement of water into the cells and reduces water efflux from cells. It helps to maintain cellular turgor at a given leaf water potential and thus delays wilting of leaves and enables sustained growth at lower plant water status. Osmotic adjustment is one of the most widely used selection criteria in breeding for drought-tolerant plants in various crop species, but breeding efforts using this trait is limited in turfgrass drought tolerance improvement. A study that examined the heritability of osmotic adjustment in perennial ryegrass reported that mature lamina solute potential and meristem solute potential values of drought-stressed plants were highly heritable, and suggests that divergent breeding selection for increasing osmotic adjustment is feasible (Thomas 1990).

Osmotic adjustment is also crucial for maintaining meristem viability under desiccation, which aids in the recovery of function upon dehydration. Upon rehydration, the various solutes are recycled and metabolized which is considered an important energy resource for growth recovery. Species varied with the magnitude of osmotic adjustment, with the ranking of buffalograss being the equal to zoysiagrass, bermudagrass greater than zoysiagrass, and tall fescue greatest of all (Qian and Fry 1997). Qian and Fry found that the recuperative ability of turf quality following rewatering was positively correlated with magnitude of osmotic adjustment.

Plant growth regulators and water use

Plant growth regulators (PGRs), such as growth inhibitors, are widely used in turfgrass management to suppress shoot growth and inflorescence. Plant growth regulators that contribute to the development of a short, compact turf have been shown to reduce ET rates in turfgrass, including trinexapac-ethyl (TE); flurprimidol, alpha-(1-methylethyl)-alpha-[4-(trifluoromethyoxy) phenyl]-5-pyrimidinemethanol; and mefluidide *N*-[2,4-dimethyl-5-[[(trifluoromethyl)sulfonyl]amino] phenyl] acetamide.

Trinexapac-ethyl is one of the most widely used PGRs in the management of both cool-season and warm-season turfgrass species. TE is absorbed quickly by foliage and slows cell elongation by stopping the conversion of one gibberellic acid (GA20) to another [GA1], which is the final step in GA production. The primary sites of GA and subsequent cell elongation inhibition are shoot growing points (shoot basal and intercalary meristems) (Fagerness and Penner 1998). Therefore, TE has been traditionally used to suppress turf vertical growth. Recent research has reported that along with growth inhibition, TE affects a number of other turf morphological and physiological characteristics. Turf density may increase with repeated applications in some turfgrass species (Stier and Rogers 2001), which could be due to enhanced lateral growth of stolons and rhizomes (McCullough et al. 2006) and increased tiller production (Beasley and Branham 2007). Turf treated with TE normally turns darker green; researchers have determined that the chlorophyll content increases, and there is a higher concentration in the smaller, more compact leaves (Stier and Rogers 2001; Ervin and Koski 2001; Heckman et al. 2001; McCullough et al. 2006). It has been reported that TE may increase overall photochemical activity in creeping bentgrass (Zhang and Schmidt 2000). TE regulation of growth and physiological characteristics of turfgrass may contribute to its positive effects on the reduction in water use in turfgrass.

Research has shown that application of TE may reduce water consumption in various turf species, possibly resulting from effects on growth inhibition. The ET rate in Kentucky bluegrass and tall fescue was reduced when TE was applied to well-irrigated turfgrass (Ervin and Koski 2001; Marcum and Jiang 1997). Foliar TE treatments prior to the onset of drought increased the turf quality of perennial ryegrass during dry-down in a greenhouse study by slowing water depletion from the containers; however, the authors did not observe the positive effects of TE in a nonirrigated field trial (Jiang and Fry 1998). A growth chamber study that examined effects of preconditioning of creeping bentgrass following three applications of TE (applied biweekly) on drought responses found that TE pretreatment prolonged turfgrass survival of drought stress by suppressing shoot vertical growth and slowing soil water depletion prior to stress, as well as by sustaining growth and photosynthetic activity during drought stress (McCann and Huang 2008). However, under combined heat and drought stress conditions, TE-treated turf had a higher ET rate than untreated turf (McCann and Huang 2007). Higher ET may help plants maintain the transpirational cooling mechanism and avoid heat stress. Improved water relations under TE were also demonstrated by the maintenance of a higher leaf relative water content in TE-treated turf than in untreated turf. TE pre-treated creeping bentgrass also maintained better leaf hydration through osmotic adjustment.

The positive effects of TE on turf performance in water-limiting environments may not be related to changes in root growth and water uptake, because the data on root growth are inconsistent. Several studies have reported no effects on rooting of perennial ryegrass (Jiang and Fry 1998) and creeping bentgrass (Fagerness and Yelverton 2001), a reduction in tall fescue (Marcum and Jiang 1997) and Kentucky bluegrass (Beasley and Branham 2007), and increases in root growth in zoysiagrass (Qian and Engelke 1999) and bermudagrass (Baldwin et al. 2006).

Field research investigating TE effects on turfgrass water use is limited, and most of the studies were conducted in controlled-environment conditions. A greenhouse study examining ET rate for tall fescue treated with TE at 370 mg l^{-1} showed significant reduction (11%) in ET over a 6-week period (Marcum and Jiang 1997). In another greenhouse study, it was found that a mixed stand of Kentucky bluegrass and tall fescue used 20% less water than the control within a 4-week period (King et al. 1997). A field study using lysimeters showed that application of TE (0.27 kg a.i./ha^{-1}) three times per year at 6-week intervals reduced weekly ET in Kentucky bluegrass in 5 out of a total of 34 weeks (Ervin and Koski 2001).

Current studies suggest that TE could be a potentially effective tool for managing turf with limited irrigation. Prestress conditioning of turf with TE seems to be more effective than applying TE at the onset of or during drought stress. TE can be applied to turf at reduced rates more frequently before a dry period is anticipated or prior to reducing irrigation. The influence of TE on turf water use rates seems to be mainly related to the reduction in water demand due to the inhibition of vertical shoot growth and the production of smaller and more compact leaves, which may reduce water loss through transpiration. However, more investigation is needed to reveal other possible explanations that may exist.

RESEARCH METHODS AND TECHNIQUES FOR THE ASSESSMENT OF PLANT WATER RELATIONS

Quantification of plant water relations is important for understanding physiological processes controlling water status and water movement through the soil-plant-atmosphere continuum. Many methods and instruments have been developed for measuring water status, water uptake, and water requirements of plants. The theories of operation and pros and cons of different methods have been described in detail (see Kirkham 2005). This section introduces several methods that are applicable to turfgrasses.

Plant Water Status

The water status of plant tissues is an important indicator for plant heath, especially under environmental stress conditions. Various methods are used to evaluate plant water status. Water potential and relative water content (RWC) are the two most widely used parameters for the measurement of plant water status.

Water potential (ψ) is the measure of the chemical potential or free energy of water in a system relative to pure water (chemical potential = 0). Water potential consists of three components: osmotic potential (ψ_o), turgor pressure (ψ_p), and matric potential (ψ_m). Osmotic potential is regulated by the accumulation of dissolved solutes, which reduce the free energy of water and therefore contribute to lowering ψ. Turgor pressure is determined by water availability and cell wall elasticity, which is positively related to ψ. Matric potential results from the surfaces of macromolecules (e.g., cellulose) exerting an attractive force on water, which lowers the free energy of water and thus leads to lower ψ. Matric potential is usually a minor component of ψ and is often ignored. The absolute level of water potential is used to measure the water status of plant tissues. Water potentials in plant tissues are usually negative because of the large quantities of dissolved solutes in cells. Water potential gradient is the driving force for water fluxes through a plant, which has proved especially useful in understanding water movement within plants, between the soil and roots for water uptake, and between the leaves and the atmosphere for transpiration.

Two commonly used techniques for measuring plant water potential are the pressure chamber and the thermocouple psychrometer (Kirkham 2005). A pressure chamber is a steel chamber that can be pressurized, usually with nitrogen. This instrument may be used to measure the water potential of leaves, stems, and taproot systems, but in turf it is used primarily for measuring the water potential of leaves. An excised leaf is placed in the chamber with the open end of the leaf exposed through a hole in the lid. The sample is pressurized, and the pressure that is required to force water to appear on the open end of the leaf is assumed to be equivalent to the water potential of the tissue.

Thermocouple psychrometry is a technique that infers the water potential of the liquid phase of a sample from measurements within the vapor phase that is in equilibrium with the sample. When plant tissues are sealed into a thermocouple chamber containing air, water from the tissues will evaporate until the partial pressure of the vapor in the air equals the vapor pressure of the tissue. By measuring the humidity of the air, the vapor pressure of the tissue can be determined and the tissue water potential can be estimated. Thermocouple psychrometers can be used to measure water potential of any plant parts, as well as soil or any substances containing water. Typical leaf water potential values are between 0 and –1.0 MPa for well-watered plants and from –1.0 to –2.0 MPa under mild water stress. The leaf water potential of several warm-season grass species was found to be between –0.5 and –1.5 MPa under well-watered conditions (Barker et al. 1993). The leaf water potential at zero turgor for zoysiagrass ranges from –1.76 to –2.59 MPa (White et al. 2001).

Relative water content is a good indicator of plant water status. It represents the absolute content of water in fresh plant tissues relative to the maximum water content in the tissues at full turgidity. It is the most widely used indicator of water status for leaves. Leaf RWC is calculated using the following formula:

$$\text{RWC (\%)} = [(\text{fresh weight} - \text{dry weight}) \div (\text{turgid weight} - \text{dry weight})] \times 100$$

with turgid weight being determined after leaves reach full hydration by soaking them in water for a certain time. Typical values of leaf RWC are between 85 and 95% in turgid and transpiring leaves. Leaf RWC declines to 40 to 50% in severely desiccated leaves and even lower levels in dying leaves. Leaf wilting has been observed in some turfgrass species when RWC drops to below 70 to 80%. In Kentucky bluegrass, turf growth could not be fully recovered upon rewatering if RWC declined to below 25% during drought stress (Huang and Wang 2005). The values of RWC indicating the severity of water deficit may vary with turfgrass species and cultivars due to genetic variations in drought resistance.

Water Use Rate

Transpiration rate

The transpiration rate is often used to determine the water use rate of individual leaves or single plants. The transpiration rate is also a good indicator of the physiological status of individual leaves or the entire plant, because only actively growing plants or fully turgid leaves exhibit maximum transpiration.

The most widely used technique for transpiration measurement is the steady state porometer. Steady state porometers measure the flow rate of dry air with a fixed relative humidity that is just sufficient to balance the transpirational water flux out of a leaf that is placed in a cuvette. The transpiration rate is calculated as:

T = [(water vapor density in cuvette – water vapor density of dry air entering cuvette) × volumetric flow rate of dry air] ÷ by leaf area enclosed in cuvette.

Steady state porometers also measure stomatal conductance, an indicator of stomatal opening or closure. It should be noted that steady state porometers are limited to measuring the transpiration rate and stomatal conductance of individual leaves and are not suitable for taking measurements of the turf canopy.

When stomata are open in well-watered plants, transpirational water loss leads to cooling and a lower canopy temperature of the plant. In contrast, when a plant suffers water deficit, stomata are closed and evaporative cooling via transpiration is significantly reduced, leading to an increase in canopy temperature. Therefore, canopy temperature can also be used as an indicator of transpiration and the water status of a plant (Kirkham 2005). Canopy temperature can be measured using infrared thermometers. Indexes such as the crop water stress index (CWSI) have been developed using canopy air temperature differences to quantify crop water stress and to provide guidelines for irrigation scheduling. The CWSI is an index of the level of water deficit using a measure of plant temperature. When a plant is transpiring fully, the leaf temperature is 1° to 4°C below air temperature and CWSI is 0. As the transpiration decreases, the leaf temperature rises and can reach 4° to 6°C above the air temperature; when the plant is no longer transpiring, the CWSI is 1. Several studies have suggested that CWSI could be used for irrigation scheduling in turfgrass species such as Kentucky bluegrass (Throssell et al. 1987), bermudagrass (Jalali-Farahani et al. 1993), and tall fescue (Al-Faraj et al. 2001). However, CWSI values vary with plant species, cultural practices, and climatic conditions.

Evapotranspiration rate

The most widely used parameter for quantifying turfgrass water use is the ET rate, which is the sum of water loss from transpiration of the plants and from evaporation of the soil. Several techniques are available for measuring ET: lysimeters, atmometers, and empirical models.

Lysimeters are considered the standard for making ET measurements. A lysimeter is a container, which can vary in size, that is filled with soil whose surface is cultivated. Lysimeters may be placed above the ground or buried into the ground with its turf canopy level with the turf canopy of the field. The turf in the lysimeter is managed with the same practices as the surrounding turf in the field. The evapotranspiration rate can be estimated from the change in the weight of the lysimeter within a given time interval.

Lysimeters directly measure actual ET for a given area of turf; atmometers measure evaporation of water and then correlate this to estimate turf ET. The most well-known atmometer is an evaporation pan filled with water. Daily measurements of water loss from the pan can be converted to turf ET using a crop coefficient. Coefficients vary greatly depending on turf species and environmental conditions. The evaporation pan method tends to overestimate ET, since it does not include the resistance of water loss from the turf canopy. A second type of atmometer commonly used to estimate turf ET is the Bellani plate. This apparatus consists of a container filled with water and capped with a porous porcelain plate. As water evaporates from the porous plate, the volume of water in the container decreases. The change in water volume in the container gives an estimate of ET for the turf surface where the apparatus is installed. Bellani plates are portable and make it possible to monitor ET in multiple locations.

The ET rate can also be estimated using empirical models, such as Penman model, that typically come with weather stations. These models are equations that incorporate climatic data, such as temperature, soil radiation, relative humidity, and wind speed to generate a predicted ET value. Weather-station-estimated empirical ET estimates may differ from turf ET readings primarily because of microclimatic differences between the weather station site and areas where turf is maintained. Weather-station-estimated empirical ET from the Penman model was higher than ET estimated from atmometer evaporation, particularly when ET was more than 4 mm/day^{-1} (Jiang et al. 1998).

Soil Water Availability and Water Uptake

Plant water status, water uptake, and water use rate are largely controlled by the availability of soil water. Knowledge of the soil water content provides guidelines on when and how much water to use in turfgrass irrigation. The water uptake or depletion rate of individual plants or a turf canopy can be estimated using the changes in soil water content within a given time interval.

The soil water content can be measured using tensiometers, gypsum blocks, or time domain reflectometry (TDR) (Kirkham 2005). Tensiometers consist of a porous ceramic cup that is fed by a column of water. The ceramic end is buried in the soil at the preferred depth and allowed to reach equilibrium with the soil water content. In a drier soil, more water exits the ceramic cup, creating a vacuum that is recorded by a gauge on the opposite end of the device. Tensiometers are not effective when the soil dries extensively and are better for use on relatively high-maintenance turf. Gypsum blocks use electrical conductivity to provide an estimate of soil water content. Two electric probes are buried in a block of gypsum, which is set at the preferred soil depth. In time, the gypsum block comes into equilibrium with the soil water. The soil water content can be positively correlated to electrical conductivity readings. Time domain reflectometry (TDR) is one of the newest technologies becoming widely used for the measurement of soil water content. It provides accurate measurements over a wide range by measuring the dielectric constant of soil, which is directly affected by its water content. TDR probes of various lengths may be buried in the soil at different depths, which allows the soil water content to be measured nondestructively. The dynamic change in soil water content can be used to calculate water uptake or depletion rate of plants.

CONCLUSION

Plant water relations are a dynamic process that involves absorption of water from the soil, water translocation throughout the plant, and water loss to the environment principally in transpiration from individual plants or evapotranspiration from a turfgrass canopy. Maintaining a balance between water absorption and water loss, or water use, is critical for cellular hydration that controls cell growth and elongation. Competition for water is most effective with an extensive, highly conductive, viable root system. In a drought-prone environment where turfgrass plants rely heavily on water stored deep in the soil profile, plants must use water sparingly so that sufficient water is left in the soil to ensure long-term survival. Stomatal regulation, growth control, and osmotic adjustment are major traits associated with water conservation. Understanding the basic concepts and principles for plant water relations and a knowledge of the methodologies for the evaluation of various physiological processes controlling water uptake and water use are critical for developing water conservation strategies in turfgrass management, as well as for genetic modification of turfgrasses to develop water-saving turfgrass species and cultivars through genetic engineering or traditional breeding.

REFERENCES

Al-Faraj, A., G. E. Meyer, and G. L. Horst. 2001. A crop water stress index for tall fescue (*Fetusca arundinacea* Schreb.) irrigation decision-making: A traditional method. Computers and Electronics in Agriculture 31:107–124.

Baldwin, C. M., H. Liu, L. McCarty, and W. L. Bauerle. 2006. Effects of trinexapac-ethyl on the salinity tolerance of two ultradwarf bermudagrass cultivars. HortScience 41:808–814.

Barker, D. J., C. Y. Sullivan, and L. E. Moser. 1993. Water deficit effects on osmotic potential, cell wall elasticity, and proline in five forage grasses. Agronomy Journal 85:270–275.

Beard, J. B. 1973. Turfgrass: Science and culture. Englewood Cliffs, NJ: Prentice-Hall.

Beard, J. B., and S. I. Sifers. 1997. Genetic diversity in dehydration avoidance and drought resistance within the *Cynodon* and *Zoysia* species. International Turfgrass Society Research Journal 8:603–610.

Beard, J. B., R. L. Green, and S. I. Sifers. 1992. Evapotranspiration and leaf extension rates of 24 well-watered turf-type *Cynodon* genotypes. HortScience 27:986–998.

Beasley, J. S., and B. E. Branham. 2007. Trinexapac-ethyl and paclobutrazol affect Kentucky bluegrass single-leaf carbon exchange rates and plant growth. Crop Science 47:132–138.

Blackman, P. G., and W. J. Davies. 1985. Root to shoot communication in maize plants of the effects of soil drying. Journal of Experimental Botany 36:39–48.

Blum, A. 1988. Plant breeding for stress environments. Boca Raton, FL: CRC Press.

Bonos, S., and J. A. Murphy. 1999. Growth responses and performance of Kentucky bluegrass under summer stress. Crop Science 39:770–774.

Carrow, R. N. 1996. Drought avoidance characteristics of diverse tall fescue cultivars. Crop Science 36:371–377.

Chaves, M. M., J. P. Maroco, and J. S. Pereira. 2003. Understanding plant responses to drought from genes to the whole plant. Functional Plant Biology 30:239–264.

DaCosta, M., and B. Huang. 2006. Osmotic adjustment associated with variation in bentgrass tolerance to drought stress. Journal of the American Society for Horticultural Science 131:338–344.

Ebdon, J. S., and A. M. Petrovic. 1998. Morphological and growth characteristics of low- and high-water-use Kentucky bluegrass cultivars. Crop Science 38:143–152.

———. 1998. Drought avoidance aspects and crop coefficients of Kentucky bluegrass and tall fescue turfs in the semiarid West. Crop Science 38:788–795.

Ervin, E. H., and A. J. Koski. 2001. Trinexapac-ethyl effects on Kentucky bluegrass evapotranspiration. Crop Science 41:247–250.

Fagerness, M. J., and D. Penner. 1998. Evaluation of V-10029 and trinexapac-ethyl for annual bluegrass seedhead suppression and growth regulation of five cool-season turfgrass species. Weed Technology 12:436–440.

Fagerness, M. J., and F. H. Yelverton. 2001. Plant growth regulator and mowing height effects on seasonal root growth of Penncross creeping bentgrass. Crop Science 41:1901–1905.

Fu, J., and B. Huang. 2004. Leaf characteristics associated with drought resistance in tall fescue cultivars. Acta Horticulturae 661:233–240.

Green, R. L., S. I. Sifers, and J. B. Beard. 1991. Evapotranspiration rates of eleven zoysiagrass genotypes. HortScience 26:264–266.

Heckman, N. L., T. E. Elthon, G. L. Horst, and R. E. Gaussoin. 2001. Influence of trinexapac-ethyl on respiration of isolated wheat mitochondria. Crop Science 42:423–427.

Hopkins, W. G. 1999. Introduction to plant physiology. 2nd ed. New York: Wiley.

Huang, B. 1999. Water relations and root activities of *Buchloe dactyloides* and *Zoysia japonica* in response to localized soil drying. Plant and Soil 208:179–186.

———. 2000. Role of root morphological and physiological characteristics in drought resistance of plants. In R. E. Wilkinson, ed., Plant-environment interactions. New York: Marcel Dekker.

———. 2008. Turfgrass water requirements and factors affecting water usage. In J. B. Beard and M. Kenna, eds., Water quality and quantity issues for turfgrasses in urban landscapes. Ames, IA: Council for Agricultural Science and Technology. 193–204.

Huang B., and J. D. Fry. 1998. Root anatomical, physiological and morphological responses to drought stress for tall fescue cultivars. Crop Science 38:1017–1022.

———. 1999. Turfgrass evapotranspiration. In M. B. Kirkham, ed., Water use in crop production. New York: Food Products Press.

Huang, B., and H. Gao. 2000. Root physiological characteristics associated with drought resistance in tall fescue cultivars. Crop Science 40:196–203.

Huang, B., and Z. Wang. 2005. Physiological recovery of Kentucky bluegrass from drought stress. International Turfgrass Society Research Journal 10:867–873.

Huang, B., R. R. Duncan, and R. N. Carrow. 1997. Drought-resistance mechanisms of seven warm-season turfgrasses under surface soil drying. II: Root aspects. Crop Science 37:1863–1869.

Jalali-Farahani, H. R., D. C. Slack, D. M. Kopec, and A. D. Matthias. 1993. Crop water-stress index models for bermudagrass turf: A comparison. Agronomy Journal 85:1210–1217.

Jiang, H., and J. D. Fry. 1998. Drought responses of perennial ryegrass treated with plant growth regulators. HortScience 33:270–273.

Jiang, Y., and B. Huang. 2001. Osmotic adjustment associated with drought-preconditioning enhanced heat tolerance in Kentucky bluegrass. Crop Science 41:1168–1173.

Jiang, H., J. D. Fry, and S. C. Wiest. 1998. Variability in turfgrass water requirements on a golf course. American Society of Horticultural Science 33:590–606.

———. 2002. Protein alterations in tall fescue in response to drought stress and abscisic acid. Crop Science 42:202–207.

Keeley, S. J., and A. J. Koski. 2002. Root distribution and ET as related to drought avoidance in *Poa pratensis.* In E. Thain, ed., Science and golf IV: Proceedings of the World Scientific Congress of Golf, St Andrews, Scotland. London: Routledge. 555–563.

Kim, K. S., and J. B. Beard. 1988. Comparative turfgrass evapotranspiration rates and associated plant morphological characteristics. Crop Science 28:328–331.

King, R. W., C. Blundell, L. T. Evans, L. N. Mander, and T. J. Wood. 1997. Modified gibberellins retard growth of cool-season turfgrasses. Crop Science 37:1878–1883.

Kirkham, M. B. 2005. Principles of soil and plant water relations. New York: Academic Press.

Kjelgren R., L. Rupp, and D. Kilgren. 2000. Water conservation in urban landscapes. HortScience 35:1037–1040.

Lackman, P. G., and W. J. Davies. 1985. Root to shoot communication in maize plants of the effects of soil drying. Journal of Experimental Botany 36:39–48.

Marcum, K. B., and H. Jiang. 1997. Effects of plant growth regulators on tall fescue rooting and water use. Journal of Turfgrass Management 2:13–27.

McCann, S., and B. Huang. 2007. Effects of trinexapac-ethyl foliar application on creeping bentgrass responses to combined drought and heat stress. Crop Science 47:2121–2128.

———. 2008. Drought responses of Kentucky bluegrass and creeping bentgrass as affected by abscisic acid and trinexapac-ethyl. Journal of American Society of Horticultural Science 133:20–26.

McCullough, P., P. Liu, L. McCarty, T. Whitwell, and J. E. Toler. 2006. Bermudagrass putting green growth, color and nutrient partitioning influenced by nitrogen and trinexapac-ethyl. Crop Science 46:1515–1525.

Moreshet, S., B. Huang, and M. Huck. 1995. Water permeability of plant roots. In Y. Waisel, A. Eshel, and U. Kafkafi, eds., Plant roots: The hidden half. 2nd ed. New York: Marcel Dekker. 659–678.

Nilsen, E. T., and D. M. Orcut. 1996. Physiology of plants under stress: Abiotic factors. New York: Wiley.

Qian, Y. L., and M. C. Engelke. 1999. Influence of trinexapac-ethyl on diamond zoysiagrass in a shade environment. Crop Science 39:202–208.

Qian, Y. L., and J. D. Fry. 1997. Water relations and drought tolerance of four turfgrasses. Journal of the American Society for Horticultural Science 122:129–133.

Qian, Y. L., J. D. Fry, and W. S. Upham. 1997. Rooting and drought avoidance of warm-season turfgrasses and tall fescue in Kansas. Crop Science 37:905–910.

Richardson, M. D., G. W. Chapman, C. S. Hoveland, and C. W. Bacon. 1992. Sugar alcohols in endophyte-infected tall fescue under drought. Crop Science 32:1060–1061.

Shearman, R. C. 1986. Kentucky bluegrass cultivar evapotranspiration rates. HortScience 24:767–769.

———. 2008. Turfgrass cultural practices for water conservation. In J. B. Beard and M. Kenna, eds., Water quality and quantity issues for turfgrasses in urban landscapes. Ames, IA: Council for Agricultural Science and Technology. P. 205–222.

Shearman, R. C., and J. B. Beard. 1973. Environmental and cultural preconditioning effects on the water use rate of *Agrostis palustris* Huds., cultivar Penncross. Crop Science 13:424–427.

Sheffer, K. M., J. H. Dunn, and D. D. Minner. 1987. Summer drought response and rooting depth of three cool-season turfgrasses. HortScience 22:296–297.

Stahnke, G. K., and J. B. Beard. 1982. An assessment of antitranspirants on creeping bentgrass and bermudagrass turfs. In Texas turfgrass research. College Station: Texas Agricultural Experiment Station. 36–37.

Stier, J. C., and J. N. Rogers. 2001. Trinexapac-ethyl and iron effects on supine and Kentucky bluegrasses under low irradiance. Crop Science 41:457–465.

Thomas, H. 1990. Osmotic adjustment in *Lolium perenne*; its heritability and the nature of solute accumulation. Annals of Botany 66:521–530.

Throssell, C. S., R. N. Carrow, and G. A. Milliken. 1987. Canopy temperature based irrigation scheduling indices for Kentucky bluegrass turf. Crop Science 27:126–131.

Wang, Z., and B. Huang. 2003. Genotypic variation in abscisic acid accumulation, water relations, and gas exchange for Kentucky bluegrass exposed to drought stress. Journal of the American Society for Horticultural Science 128:349–355.

Wang, Z., B. Huang, and Q. Xu. 2003. Effects of abscisic acid on drought responses of Kentucky bluegrass. Journal of the American Society for Horticultural Science 128:36–41.

White, R. H., M. C. Engelke, S. J. Morton, and B. A. Ruemmele. 1993. Irrigation water requirements of zoysiagrass. International Turfgrass Society Research Journal 7:587–593.

White, R. H., M. C. Engelke, S. J. Anderson, B. A. Ruemmele, K. B. Marcum, and G. R. Taylor. 2001. Zoysiagrass water relations. Crop Science 41:133–138.

Youngner, V. B. 1985. Physiology of water use and water stress. In V. A. Gibeault and S. T. Cockerham, eds., Turfgrass water conservation. Oakland: University of California Division of Agriculture and Natural Resources Publication 21405. 37–43.

Zhang, X., and R. E. Schmidt. 2000. Application of trinexapac-ethyl and propiconazole enhances photochemical activity in creeping bentgrass. *(Agrostis stoloniferous* var. *palustris)*. Journal of the American Society for Horticultural Science 125:47–51.

6

Modified Root Zones for Efficient Turfgrass Water Use

Paul E. Rieke and James A. Murphy

SOILS AND TURF

Manipulated soil profiles are common in the construction of landscapes. The resultant soil physical properties of manmade profiles can affect water use. Much research on soil physical properties in turfgrass systems has focused on drainage, and for good reason. Soil surface compaction and poor drainage can dramatically affect the use and maintenance of turf areas, particularly those that are highly trafficked (Waddington 1992). More limited attention has been given to the manipulation of soil physical properties for water conservation in turfgrass systems.

One important component of a quality turf is uniformity. Several factors contribute to turf uniformity, among which are the physical properties of the soil. Uniform soil conditions make it easier to provide uniform turf and thus more efficient use of irrigation. While turf sites may have uniform soils if there was little movement of native soil or if soils were intentionally modified, many sites have highly variable soil conditions. Soils modified by humans are referred to as anthropogenic soils (Evans et al. 2000). Examples include home lawns or grounds around buildings where topsoil has been removed or mixed with subsoil, cemeteries, and roadsides. Parks and sports fields can have uniform soils, depending on the natural lay of the land and whether significant amounts of soil were moved during establishment.

Golf course fairway soils could be highly variable if the native soil varies across the entire course or if a large amount of soil was moved during shaping, especially in the more dramatic designs followed in recent years. When soil variability exists on any site, greater attention must be given to site-specific irrigation planning, using knowledge of soil properties such as texture, structure, organic matter content, compaction, drainage, slope, fertility and pH, as well as shade and air movement.

Soils on home lawns and grounds around buildings often present challenges due to variability because of compaction of soil during construction (Craul 1992), variable mixing of topsoil and subsoil, and removal of all topsoil, leaving subsoils in which to grow turf and landscape plants. In addition, sloping sites and landscapes with unusual shapes create a challenge for the design and operation of an efficient irrigation system. Sod is frequently established on compacted subsoils, resulting in limited rooting into the underlying soil. Under these conditions a significant thatch layer can develop, particularly when excess water is applied. Roots tend to grow in the thatch layer rather than into the soil, reducing the amount of water available for turf use.

Water relations in soils depend on the retention and transmission properties of a given soil (McIntyre and Jakobsen 2000; Carrow and Duncan 1998; McCoy 2008). Water is held in pore spaces by the forces of adhesion (water attracted to soil particles) and cohesion (water layers attracted to adjacent water layers). The outer water layers are held less strongly and are more subject to the forces of gravity (fig. 6.1). This can be more scientifically described using the concept of soil water potential: the energy with which soil holds water. The water potential is a sum of the matric potential (the energy with which the water is held by the soil), the osmotic potential (the impact of soluble salts that can reduce availability of water to plants), and the pressure potential (0 in unsaturated soils). Thus, in most soils the matric potential and the effect of soluble salts control how much water is available to roots.

Sand-based profiles are widely used for highly trafficked turf areas such as golf putting greens and other sports turfs (Waddington 1992). Sand particle size distribution and materials for amending root zones should normally be evaluated for use in constructing highly trafficked sites to ensure adequate water flow (i.e., infiltration, percolation, and drainage) and appropriate amounts of water retention (Davis et al. 1970; USGA Green Section Staff 1993, 2004). Water conservation is the purpose of profile designs that encourage development of a water table (Miller 1964, 1969; Miller and Bunger 1963); however, this purpose is often poorly understood by many practitioners. Water distribution within these sand-based profiles varies dramatically over relatively small distances (Bigelow et al. 2001). Under idealized conditions of limited slope, these root zones, when drained to field capacity, will have water content distribution ranging from unsaturated and well-aerated at surface depths to nearly saturated conditions at the lowest depths.

PUTTING GREEN CONSTRUCTION

Soils are typically modified for most putting greens, some tees on golf courses, and some sports fields. Putting green soils have been modified for many years. A good review of the history of construction methods for improving putting green soils (Hurdzan 2004) describes early attempts at layering soils to impact water retention and movement in soils. Dr. Marvin Ferguson was instrumental in developing ideas about soil and water relationships in putting greens (Ferguson 1965). He and several others at

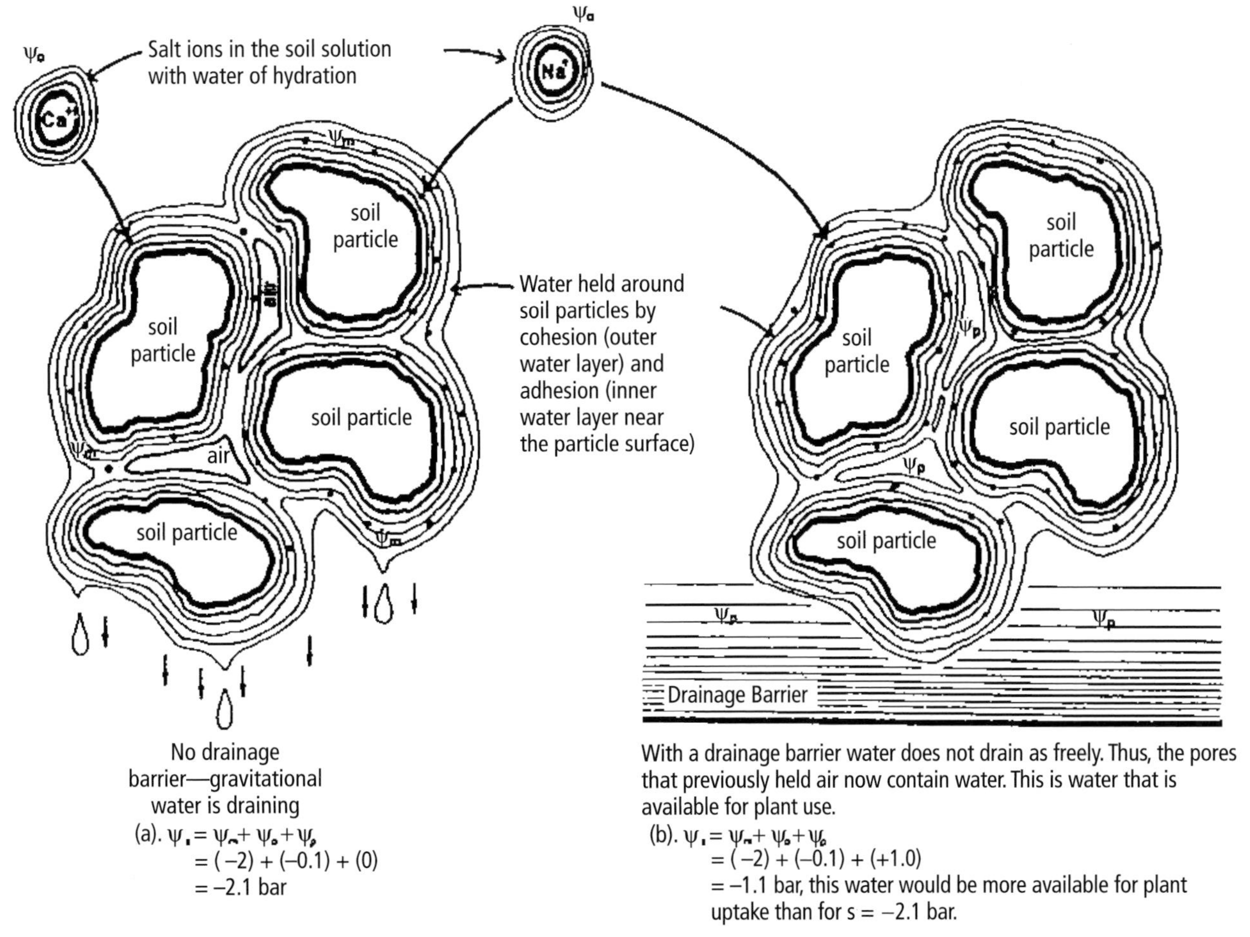

FIGURE 6.1. ■ Soil water potential (ψ_s) and its components: ψ_m = matric potential (water is less free due to cohesive and adhesive forces associated with the soil particles); ψ_o = osmotic potential (water is less free due to cohesive and adhesive forces associated with the soil solutes or ions); and ψ_p = pressure potential (water is more available or free for plant use since it is not being retained by any forces attracting individual water molecules). $\psi_s = \psi_m + \psi_o + \psi_p$. *Source:* Carrow and Duncan 1998, 9.

Texas A&M University (Kunze et al. 1957; Ferguson et al. 1960) expanded on the concept of placing a finer-textured sand over coarser material (sand or gravel) to impact the water status of soils. The principle is based on the fact that finer-textured soil particles hold water so strongly that gravitational forces are unable to pull the water downward until the soil approaches a saturated condition. This zone of higher water content in the top mix at the interface with the gravel layer has been called a perched or suspended water table. Soil physicists prefer the terms "textural discontinuity" or "layered profile" since this wet zone is not truly saturated.

Under the leadership of Dr. Ferguson the first USGA specifications were developed for construction of putting greens (Ferguson 1965), prescribing a 3-layer profile: top mix, an intermediate sand layer, and gravel. Other iterations followed. Based on research at a number of institutions and on field observations, the latest specifications (USGA Green Section Staff 2004; Moore 2004) were developed using a 2-layer profile specifying a sand root zone mix meeting particular ranges in physical properties. The mix is placed over appropriately sized gravel. Newer flat drainage pipe may be installed in the gravel layer, but traditional round tile must be installed in trenches in the subgrade and covered by the gravel layer. The USGA specifications have been used with success in the construction and maintenance of thousands of new putting greens. The details are sometimes followed carefully, sometimes not; if not, changes can occur in how much water is available to turf and in drainage patterns in the greens.

Based on the water movement visuals (Gardner 1960) that have been used in teaching soils for years, many have assumed that a true perched water table develops at the interface between the root zone mix and the underlying layer. In a flat landscape or green, a case can be made that a suspended water table can exist, holding some water that is available to roots depending on the particle size and depth of the mix. However, if the root zone mix is too deep, very little to no water held above the gravel layer would be directly accessible to roots. Capillary rise can provide limited upward movement of water to roots in finer sands depending on depth of the sand; capillary rise is limited in coarser sands (McCoy 2008).

Among scientists addressing the matter of simplifying green construction as it affects soil moisture were Davis and Madison at the University of California, Davis. Their approach has a 1-layer system consisting of well-draining sand matching specific physical properties that is placed over subsoil (Davis et al. 1990). Drain tile is installed in trenches in the subsoil and covered with pea gravel. The water held at the bottom of the root zone is more typical of a perched water table if there is very limited or no drainage into the underlying soil. Many greens have been successfully constructed at cheaper cost using this technique.

Ed McCoy and coworkers at Ohio State University have provided good insight into what happens to water in these putting greens and how much water is available to plants. They studied water retention in and drainage from 1- and 2-layer profiles using long metal drainage beds equipped with drain lines across the slope and soil water monitoring devices (Prettyman and McCoy 2002). Two sand mixes meeting USGA specifications were used, one at the finer end of the range, and one coarser. In addition they compared water relations in beds either level or sloped at 4%. The 2-layer bed met the USGA specifications, while the 1-layer bed did not completely fit the California green specifications. When the beds were flat the USGA profiles drained faster and had more uniform soil water levels across the drainage beds than did the 1-layer construction. The 1-layer profiles showed the effect of tile spacing, with less water available in the surface directly above the tile lines. Water retention in the root zone was most uniform in both construction types when the beds were flat.

Imposing slope on the beds increased the rate of drainage from both 1- and 2-layer systems (Prettyman and McCoy 2002, 2003a, 2003b). The 1-layer beds drained more slowly than the 2-layer system. When sloped, some water moved downslope because of the hydraulic gradient. This resulted in the greatest volume of water draining from tile in the beds occurring at the lowest elevation of the beds. Drainage from the 2-layer (USGA) greens tended to be independent of the sand mix, while the 1-layer system drained slower with the finer sand mix. Turf suffered water stress first at the highest elevations with the coarser sand in beds with a slope of 4%. When sloped, soil water levels were again more uniform in the 2-layer profile. Prettyman and McCoy proposed that the 1-layer profile holds more water for turf than does the 2-layer profile, and that in sloping USGA greens there is only a short-term perched water table effect because of the downslope movement of water. An interesting animated computer simulation has been created that predicts water flow in layered and in nonlayered (native soil) greens (McCoy and McCoy 2006). From a practical perspective, the 2-layer USGA construction could be especially useful when rapid drainage is desired, such as in regions where high-rainfall events occur or where leaching of soluble salts is necessary. For lower-cost construction or in low-rainfall areas, the 1-layer California construction could be employed.

Unfortunately, some golf course architects have taken liberties with the depth of the top mix in order to achieve a final creative touch when shaping greens. Sandy root zone depths have been found to vary from 200 to over 500 mm (Kussow 2000). The deepest mix is usually at the highest location on the green, resulting in greater water stress and development of localized dry spots. If the top mix is too shallow there can be practical difficulty in properly placing the cup (hole liner). From a soils perspective, if the sand top mix is too shallow in the lowest parts of the green, wet areas could develop due to limited drainage: there is not adequate depth for the effect of gravity to pull water from the surface layer. In such areas the lack of adequate oxygen (anaerobiosis) enhances the development of the condition black layer (see the section later in this chapter). To address the effect of variable depth of the root zone mix, water relations were studied in 2-layer (USGA) sloping profiles with either the standard 300 mm depth or a modified profile with 200 mm of top mix at the apex of the slope and 400 mm at the lowest elevation of the root zone (Leinauer et al. 2001a; Frank et al. 2005). Soil water was monitored during dry-down periods following saturation. Water contents in the surface 100 mm in the modified profile were more uniform across the slope than in the standard construction design (fig. 6.2). Some of the water moved down to the toe slope at the lowest elevation of the modified root zone profile. The greater depth of soil mix in the areas of lowest elevation in the modified construction allowed sufficient air entry into the surface 100 mm, resulting in greater water uniformity across the green. Adding peat or soil to sand resulted in less variation in soil water levels compared with pure sand greens (Frank et al. 2005).

Theoretically, this modification of the USGA specifications could result in more efficient use of water on putting greens. Objections to following these modifications of USGA specifications have been raised by golf course architects and builders, but the principle could be applied by simply making the top mix 350 to 400 mm deep only in the lowest area of the green. This would allow for some artistic change in putting green shape, yet retain adequate depth of root zone mix for drainage.

Systems that can either move air into the base of a sand root zone or provide a vacuum that pulls water from the root zone have been installed in putting greens. Water content was reduced across the 0 to 270 mm depth, with greater reductions near the bottom of the rooting media when vacuum was applied (Bigelow et al. 2001).

Some of the earliest ideas in putting green construction before sprinkler irrigation was widely available included subirrigation (Hurdzan 2004). This concept has received more study recently (Leinauer 1998; Leinauer et al. 2004; Leinauer and Makk 2007; Park et al. 2005). Subirrigation reduced irrigation requirements 70% or more compared with surface irrigation (Park et al. 2005; Leinauer 1998). If desired, a subirrigation system could be closed, preventing leaching losses. If the root zone profile is level it may be possible to raise and lower the water table as needed. Subirrigation resulted in development of a more extensive root system in creeping bentgrass (Leinauer 1998). The particle size range and the depth of sand dictate the degree of capillary rise of water (Hillel 1982). Issues to be solved with subirrigation of putting greens include how to manage high levels of soluble salts and sodium, as well as maintaining uniform water levels in soil on sloping greens.

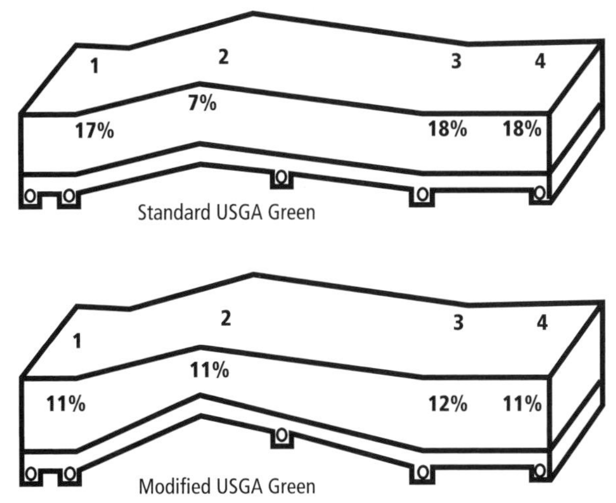

FIGURE 6.2. ■ Mean volumetric water content in the 0 to 100 mm depth root zone on day 3 of a dry-down period. Standard USGA (uniform 300 mm depth, top) and modified (variable depth) construction, 2000–2003.

W. H. Daniel and his students proposed putting green construction with dune sands (PURR [Purdue Underground Root Reservoir]-WICK) (Daniel and Freeborg 1979). Dune sands are finer-textured than the USGA specifications and have a narrow particle size range. The greens were underlain by plastic to hold water in the mix. With this construction, significant amounts of water moved down slope, and too much water frequently accumulated at the bottom of the slope. Few greens were constructed with this technique, but some tees, being flat, have performed well.

Two other approaches to constructing greens or sports fields are the Airfield sand system and the Evaporative Control System. A comparison was made between the construction of an Airfield system and a USGA green (Xiong et al. 2006). The Airfield system specifies a concrete sand (coarser than USGA specifications) placed over a geotextile, which overlays PVC grid support structures. Soil water content in the 0 to 7.6 cm and the 7.6 to 15 cm depths was similar for both the Airfield and the USGA greens. The wider sand particle size range used in the Airfield system would reduce the cost of sand in construction, but the reduction may be offset by the cost of other construction materials. The wide particle size range of concrete sand could also result in a harder playing surface than the USGA construction (Crum et al. 2003).

Recent research (Leinauer and Makk 2007) examined the Evaporative Control System (ECS), in which USGA-specification sand is placed on PVC trays; slotted pipes in the trays provide subirrigation and drainage. Creeping bentgrass established more rapidly on the ECS plots than on a USGA sprinkler-irrigated green. Leinauer and Makk proposed that this occurred because the permanent perched water table maintained with the ECS system provided more consistent water content at the surface during establishment. Further research is needed to determine whether this system would provide significant water savings that would offset construction costs.

SPORTS TURFS

In recent years much attention has been given to modifying sports turf fields. One of the early ideas proposed was called PAT (prescription athletic turf) (Daniel et al. 1974). This design uses sands placed in a plastic-lined system with tile placed on top of the plastic. The tile is attached to pumps installed to either draw water from or to pump water into the sand profile (subirrigation). A number of sports fields using this or similar techniques have been successfully developed, although the appropriate size range of sand must be used.

Attempts have been made to mix sand into existing soil (Puhalla et al. 1999), usually with poor results. Effective soil modification can be achieved, however, if careful attention is given to the properties of sand and topsoil used in a mix (Henderson 2007; Henderson et al. 2005). Generally, a mix with a minimum of 90% sand and about equal amounts of silt and clay has proven acceptable. Turfgrass established on this type of root zone has been grown on modules outdoors and moved into sports stadia at Michigan State University and on Olympic fields (Carson 2008). The costs of materials, mixing, and transportation limit using such technology to higher-budget programs.

TOPDRESSING NATIVE SOIL TURFS

Most putting greens on older golf courses were constructed with native soils. In earlier golf course construction in the United States, native soils containing adequate silt and clay to hold water and nutrients were preferred. These putting greens had adequate slope to permit runoff of rain, and little irrigation was used. Sand topdressing of these greens has resulted in a layer of sand over the native soil, some as deep as 100 to 150 mm. One study (Schleicher et al. 2007) sampled topdressed putting greens and determined that there was more sand (80%) in the 0 to 15 mm depth than in the 15 to 30 mm depth (64%), suggesting soil from cultivation has mixed with the sand from topdressing.

As topdressing continues over time a layer of sand accumulates that enhances infiltration on putting greens made of native soil. In some cases the putting greens now hold water in the sand layer that had previously run off the surface. This practice has changed drainage patterns and impacted irrigation management. With continued topdressing the sand layer will eventually simulate a sand putting green profile. Questions remain about how deep the sand topdressing layer over the underlying native soil needs to be in order to provide physical conditions similar to sand putting greens, and about the effect of the water movement down to the front (or other slope area) of the green. The latter can result in the accumulation of excess water, requiring additional drainage and changes in irrigation management.

Topdressing of fairways growing on finer-textured soils has gained popularity in some climates. Positive results have been observed on golf courses whose fairways have been topdressed for several years (Gilhuly 1999). Among other advantages, the surface is drier, providing better-quality playing and maintenance conditions during wet weather. A major drawback is cost of topdressing such large areas. Questions remain about how deep the sand needs to be to achieve the desired effects under different soil and climatic conditions and what drainage practices should be addressed before initiating a sand topdressing program. While sand topdressing does not have a substantial effect on evapotranspiration, a significant sand layer can influence irrigation practices.

Most sports fields are built on native soils. More research on sand topdressing has been conducted on sports turfs than on fairways (Cockerham et al. 1993). As with fairways, sand topdressing can result in improved conditions. Sand-topdressing native soil sports fields that had good drainage provided greater firmness, less ponding, and less loss of ground cover when wet (Baker and Canaway 1990; 1992). When dry, the topdressed fields had lower surface hardness measurements. There would be little impact on evapotranspiration on these fields, but irrigation practices might need to change.

Localized Dry Spots

A frequent problem observed with sand media is the development of hydrophobicity, often referred to as localized dry spot or dry patch. Wilkinson and Miller were among the first to study this phenomenon in detail on golf courses. They reported (1978) that sand was most hydrophobic in the top 20 mm, and infiltration of the hydrophobic spots was 20% of that observed on adjacent nonhydrophobic areas.

The spatial variability of localized dry spots is typically high, with both hydrophobic and nonhydrophobic areas in close proximity. Scanning electron micrography revealed that sand grains coated with organic matter had patterns similar to fungal mycelia growth (Wilkinson and Miller 1978). A different technology was used to identify organic matter that gave the appearance of fungal mycelia (Karcher 2000).

As soils dry, organic coatings tend to polymerize (Dekker et al. 2004), increasing water repellency. Hydrophobicity typically decreases with depth and can increase with time under dry conditions (Stromqvist and Jarvis 2005). Variability was found among creeping bentgrass (*Agrostis* spp.) cultivars in their susceptibility to development of localized dry spots (Landry et al. 1997).

Hydrophilic sands typically exhibit a relatively uniform wetting front as applied water moves down in the soil. When hydrophobicity develops, water tends to flow down through narrow channels (Hendrickx et al. 1993; Nektarios et al. 2002, 2004). This phenomenon can be referred to as finger flow, preferential flow, a nonuniform wetting front, or an unstable wetting front. Preferential flow may be attributed to water draining through hydrophilic areas and avoiding hydrophobic areas; at some critical soil water content, the sand becomes hydrophobic, reducing infiltration, water use efficiency, and turf quality (Dekker et al. 2004). When preferential flow occurs, water can drain more rapidly from a sand profile, decreasing irrigation efficiency. Solutes can move faster through the soil with preferential flow (Hendrickx et al. 1993).

Localized dry spots are often observed on areas where irrigation coverage is inadequate, on slopes where water tends to run off rather than infiltrate, and on slopes facing the sun. Once hydrophobicity develops, it can be difficult to achieve adequate short-term rewetting of the soil.

Application of effective wetting agents, cultivation (aerification), thatch control, and syringing are the most common practices for controlling localized dry spots (Beard 2002). Applying a wetting agent combined with cultivation improved turf (Wilkinson and Miller 1978). The efficacy of wetting agent treatments is usually limited to weeks or months, but it has lasted as long as 13 months from a single application (Rieke 1975). Localized dry spots were reduced by both water injection cultivation and wetting agent injection through the water injection cultivation machine (Gibbs et al. 2000; Karcher and Rieke 2005).

Reported benefits of application of effective wetting agents include increased water retention in the top 10 cm of sands that is available to turf roots

(Karnok and Tucker 2001; Leinauer et al. 2001b); improvement in infiltration, turf quality, and root length (Karnok and Tucker 2001; Landry et al. 1997); up to 71% reduction in irrigation requirements (Park et al. 2005); and reduced preferential flow (Dekker et al. 2004; Nektarios et al. 2004). Management of localized dry spots in sandy media can have a significant impact on irrigation management and water use efficiency. (For a review of hydrophobic soil information, see Ritsema and Dekker 2003.)

Organic Matter Accumulation

Turfgrasses growing on sands seem particularly susceptible to the accumulation of excess organic matter in the surface layer, especially with the newer high-density, aggressive creeping bentgrass and bermudagrass cultivars used on putting greens. An effective maintenance program should keep the organic matter content at no more than 40 g/kg^{-1} in the top 50 mm of the green (Carrow 2003). This accumulating organic matter can consist primarily of relatively undecomposed thatch or, more typically, as more degraded material that can seal the surface. With further degradation this layer can form a gelatinous mass that can plug macropores, hold water that would normally drain, cause oxygen stress, and result in loss of roots (Carrow 2003). This can also make the turf more susceptible to the development of the condition commonly referred to as black layer (Carrow 2004).

Topdressing with sand has been reported to both dilute thatch with sand and enhance microbial degradation (Couillard et al. 1997). Maintaining a proper level of organic matter in the surface layer of a turf requires a range of management practices, among which is water management.

Black Layer

Although the soil condition referred to as black layer can be found on finer soil textures, the most serious cases are usually found in sand profiles. Black layer is often associated with the accumulation of organic matter that results in limited oxygen levels and anaerobiosis (Carrow 2004). Reduction of sulfur compounds to sulfides causes the typical odor associated with black layer (Berndt and Vargas 1992). Metal sulfides cause the black coloration (Berndt and Vargas 1992, 2006; Hodges 1992). What initiates the black layer is not clear. A buried layer of organic matter (thatch, mat, or grow-in layer) or a significant soil textural change have been observed as the site for black layer development. Algae and bacteria have been implicated as well (Hodges 1992). Management practices to prevent or cure black layer include reducing sulfur inputs, getting more oxygen in the affected zone through cultivation, topdressing to prevent layer formation, improving drainage, controlling organic matter, and improving irrigation practices. Reducing irrigation may reduce susceptibility to black layer, but keeping sands too dry increases the susceptibility to localized dry spots.

Soil Amendments

Evaluation of sand-based root zones varying broadly within and slightly exceeding USGA physical properties guidelines (USGA Green Section Staff 2004) indicate that turfgrass rooting exhibits an inverse relationship with water retention (Hannaford and Baker 2000; McCoy et al. 2007; Murphy et al. 2001, 2005). This inverse relationship has two plausible interpretations: greater wetness limits root growth, or greater dryness forces plant investment in root growth exploration for limited available water (Russell 1977). Moreover, rooting differences are often presumed to affect performance.

Contrary to common perceptions, better turf performance has been observed on root zones that retain more water with reduced rooting than on root zones retaining less water with greater rooting (Murphy et al. 2001, 2005). Differences in water retention and saturated hydraulic conductivity in root zones had little effect on actual evapotranspiration when turf was maintained in a well-watered condition; moreover, turf quality and evapotranspiration were uniform regardless of rooting depth (McCoy et al. 2007). Thus, within the context of sand-based root zones, greater rooting depth has not been related to better turf performance or greater efficiency in water use. Capillary recharge may be one plausible explanation for deeper root distribution not being associated with better turf performance or evapotranspiration.

Water uptake from sand-based root zones is probably associated with root distribution during daylight, creating a large water potential gradient at the surface where rooting is more extensive. This gradient provides the driving force for capillary flow of water from lower and considerably wetter root zone depths toward the surface overnight when evapotranspirational demand is low. Such processes, if broadly applicable, suggest that construction designs that sacrifice water storage (retention) in a sand-based root zone for the sake of greater water transmission could limit the soil's ability to conserve water. More study is necessary to determine whether capillary recharge is universally important in the management of golf course putting greens. Additionally, coarser-textured root zones may have a limited capacity for capillary recharge of surface depths due to greater discontinuity of water films (Hillel 1982).

Managing stored water in sand-based root zones is difficult for some practitioners, and water storage and redistribution are complicated by slope in the subgrade. However, evidence suggests that greater water conservation can be achieved with more-water-retentive sand-based root zones. The authors' unpublished observations in the humid climate of New Jersey suggest that root zones retaining the maximum amount of water (0.25 m^3/m^{-3}) based on USGA standards (capillary porosity at –3 kPa) had the lowest irrigation requirement. Increasing water retention (at –3 kPa) by 0.05 m^3/m^{-3} decreased the amount of irrigation required to maintain creeping bentgrass as putting green turf. Challenges in managing more-water-retentive root zones would be related to undesired algae and moss growth at the surface under conditions of liberal irrigation, particularly in more humid climates.

More experimental and empirical observations regarding water storage and redistribution are needed to confirm the utility of this concept in the field. Issues of capillary recharge should be assessed in coarser-textured root zones where capillarity is more limited, especially under environmental conditions of large evapotranspirational demand. And finally, more research on the effect of greater water retention in sand-based root zones on irrigation efficiency (reduced frequency of irrigation) in more arid climates is needed.

CONCLUSION

Although putting greens comprise a relatively small portion of a golf course, the quality of the surface provided for the golfer is often the basis on which the reputation of golf courses is judged. The intensity of management of putting greens has increased significantly in recent years, subjecting the turf to increased stress. Careful water management (irrigation and drainage) can aid in managing turf stress. The increased use of effluent and poorer-quality water increases the emphasis needed on proper water management. To make wise water management decisions, turf managers must understand water retention and drainage characteristics in soils, especially in modified root zones.

REFERENCES

Baker, S. W., and P. M. Canaway. 1990. The effect of sand topdressing on the performance of winter games pitches of different construction types. I: Soil physical properties and ground cover. Journal of the Sports Turf Research Institute 66:21–27.

———. 1992. The effect of sand topdressing on the performance of winter games pitches on different construction types. II: Playing quality. Journal of the Sports Turf Research Institute 68:62–72.

Beard, J. B. 2002. Turf management for golf courses. Chelsea, MI: Ann Arbor Press.

Berndt, W. L., and J. M. Vargas Jr. 1992. Elemental sulfur lowers redox potential and produces sulfide in putting green sand. HortScience 27(11): 1188–1190.

———. 2006. Dissimilatory reduction of sulfate in black layer. HortScience 41:815–817.

Bigelow, C. A., D. C. Bowman, K. K. Cassel, and T. W. Rufty Jr. 2001. Creeping bentgrass response to inorganic soil amendments and mechanically induced subsurface drainage and aeration. Crop Science 41:797–805.

Carrow, R. N. 2003. Surface organic matter in bentgrass greens. USGA Turfgrass and Environmental Research Online 2(17): 1–12.

———. 2004. Surface organic matter in creeping bentgrass greens: Controlling excessive organic matter can lead to healthy greens in summer. Golf Course Management 72(5): 96–101.

Carrow, R. N., and R. R. Duncan. 1998. Salt-affected turfgrass sites: Assessment and management. Chelsea, MI: Ann Arbor Press.

Carson, T. 2008. Olympian fields. Golf Course Management 76(7): 42.

Cockerham, S. T., V. A. Gibeault, and R. A. Kahn. 1993. Alteration of sports field characteristics using management. International Turfgrass Society Research Journal 7:182–191.

Couillard, A., A. J. Turgeon, and P. E. Rieke. 1997. New insights into thatch biodegradation. International Turfgrass Society Research Journal 8:427–435.

Craul, P. J. 1992. Urban soil in landscape design. New York: Wiley.

Crum, J. R., T. F. Wolff, and J. N. Rogers III. 2003. Agronomic and engineering properties of USGA putting greens. USGA Turfgrass and Environmental Research Online 2(15): 1–9.

Daniel, W. H., and R. P. Freeborg. 1979. Turf managers handbook. Cleveland, OH: Harvest.

Daniel, W. H., R. P. Freeborg, and J. J. Roby. 1974. Precision athletic turf system. In E. C. Roberts, ed., Proceedings of the 2nd International Turfgrass Research Conference, Blacksburg, VA. 277–280.

Davis, W. B., J. L. Paul, J. H. Madison, and L. Y. George. 1970. A guide to evaluating sands and amendments used for high-trafficked turfgrass. Oakland: University of California Agricultural Extension Publication AXT-n113.

Davis, W. B., J. L. Paul, and D. Bowman. 1990. The sand putting green: Construction and management. Oakland: University of California Division of Agriculture and Natural Resources Publication 21448.

Dekker, L. W., C. J. Ritsema, and K. Oostindie. 2004. The impact of water repellency on soil moisture variability and preferential flow. Acta Horticulturae 661:99–104.

Evans, C.V., D. S. Fanning, and J. R. Short. 2000. Human influenced soils. In R. B. Brown, J. H. Huddleston, and J. L. Anderson, eds., Managing soils in an urban environment. Agronomy Monograph 39. Madison, WI: American Society of Agronomy. 33–67.

Ferguson, M. H. 1965. The Green Section specifications for a putting green. USGA Green Section Record 2(4): 1–7.

Ferguson, M. H., L. Howard, and M. E. Bloodworth. 1960. Laboratory methods for evaluation of putting green soil mixtures. USGA Journal and Turf Management 13(5): 30–32.

Frank, K. W., B. E. Leach, J. R. Crum, P. E. Rieke, B. R. Leinauer, T. A. Nikolai, and R. N. Calhoun. 2005. The effects of a variable depth root zone on soil moisture in a sloped USGA putting green. International Turfgrass Society Research Journal 10:1060–1066.

Gardner, W. H. 1960. Water movement in soil. Film. Washington State University.

Gibbs, R. J., C. Liu, M.-H. Yang, and M. P. Wrigley. 2000. Effect of rootzone composition and cultivation/aeration treatment on surface characteristics of golf greens under New Zealand conditions. Journal of Turfgrass Science 76:37–52.

Gilhuly, L. 1999. A decade of piling it on: Has fairway topdressing worked? USGA Green Section Record 37(6): 1–4.

Hannaford, J., and S. W. Baker. 2000. The effect of rootzone composition and compaction on root development in sand-dominated golf green profiles. Journal of Turfgrass Science 76:24–36.

Henderson, J. 2007. Right rootzone recipe maximizes performance. SportsTurf 23(1): 14, 16–18.

Henderson, J. J., J. R. Crum, and J. N. Rogers III. 2005. Effects of particle size distribution and water content at compaction on saturated hydraulic conductivity and strength of high sand content root zone materials. Soil Science 170(5): 315–324.

Hendrickx, J. M. H., L. W. Dekker, and O. H. Boersma. 1993. Unstable wetting fronts in water-repellent soils. Journal of Environmental Quality 22:109–118.

Hillel, D. 1982. Introduction to soil physics. New York: Academic Press.

Hodges, C. F. 1992. Interaction of cyanobacteria and sulfate-reducing bacteria in subsurface black layer formation in sand content golf greens. Soil Biology and Biochemistry 24(1): 15–20.

Hurdzan, M. J. 2004. Golf greens: History, design and construction. Hoboken, NJ: Wiley

Karcher, D. E. 2000. Investigations on statistical analysis of turfgrass rating data, localized dry spots of greens, and nitrogen application techniques for turf. PhD dissertation. Crop and Soil Sciences Department, Michigan State University.

Karcher, D. E., and P. E. Rieke. 2005. Water injection cultivation of sand topdressed putting green. International Turfgrass Society Research Journal 10:1094–1098.

Karnok, K. J., and K. A. Tucker. 2001. Wetting-agent-treated hydrophobic soil and its effect on color, quality and root growth of creeping bentgrass. International Turfgrass Society Research Journal 9(2): 537–541.

Kunze, R. J., M. H. Ferguson, and J. B. Page. 1957. The effects of compaction on golf green mixtures. USGA Journal and Turfgrass Management 10(6): 24–27.

Kussow, Wayne R. 2000. Understanding soil water. Grass Roots 29(6): 16, 17, 19–23.

Landry, G., K. Karnok, C. Raikes, and K. Mangum. 1997. Bentgrass (*Agrostis* spp.) cultivar performance on a golf course putting green. International Turfgrass Research Society Journal 8:1230–1239.

Leinauer, B. 1998. Water savings through subirrigation. Golf Course Management 66(10): 65–69.

Leinauer, B., and J. Makk. 2007. Establishment of golf greens under different construction types, irrigation systems, and root zones. USGA Turfgrass and Environmental Research Online 6(7): 1–7.

Leinauer, B., P. Rieke, and J. Crum. 2001a. Retaining moisture in USGA putting greens: Modifying root-zone depths may be the solution to protecting against black layer and localized dry spots in USGA putting greens. Golf Course Management 69(7): 65–69.

Leinauer, B., P. E. Rieke, D. VanLeeuwen, R. Sallenave, J. Makk, and E. Johnson. 2001b. Effects of soil surfactants on water retention in turfgrass rootzones. International Turfgrass Research Society Journal 9(2): 542–547.

Leinauer, B. R. Sallenave, and H. Schulz. 2004. A comparison of construction types and their associated systems: Effect on turfgrass quality, drought avoidance, and irrigation water use. Acta Horticulturae 661:123–129.

McCoy, E. 2008. Soil water in managed turfgrass landscapes. In J. B. Beard and M. P. Kenna, eds., Water quality and quantity issues for turfgrasses in urban landscapes. Ames, IA: Council for Agricultural Science and Technology. 91–106.

McCoy, E., and K. McCoy. 2006. Dynamics of water flow in putting greens via computer simulations. USGA Turfgrass and Environmental Research. September 1.5(17): 1–15.

McCoy, E. L., P. Kunkel, G. W. Prettyman, and K. R. McCoy. 2007. Root zone composition effects on putting green soil water. Applied Turfgrass Science Online, http://www.plantmanagementnetwork.org/ats/, doi:10.1094/ATS-2007-1119-02-RS.

McIntyre, K., and B. Jakobsen. 2000. Practical drainage for golf, sportsturf and horticulture. Chelsea, MI: Sleeping Bear Press.

Miller, D. E. 1964. Estimating moisture retained by layered soils. Journal of Soil Water Conservation 19:235–237.

———. 1969. Flow and retention of water in layered soils. USDA-ARS Conservation Research Report 13. Washington, DC: U.S. Government Printing Office.

Miller, D. E., and W. C. Bunger. 1963. Moisture retention by soil with coarse layers in the profile. Soil Science Society of America Proceedings 27:586–589.

Moore, J. F. 2004. Revising the USGA's recommendations for a method of putting green construction. USGA Green Section Record (42)3: 26–28.

Murphy, J. A., J. A. Honig, H. Samaranayake, T. J. Lawson, and S. L. Murphy. 2001. Creeping bentgrass establishment on root zones varying in sand sizes. International Turfgrass Research Society Journal 9:573–579.

Murphy, J. A., H. Samaranayake, J. A. Honig, T. J. Lawson, and S. L. Murphy. 2005. Creeping bentgrass establishment on amended-sand root zones in two microenvironments. Crop Science 45:1511–1520.

Nektarios, P. A., A. M. Petrovic, and T. S. Steenhuis. 2002. Effect of surfactant on fingered flow in laboratory golf greens. Soil Science 167:572–579.

———. 2004. Aeration type affects preferential flow in golf putting greens. Acta Horticulturae 66:421–442.

Park, D. M., J. L. Cisar, D. K. McDermitt, K. E. Williams, J. J. Haydu, and W. P. Miller. 2005. Using red and infrared reflectance and visual observation to monitor turf quality and water stress in surfactant-treated bermudagrass under reduced irrigation. International Turfgrass Society Research Journal 10:115–120.

Prettyman, G. W., and E. L. McCoy. 2002. Effect of profile layering, root zone texture, and slope on putting green drainage rates. Agronomy Journal 94:358–364.

———. 2003a. Localized drought on sloped putting greens with sand-based root zones. USGA Turfgrass Environmental Research Online 2(4): 1–8.

———. 2003b. Profile layering, root zone permeability, and slope on putting green drainage rates. Crop Science 43:985–994.

Puhalla, J., J. Krans, and M. Goatley. 1999. Sports fields: A manual for design, construction and maintenance. Chelsea, MI: Ann Arbor Press.

Rieke, P. E. 1975. Soils research: Nitrogen carriers, potassium studies and rewetting a hydrophobic soil. In Proceedings of the [45th] Michigan Turfgrass Conference. Vol. 4. 3–5.

Ritsema, C. J., and L. W. Dekker. 2003. Soil water repellency. Wageningen, The Netherlands: Elsevier.

Russell, R. S. 1977. Plant root systems: Their function and interaction with the soil. London: McGraw-Hill.

Schleicher, L., J. J. Doolittle, and E. M. Nielsen. 2007. Survey of root zone properties in amended native soil pushup greens. American Society of Agronomy Abstracts 268: 25.

Stromqvist, J., and N. Jarvis. 2005. Sorption, degradation, and leaching of the fungicide iprodione in a golf green under Scandinavian conditions: Measurements, modeling and risk assessment. Pest Management Science 61:1168–1178.

USGA Green Section Staff. 1993. USGA recommendations for a method of putting green construction. USGA Green Section Record 31(2): 1–3.

———. 2004. USGA recommendations for a method of putting green construction. USGA Web site, http://www.usga.org/.

Waddington, D. V. 1992. Soils, soil mixtures, and soil amendments. In D. V. Waddington, R. N. Carrow, and R. C. Shearman, eds., Turfgrass. Agronomy Monograph 32. Madison, WI: American Society of Agronomy. 331–383.

Wilkinson, J. P., and R. H. Miller. 1978. Investigations and treatment of localized dry spots on sand golf greens. Agronomy Journal 70:299–304.

Xiong, X., G. E. Bell, M. W. Smith, and B. Martin. 2006. Comparison of the USGA ANS Airfield sand systems for sports turf construction. Applied Turfgrass Science Online, http://www.plantmanagementnetwork.org/ats/, doi:10.1094/ATS-2006-0531-02-RS.

7 Irrigation Water Quality, Management, and Policy Issues

Laosheng Wu and M. Ali Harivandi

THE DEMAND FOR HIGH-QUALITY WATER DUE TO URBANization, climate change, and environmental water use has increased rapidly and has required agriculture and landscaping to use waters of lower quality for irrigation. These waters can come from saline or brackish groundwater, drainage water, irrigation return water, and to a large extent, from reclaimed wastewater. These waters usually contain one or more constituents at undesirably high levels.

Water can be assessed in terms of physical, chemical, and biological quality. Depending on the intended use, water quality requirements may differ significantly. Some quality parameters are of agronomic importance; others are of environmental and human health importance. For example, a nitrate level of greater than 10 ppm is considered unhealthy (EPA 2009) for drinking water; water with this level of nitrate will be unsuitable for groundwater recharge since many places use groundwater as drinking water. However, the same water is suitable for irrigating crops.

This chapter focuses mainly on the agronomic significance of water quality for turfgrass irrigation, with less reference to the environmental and human health implications of using water containing undesirably high levels of dissolved salts and other contaminants for irrigating turfgrass.

WATER QUALITY PARAMETERS AND THEIR EFFECT ON SOIL AND TURFGRASS

Salinity

All irrigation waters contain dissolved mineral salts and chemicals. Some of these minerals may be phytotoxic when present in the water in high concentrations. The rate at which salts accumulate to undesirable levels in a soil depends on their concentration in the irrigation water, the amount of water applied annually, annual precipitation (rain plus snow), and the physical and chemical characteristics of the soil.

Water salinity is reported quantitatively as total dissolved solids (TDS) in units of parts per million (ppm) or milligram per liter (mg l^{-1}); it may also be reported as electrical conductivity (EC_w) in units of millimhos per centimeter (mmhos cm^{-1}), micromhos per centimeter (μmhos cm^{-1}), decisiemens per meter (dS m^{-1}), or siemens per meter (S m^{-1}). Some laboratories may also report the individual components of salinity (e.g., sodium) in milliequivalents per liter (meq l^{-1}). The following equations may be used to convert results from one set of units to another, enabling comparisons of data from differently formatted reports:

$$1 \text{ ppm} = 1 \text{ mg } l^{-1}$$
$$1 \text{ mg } l^{-1} = \text{meq } l^{-1} \times \text{equivalent weight}$$
$$1 \text{ mmhos cm}^{-1} = 1 \text{ dS m}^{-1} = 0.1 \text{ S m}^{-1}$$

The most common method of reporting salinity by laboratories is electrical conductivity, which is directly related to the salt content of the water. Regardless of how salinity is reported, the relationship between EC_w and TDS is approximately

$$EC_w \text{ (mmhos cm}^{-1} \text{ or dS m}^{-1}) \times 640 = \text{TDS (ppm or mg } l^{-1})$$

Note that the multiplier of 640 is a general average factor and may need adjusting in special circumstances. For example, for water containing substantial amount of sulfate, a higher conversion factor (700 or more) should be used.

TABLE 7.1. Relative tolerances of turfgrass species to saturated soil paste extract salinity (EC_e)

Sensitive (<3 dS m^{-1})	Moderately sensitive (3–6 dS m^{-1})	Moderately tolerant (6–10 dS m^{-1})	Tolerant (> 10 dS m^{-1})
annual bluegrass	annual ryegrass	perennial ryegrass	alkaligrass
bahiagrass	buffalograss	creeping bentgrass (cultivars Mariner and Seaside)	bermudagrass
carpetgrass	creeping bentgrass	coarse-leaf (Japonica type) zoysiagrasses	fineleaf (Matrella type) zoysiagrasses
centipedegrass	slender creeping, red, and Chewings fescue	tall fescue	saltgrass
colonial bentgrass			seashore paspalum
hard fescue			St. Augustinegrass
Kentucky bluegrass			
rough bluegrass			

Source: Harivandi et al. 2007.

Most water of acceptable quality for turfgrass irrigation contains from 200 to 800 ppm soluble salts. Soluble salt levels above 2,000 ppm may injure turfgrass; irrigation water with salt levels up to 2,000 ppm may still be tolerated by some turfgrass species, but only on soils with high permeability and subsoil drainage. Good permeability and drainage, such as sand-based sport fields and golf greens, allow a turfgrass manager to leach excessive salt from the root zone by periodic heavy irrigations.

The salt tolerance of turfgrass and other plants is expressed in terms of electrical conductivity of saturated paste extract (EC_e) of the root zone soil. Table 7.1 is a general guide to the salt tolerance of selected turfgrass species. As indicated, soils with an EC_e below 3 dS m^{-1} are considered satisfactory for growing most turfgrass species. Soils with EC_e between 3 and 10 dS m^{-1} indicate that only a few salt-tolerant turfgrass species could survive in such soils.

Table 7.2 gives the parameters that should be considered when evaluating irrigation water quality (Harivandi 1999). When the electrical conductivity of water (EC_w) is above 0.7 dS m^{-1} (or about 450 mg l^{-1}), it presents increased salinity problems. Only

TABLE 7.2. ■ Guidelines for the interpretation of water quality for irrigation

Water quality factor	Unit of measure	Degree of problem: Negligible	Slight to moderate	Severe
		Salinity		
EC_w	dS m^{-1} or mmhos cm^{-1}	< 0.7	0.7–3.0	> 3.0
TDS	mg l^{-1} or ppm	< 450	450–2,000	> 2,000
		Soil water infiltration (evaluate using SAR and EC_w together)		
SAR = 0–3 and EC_w =	dS m^{-1}	> 0.7	0.7–0.2	< 0.2
SAR = 3–6 and EC_w =	dS m^{-1}	> 1.2	1.2–0.3	< 0.3
SAR = 6–12 and EC_w =	dS m^{-1}	> 1.9	1.9–0.5	< 0.5
SAR = 12–20 and EC_w =	dS m^{-1}	> 2.9	2.9–1.3	< 1.3
SAR = 20–40 and EC_w =	dS m^{-1}	> 5.0	5.0–2.9	< 2.9
		Specific ion toxicity		
sodium (Na)				
root absorption	SAR	< 3	3–9	> 9
foliar absorption	meq l^{-1}	< 3	> 3	—
	meq l^{-1}	< 70	> 70	—
chloride (Cl)				
root absorption	meq l^{-1}	< 2	2–10	> 10
	meq l^{-1}	< 70	70–355	> 355
foliar absorption	meq l^{-1}	< 3	> 3	—
	meq l^{-1}	< 100	> 100	—
boron (B)	meq l^{-1}	< 1	1–2	> 2
		Miscellaneous effects		
bicarbonate (HCO_3)	meq l^{-1}	< 1.5	1.5–8.5	> 8.5
(unsightly foliar deposits)	meq l^{-1}	< 90	90–500	> 500
pH		common range	6.5–8.4	
residual chlorine (Cl_2)	meq l^{-1}	< 1	1–5	>5

Source: Adapted from Westcot and Ayers 1984; Farnham et al. 1985; and Harivandi 1999.

careful irrigation and water management will prevent deleterious salt accumulation in the soil if water with a high EC_w is used for irrigation. Water with an EC greater than 3 dS m^{-1} should be avoided. Soil physical characteristics and drainage, both important factors in determining root zone salinity, must also be considered when determining the suitability of a given irrigation water. As an example, water with an EC_w of 1.5 dS m^{-1} may be successfully used on grass grown on sandy soil with good drainage (and thus high natural leaching), but it may prove injurious within a very short time period if used to irrigate the same grass grown on a clay soil or soil with limited drainage due to salt buildup in the root zone.

Sodium

Sodium content is an important factor in irrigation water quality evaluation. Plant roots absorb sodium and transport it to leaves, where it can accumulate and cause injury. Thus, symptoms of sodium toxicity resemble those of salt burn on leaves. In some plants, sodium may cause root toxicity through root cell deterioration.

Irrigation water with high levels of sodium can be particularly toxic if applied to plant leaves by overheard sprinkler since salts can be absorbed directly by leaves. Sodium toxicity is often of more concern on plants other than turfgrasses, primarily because accumulated sodium is removed when grass is mowed. Among grasses grown on golf courses, annual bluegrass and bentgrass are the most susceptible to sodium phytotoxicity. Mowing may not provide protection to these grasses since they are generally cut very short (a stress in itself), and any sodium accumulation will comprise a large proportion of the small quantity of remaining leaf tissue.

As indicated in table 7.2, the level of sodium tolerated by nonturf plants varies with irrigation application method. Most landscape plants will tolerate up to 70 ppm (mg l^{-1}) sodium when irrigated by overhead sprinkler.

Although sodium can be directly toxic to plants, its most frequent deleterious effects on plant growth are indirect due to its effect on soil structure (fig. 7.1). This latter effect is most often of concern to golf course superintendents and other professional managers of intensely used turfgrasses. For irrigation management, the best indicator of sodium effect is the sodium adsorption ratio (SAR) of the irrigation water:

$$SAR = Na^+ \div \sqrt{[(Ca^{2+} + Mg^{2+}) \div 2]}$$

where Na^+, Ca^{2+}, and Mg^{2+} denote the concentrations of respective cations of the water (meq l^{-1}). High sodicity in irrigation water is due to a high ratio of Na^+ versus Ca^{2+} plus Mg^{2+} and low salinity, or it is induced by the precipitation of calcium with bicarbonate (HCO_3^-) to form calcium carbonate ($CaCO_3$).

A high SAR can reduce soil infiltration. Generally, irrigation water with high SAR value (i.e., SAR > 9) can cause severe restrictions on permeability when applied to fine-textured clay soils over a period of time. However, the sodic (SAR) effect of water is often evaluated together with salinity. At the same SAR level, soil is more susceptible to dispersion in a low-salinity water than in a high-salinity water (fig. 7.2). In coarse-textured (sandy) soils, restrictions on permeability would be less severe, and water with this magnitude of SAR may be tolerated. Golf greens and sports fields constructed with high-sand-content root zone mixes, for example, can be successfully irrigated with high-SAR water because their drainage is good.

For water high in bicarbonate, some laboratories adjust the calculation of SAR, yielding a parameter called "adjusted SAR" or "Adj. SAR," because soil calcium and magnesium concentrations are affected by

FIGURE 7.1. Soil or water sodicity reduces irrigation water infiltration and creates waterlogging. *Photo:* A. Haravandi.

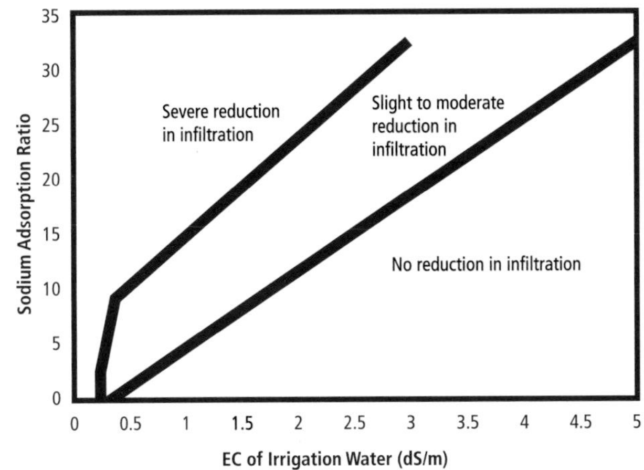

FIGURE 7.2. ■ Effect of sodium adsorption ratio (SAR) and electrical conductivity of irrigation water (EC_w) on infiltration. *Source:* Adapted from Ayers and Westcot 1985.

bicarbonate in the water. In simplest terms, adjusted SAR reflects the calcium, magnesium, sodium, and bicarbonate, as well as the total salinity of the water. Other laboratories adjust the SAR value using a newly introduced method and report the adjusted value as R_{NA}. Since not all laboratories have adopted this new method for properly adjusting the SAR to account for either the precipitation or dissolution of calcium carbonate, the unadjusted SAR value will suffice.

Bicarbonate and pH

The bicarbonate, and to a lesser degree carbonate, content of irrigation water also deserves careful evaluation. A high bicarbonate level in irrigation water can increase soil pH and, in combination with carbonate, may affect soil permeability. In addition, bicarbonate content may cause white lime ($CaCO_3$) deposits to appear on leaves of plants irrigated by overhead sprinklers during hot, dry periods due to evaporation. Although high levels of bicarbonate in water can raise soil pH to undesirable levels, the negative impact of bicarbonate on soil permeability is more often a concern. As mentioned above, the bicarbonate ion may combine with calcium or magnesium and precipitate as calcium carbonate or magnesium carbonate. This precipitation increases the SAR in the soil solution because it lowers the dissolved calcium concentration.

Tolerable levels of bicarbonate in irrigation waters are given in table 7.2. The bicarbonate hazard of water may be expressed as residual sodium carbonate (RSC):

$$RSC = (HCO_3^- + CO_3^{2-}) - (Ca^{2+} + Mg^{2+})$$

where concentrations of ions are expressed in meq l^{-1}. Generally, water with an RSC value of 1.25 meq l^{-1} or lower is safe for irrigation, water with an RSC between 1.25 and 2.5 meq l^{-1} is marginal, and water with an RSC of 2.5 meq l^{-1} and above is probably not suitable for irrigation.

The pH value (hydrogen ion activity) is a measure of the acidity or alkalinity of a water. Most irrigation water is in a pH range of 6.5 to 8.4, although the desirable soil pH for most turfgrasses is 5.5 to 7.0. Water with a pH outside the desirable range must be carefully evaluated. A very high or low pH warns the users that the water needs evaluation for other constituents, although pH itself seldom is a problem.

Boron, Chloride, and Heavy Metals

Irrigation water with high levels of boron and chloride may be harmful to plants. Heavy metal elements contained in irrigation water are generally not toxic to turfgrasses.

Boron (B) is an essential micronutrient for plant growth, though required in very small amounts. At even very low concentrations (as low as 1 to 2 mg l^{-1}) in irrigation water, it is phytotoxic to most ornamental plants and capable of causing leaf burn (see table 7.2). Turfgrasses are generally more tolerant of boron than are any other plants grown in a landscape. Most turfgrass species will grow in soils with boron levels as high as 10 ppm.

In addition to contributing to the total soluble salt concentration of irrigation water, chloride (Cl^{-1}) may be directly toxic to plants grown on a golf course, park, or other landscape site. Although chloride is not particularly toxic to turfgrasses, many trees, shrubs, and ground covers are quite sensitive to it. Chloride is absorbed primarily by plant roots and translocated to leaves, where it accumulates. In sensitive plants, this accumulation leads to necrosis or leaf margin scorch in minor cases, or total leaf kill and abscission in severe situations. Similar symptoms may occur on sensitive plants if water high in chloride is applied by overhead sprinklers, since chloride can be absorbed by leaves as well as roots. As indicated in table 7.2, irrigation water with a chloride concentration above 355 mg l^{-1} is toxic when absorbed by roots, while a chloride concentration higher than 100 mg l^{-1} can damage sensitive ornamental plants if applied to foliage. Turfgrasses tolerate all but extremely high levels of chloride as long as they are regularly mowed. Chloride salts are quite soluble and may be leached from soils that have good subsurface drainage.

RECLAIMED WATER QUALITY

The following water quality parameters are specific to reclaimed water and not to other nonpotable waters.

Chlorine Residue

Irrigation water originating from municipal reclaimed water may contain excessive residual chlorine (Cl_2), a potential plant toxin. Chlorine toxicity is associated only with reclaimed water sources that have been disinfected with chlorine-containing compounds. Chlorine toxicity will occur if high levels of chlorine are sprayed directly onto foliage, a situation likely to occur only where reclaimed water goes straight from a treatment plant to an overhead irrigation system. Free chlorine is very unstable in water; it dissipates rapidly if stored for even a short period of time between treatment and application. As indicated in table 7.2, residual chlorine is of concern at levels above 5 mg l^{-1}.

Pharmaceutically Active Chemicals and Endocrine Disruptors

Residues of over-the-counter and prescription drugs including antiphlogistics (e.g., ibuprofen and naproxen), lipid regulators, and beta-blockers have been found in treated wastewater effluents. Among the pharmaceutically active ingredients, the residues of antibiotics and hormonelike compounds have attracted the most attention. Although conventional wastewater treatment is not specifically designed to remove these potentially harmful chemicals, treatment processes nevertheless effectively reduce their concentrations in the treated effluents, usually to less than 10 ng l^{-1} (Hirsh et al. 1999; Huang et al. 2001; Mulroy 2001). In treated wastewater effluents, concentrations of drug and non-drug-related estrogenic chemicals have been reported in the ranges of 1 to 100×10^{-9} g l^{-1} and 0.1 to 30×10^{-6} g l^{-1}, respectively (Arcand-Hoy and Benson 1998).

Some substances are not hormones themselves but can disrupt the hormone (endocrine) system in humans and other mammals (most notably aquatic organisms such as fish and amphibians). These endocrine disruptors (EDC_s) are primarily synthetic chemicals that interact with endocrine systems to disrupt normal biological functions such as growth, development, and maturation. When interacting with the endocrine system of an organism, these substances may act like a natural hormone and bind to a receptor, interfere with the normal hormonal responses by binding and therefore blocking the receptor, or interfere with the organism's synthesis and control of natural hormones. Substances exhibiting endocrine-disrupting properties include organochlorine pesticides (e.g., DDT, dieldrin, lindane, atrazine, trifluralin, and permethrin), surfactants (e.g., alkylphenols and their degradation products nonylphenol and octylphenols), plasticizers (e.g., dibutyl phthalate, butylbenzylphthalate, diethylhexylphthalate, and polyethylphthalate), PCBs, dioxins, and tributyltin. When exposed to high concentrations, adverse effects of select chemicals on the development and reproduction, cognitive and neurological behavior, and immunoresponses of exposed organisms such as fishes have been demonstrated (NRC 1999).

There is inadequate technical information to assess the potential adverse impacts of endocrine-disrupting chemicals released when irrigating turfgrass and landscape with reclaimed wastewater. When present in the soil, certain linear alkylsulfanate surfactants (LAS) and their degradation byproducts, nonylphenols, are subject to rapid microbial degradation. They are also expected to be adsorbed to the soil organic matter. As a result, they are not likely to enter the plant tissue through root absorption. However, if they are released to natural water bodies, their potential ecotoxicological consequences cannot be overlooked.

When reclaimed wastewater is disinfected, the chemical oxidation process will also produce disinfection byproducts (DBPs) that are primarily dissolved organohalogens derived from the oxidative breakdown of dissolved low-molecular-weight organic substances in water. Chlorination, the most commonly used disinfection process, produces more DBPs with relatively high concentrations than do other methods of disinfection. When reclaimed wastewater is chlorinated, it requires a high chlorine dosage and long contact time, conditions especially conducive to the formation of DBPs.

In chlorinated wastewater effluents, there may be hundreds of DBPs, of which only a small fraction has been identified. In general, DBPs may be grouped into the trihalomethanes, haloacetonitriles, haloketones, haloacetic acids, chlorophenols, aldehydes, trichloronitromethane, chloral hydrate, and cyanogen chloride. Among them, trihalomethanes and haloacetic acids are by far the most common DBPs, and they often present at higher concentrations than the other less frequently found DBPs. Under the most conducive conditions for DBP production (fully nitrified secondary effluents), the total DBPs in chlorinated reclaimed wastewater were found to be as high as 3,000 ng Cl l^{-1}.

Human long-term exposure to DBPs may cause cancers or result in spontaneous abortion in the early trimesters of pregnancy. The likelihood of harm caused by DBPs is derived primarily from direct ingestion of chlorinated water. In crop irrigation, consumers may be indirectly exposed to DBPs through food chain transfer or contamination of the underlying groundwater. When turfgrasses are irrigated with reclaimed water, the concern with DBPs relate only to the groundwater (and to a lesser extent surface water) contamination.

Disinfection byproducts are subject to volatilization in the ambient environment and are readily degraded through chemical and biological reactions. Because chlorinated reclaimed wastewater is typically stored until the time of irrigation, DBPs formed during disinfection are expected to decay during storage (fig. 7.3). After irrigation, DBPs that are still present in the water will continue to degrade in the soil and turfgrass thatch and are not expected to accumulate.

It is also unlikely that DBPs pose a serious threat to groundwater underneath the irrigated site. Unless nonvolatile and refractory DBPs are found in chlorinated reclaimed water, DBPs are not likely to be a limiting factor in reclaimed wastewater irrigation. However, one must be aware of the potential environmental harm of DBPs and reassess the merit of reclaimed water irrigation if new information on the environmental fate of DBPs becomes available.

Recently, a field study was conducted at the University of California, Riverside, Turf Research Facility to assess the environmental behavior of 12 pharmaceutical and personal care products (PPCPs) and DBPs in turfgrass soil receiving reclaimed wastewater irrigation (Xu et al. 2008). In this study, the 12 selected compounds were spiked in the irrigation water. Two irrigation rates (1.1 to 1.2 and 1.5 to 1.6 times reference crop evapotranspiration, ET_o) were applied on plots with two types of soils (sandy loam and loamy sand), and the leachates were collected after each irrigation and analyzed for the targeted compounds. The control treatment of four plots (two of each soil type) was established by removing the turfgrass and irrigating it at 1.1 to 1.2 times ET_o. Four months after the experiment, soil samples from each plot were collected to a depth of 89 cm. None of the compounds were detected in the leachates after 4 months of irrigation. Most compounds were found in the surface layers (0 to 15 cm depth).

FIGURE 7.3. ■ Creative lake design can further aerate and reduce potential storage problems associated with reclaimed water. *Photo:* A. Harivandi.

Pathogens

Untreated wastewater contains high levels of human pathogens. Through proper treatment and disinfection of wastewater, pathogens are destroyed. Reclaimed wastewater has been used for irrigation for many decades and thus far no report has found that reclaimed wastewater irrigation has contributed to human illness. The potential for disease transmission through reclaimed water reuse, however, has not been completely eliminated. Thus, proper management is necessary to prevent potential disease transmission to human beings by the pathogens in reclaimed water: bacteria, parasites, and viruses (FAO 1997).

Epidemiological data that show a relationship between the quality of water actually applied at the field level and disease transmission or infection are not available. The U.S. Environmental Protection Agency's guideline uses the maximum acceptable level for irrigation with natural surface water, including river water, at 800 fecal coliforms per 100 ml (EPA 2004). The World Health Organization's recommendation for wastewater use in agriculture is listed in table 7.3. All the pathogens have the potential to reach the field, but many factors, including crop type, irrigation method, cultural and harvesting practices, and environmental conditions (e.g., temperature, humidity) can affect transmission of disease. Proper agronomic management can reduce and minimize the potential for disease transmission.

Nutrients

Reclaimed water can serve as a source of nutrients essential for plant growth, such as nitrogen (N), phosphorus (P), and potassium (K). These nutrients are beneficial to plants, but if not properly managed, they may cause many problems, such as nutrient imbalances, eutrophication and algae blooming in surface waters, and contamination of groundwater. Among them, nitrogen is the most noteworthy because the inputs could be significant in a reclaimed wastewater irrigation operation. It is imperative that fertilization practices be adjusted to account for the added nutrient inputs from wastewater to avoid overapplication of various nutrients that may adversely impact surface water or groundwater quality.

Other Water Quality Indicators

Biodegradable organics are measured by biochemical oxygen demand (BOD), chemical oxygen demand (COD), or total organic carbon (TOC). Biodegradable organics cause aesthetic and nuisance problems, adversely affect disinfection processes, and deplete soil oxygen.

Stable (refractory) organics, including organic

TABLE 7.3. Recommended microbiological quality guidelines for wastewater use in agriculture

Type of irrigation		Required pathogen reduction by treatment (log units)	Verification monitoring level (E. coli per 100 ml)
unrestricted	root crops	4	≤ 103
	leaf crops	3	≤ 104
	drip irrigation of high-growing crops	2	≤ 105
	drip irrigation of low-growing crops	4	≤ 103
	verification level depends on the requirements of the local regulatory agency	6 or 7	≤ 101 or 100
restricted	labor-intensive agriculture	3	≤ 104
	highly mechanized agriculture	2	≤ 105
	pathogen removal in a septic tank	0.5	≤ 106

Source: WHO 2006.

compounds such as phenols, certain pesticides (see University of California Riverside 2009), and chlorinated hydrocarbons can be resistant to degradation in conventional methods of wastewater treatment. Some are toxic in the environment and may accumulate in the soil.

POLICY AND WATER MANAGEMENT ISSUES

Federal and state policies can affect the turf industry in two ways. One is the wastewater treatment requirements that affect the quality of reclaimed water for turfgrass irrigation. The other is Section 303(d) of the Clean Water Act, which requires states to identify all of its water bodies that fail to meet applicable water quality standards and to establish total maximum daily loads (TMDLs) for these impaired, polluted water bodies so that they can get cleaned up and brought into compliance with applicable water quality objectives. TMDLs may regulate the quality of water discharged from irrigated turfgrass sites.

Total Maximum Daily Load

TMDLs define how much of a pollutant a water body can tolerate (absorb) daily and still comply with applicable water quality standards. All pollutant sources in the watershed combined, including nonpoint sources, are limited to discharging no more than the TMDL. The Water Act of 1987 (§ 304(l)) provided a new round of technology standards and called for development of numerical water quality criteria. Although much progress had been made in abating point source pollution, nonpoint source pollution had become a major and growing cause of water pollution. In responding to this concern, Congress added section 309 to the act to fund and stimulate state nonpoint source programs.

Change in state regulations may also affect the turf industry. For example, agricultural discharges as nonpoint sources were specifically exempted from National Pollutant Discharge Elimination System (NPDES) permits. Over the past 20 years, all nine California Regional Water Resources Control Boards have used this authority to grant waivers to many categories of discharges, including irrigation return flows from agricultural operations. On October 10, 1999, Senate Bill 390 amended Section 13269 of the water act to require all waivers in effect as of January 1, 2000, be terminated on January 1, 2003, if not specifically renewed. Additionally, the bill required new waivers to be conditional, limited in duration to no longer than 5 years, and revocable at any time by the regional board. As a result of this action, new conditional waivers for agricultural waste dischargers are being developed and implemented in some regions, while others have chosen to work with their irrigated agricultural operators through other processes.

Wastewater Treatment Requirements

When reclaimed wastewater is used for irrigation, the federal and state wastewater treatment requirements will affect the irrigation water quality. Although no formal statute at the federal level specifically covers the use of reclaimed water, the federal Clean Water Act (CWA) of 1972 provides the umbrella legislative mandate that covers all forms of publicly owned treatment works (POTW) effluent discharges. Under the CWA, two programs that are most relevant to water treatment and reuse are the Industrial Wastewater Pretreatment Program and the NPDES.

The Industrial Wastewater Pretreatment Program requires industrial dischargers to treat their discharge water to a level that will not cause disruption of the POTW's treatment system prior to discharging to the sanitary sewer system. The enactment of this program protects the efficiency of POTW treatment and enables reclaimed water to be used without undue water quality limitations. The NPDES sets limits on water quality constituents and regulates any discharges to the nation's waterways. All federally funded wastewater treatment for reuse projects must comply with provisions listed by the NPDES. Forty-five states have been delegated the authority of issuing NPDES permits. They may elect to adopt the federally mandated requirements or impose more stringent pollutant discharge standards.

The authorized state agencies have the authority to adopt or deny a permit based on information submitted by the permit applicant. Public input through hearings may be required prior to the regulator's adoption or denial of the permit application (fig. 7.4). Permits must be renewed or reissued every 5 years. The NPDES permit or its modification is issued by the authorized state agency, such as the California State Water Resources Control Board along with its Regional Water Quality Control Boards (RWQCB); the Arizona Department of Environmental Quality (ADEQ); and the Nevada Division of Environmental Protection, Bureau of Water Pollution Control (BWPC).

Irrigation Water Quality Assessment Using Watsuit

Leaching is required to control salinity in irrigated soils. With conventional irrigation systems, the leaching requirement (LR) is the minimum leaching fraction (LF) that a plant can endure without salinity stress. One of the approaches to estimate the LR is to use the Rhoades equation (Rhoades 1974), in which the LR is related to salinity of the applied water (EC_a) by

$$LR = EC_a \div (5EC_t - EC_a)$$

where EC_t is the plant salt tolerance or threshold EC. If the average salinity of the active root zone is greater than EC_t, crop yield may start declining. However, a recent study using transient models showed that the Rhoades equation may overestimate the leaching requirement (Letey et al. 2010; personal communication).

The amount of applied water should satisfy both ET and LR. It can be calculated by

FIGURE 7.4. In many communities, purple irrigation heads inform the public about reclaimed water irrigation at the site. *Photo:* A. Harivandi.

$$\text{Applied water} = ET_c \div (1 - LR)$$

where ET_c is crop (turfgrass) evapotranspiration.

The computer model Watsuit is a useful tool that calculates the chemical composition of soil water based on the composition of irrigation water and various management practices including leaching fraction and amendment additions to the water (Wu et al. 2008). The model does not use the depth (or volume) of applied water as an input. Rather it uses leaching fraction, the ratio of the depth of subsurface drainage water divided by the depth of applied water. It is a steady-state model that assumes a particular leaching fraction remains constant over time. The model also assumes a relative water uptake of 40, 30, 20, and 10% of the total for first (upper), second, third, and fourth (bottom) quarters of the root zone, respectively. The depth of the root zone is assumed to be constant, but it is not defined. The user can define the total depth of the root zone and assume that the depth of each quarter of the root zone is one-quarter of the total depth. Or, the user can define the depth of each quarter of the root zone based on the depths at which 40% (bottom of the first quarter), 70% (bottom of the second quarter), 90% (bottom of the third quarter), and 100% (bottom of the root zone) of the water uptake has occurred.

The model calculates pH assuming a partial pressure of CO_2 that increases with depth through the soil. At the surface, the partial pressure of carbon dioxide (PCO_2) is set at 0.07 kPa and 0.5, 1.5, 2.3, and 3.0 kPa going from the upper quarter of the root zone to the last quarter. It calculates the concentrations of the major cations (Na^+, Ca^+, Mg^+, and K^+) and anions (Cl^-, HCO_3^-, CO_3^{2-}, and SO_4^{2-}) of soil water based on the composition of irrigation water and various management practices including leaching fraction and amendment additions to the water. As noted above, the model does not use the depth (or volume) of applied water as an input; it uses leaching fraction and does not consider cation exchange. The output is expressed in terms of ion concentrations as well as the concentrations of precipitated or dissolved salts because the depth or volume of applied water is not used.

Strategies for Using Low-Quality Water

Proper use of low-quality water in irrigation can reduce the amount of non-saline water use, decrease the volume of drainage water disposal, and alleviate environmental concerns of low-quality water disposal.

If two waters (for example, a saline water and non-saline water) are available, the saline water can be used through blending or cycling. Cycling uses saline water as a substitute for non-saline water. The strategies are to substitute saline for non-saline water when irrigating salt-tolerant turfgrass at their non-sensitive growth stage in the rotation, and use the non-saline water at other times. Blending involves mixing the saline and non-saline waters to obtain a composite that is still suitable for irrigation. The amount of saline water that can be used for irrigation depends on the quality of the saline and non-saline waters, the crop type, and the leaching fraction.

To facilitate the infiltration and leaching, soil and water amendments are often used. A common amendment for sodic soils is gypsum, which provides soluble calcium (Ca^{2+}) that reduces the SAR and at the same time increases the salinity of the soil water. Both help to maintain percolation rate. Common acidifying amendments used for reclaiming sodic-calcareous soils include sulfuric acid and elemental sulfur. The latter is oxidized to sulfuric acid by microorganisms before it becomes effective. The Watsuit program allows the user to test the effect of adding sulfuric acid and gypsum to the irrigation water. The amendments can be chosen on the data input page.

CONCLUSION

Societal and climate changes have and will continue to make good-quality water less available for turfgrass irrigation. As a result, turfgrass and landscape managers must use alternative water sources such as reclaimed wastewater for irrigation. The alternative water sources usually contain one or more constituents with undesirably high concentration. However, these water sources can often be successfully and safely used for turfgrass irrigation through proper management (fig. 7.5).

FIGURE 7.5. ■ Many different chemicals and irrigation water injection methods are now available to correct potential reclaimed water chemical problems. *Photo:* A. Harivandi.

REFERENCES

Arcand-Hoy, L. D., and W. H. Benson. 1998. Fish reproduction: An ecologically relevant indicator of endocrine disruption. Environmental and Toxicological Chemistry 17:49–57.

Ayers, R. S., and D. W. Westcot. 1985. Water quality of agriculture. Rome: FAO Irrigation and Drainage Paper 29.

EPA (U.S. Environmental Protection Agency). 2004. Guidelines for water reuse. EPA/625/R-04/108. Washington, DC: EPA and U.S. Agency for International Development.

———. 2009. Basic information on drinking water contaminants. EPA Web site, http://www.epa.gov/safewater/contaminants/index.html.

FAO (Food and Agriculture Organization of the United Nations). 1997. Quality control of wastewater for irrigated crop production. FAO Web site, http://www.fao.org/docrep/w5367e/w5367e00.htm#Contents.

Farnham, D. S., R. F. Hasek, and J. L. Panel. 1985. Water quality: Its effects on ornamental plants. Oakland: University of California Cooperative Extension Leaflet 2995.

Harivandi, M. A. 1999. Interpreting turfgrass irrigation water test results. Oakland: University of California Division of Agriculture and Natural Resources Publication 8009. ANR CS Web site, http://anrcatalog.ucdavis.edu/pdf/8009.pdf.

Harivandi, M. A., J. D. Butler, and L. Wu. Salinity and turfgrass culture. 1992. In D. V. Waddington, R. N. Carrow, and R. C. Shearman, eds., Turfgrass. Agronomy Monograph 32. Madison, WI: American Society of Agronomy. 208–230.

Harivandi, M. A., K. B. Marcum, and Y. Qian. 2007. Recycled, gray, and saline water irrigation for turfgrass. In J. B. Beard and M. P. Kenna, eds., Water quality and quantity issues for turfgrasses in urban landscapes. Ames, IA: Council for Agricultural Science and Technology. 243–257.

Hirsch, R., T. Ternes, K. Haberer, and K. L. Kratz. 1999. Occurrence of antibiotics in the aquatic environment. Science of the Total Environment 225:109–118.

Huang, C.-H., J. E. Renew, and K. Pinkston. 2001. Occurrence and fate of antibiotic compounds in municipal wastewater and animal waste. In WEFTEC 2001 Conference Proceedings. Alexandria, VA: Water Environment Federation.

Mulroy, A. 2001. When the cure is the problem. Water, Environment and Technology 13(2): 32–36.

NRC (National Research Council, Committee on Hormonally Active Agents in the Environment). 1999. Hormonally active agents in the environment. Washington, DC: National Academy Press.

Rhoades, J. D. 1974. Drainage for salinity control. In J. van Schilfgaarde, ed., Drainage for agriculture. Agronomy Monograph 17. Madison, WI: American Society of Agronomy. 433–462.

Tyler, C. R., S. Jobling, and J. P. Sumpter. 1998. Endocrine disruption in wildlife: A critical review of the evidence. Critical Reviews in Toxicology 28:314–361.

University of California, Riverside. 2009. PesticideWise. UC Riverside Water Quality Program Web site, http://www.pw.ucr.edu/.

Westcot, D. W., and R. S. Ayers. 1984. Irrigation water quality criteria. In G. S. Pettygrove and T. Asano, eds., Irrigation with municipal wastewater: A guidance manual. Sacramento: California State Water Resources Control Board. 3:1–3:37.

WHO (World Health Organization). 2006. Guidelines for the safe use of wastewater, excreta and grey water. Vol. 2: Wastewater use in agriculture. Geneva, Switzerland: WHO.

Wu, L., C. Amrhein, and J. Oster. 2008. Salinity assessment of irrigation water using Watsuit. In W. Wallender, ed., Agricultural salinity assessment and management. ASCE (in process).

Xu, J., W. Chen, L. Wu, and R. Green. 2008. Fate and transport of trace organic contaminants in turfgrass soils irrigated with wastewater. Agronomy Abstract. Madison, WI: American Society of Agronomy.

8

Salinity in Soils

Robert N. Carrow and Ronny R. Duncan

THE INCREASING CHALLENGE OF SALINITY MANAGEMENT

SOIL SALINITY, AN INCREASING SECONDARY CHALLENGE in the turfgrass industry, is driven by several forces. First is societal pressure for water conservation, resulting in turfgrass sites increasingly using alternative poorer-quality saline irrigation water to alleviate demand for potable water sources (Marcum 2006; Carrow et al. 2007a). Saline irrigation water sources include saline groundwater (e.g., naturally saline, salt-affected by salt leaching, reused drainage water, salt-affected by rising water tables, seawater intrusion aquifers); brackish surface water; storm water runoff; recycled water (reclaimed effluent water); and seawater or seawater blends. Recently, some states in the United States have mandated the use of reclaimed water or saline groundwater for larger turfgrass sites (Marcum 2006). This trend is expected to continue on a worldwide basis so that in the future, irrigation water applied on turfgrass and landscape sites will often be more saline than in the past (Miyamoto et al. 2005; Miyamoto and Chacon 2006).

A second driving force is the development of salt-tolerant grasses, which allows more-variable saline irrigation sources to be used (Duncan and Carrow 2000; Marcum 2001; Loch et al. 2003). Note that these genetically improved turfgrass species and cultivars are "tolerant" to salinity, not completely resistant to it; any salt deposition on the site must be continuously managed to ensure the grasses' long-term environmental sustainability.

Development of golf courses and parklands in coastal areas is a third driving force in increased salinity. In these areas, salinity results from salt water intrusion, dredged soils, acid sulfate sites, periodic flooding, high tidal influences, and wind-driven persistent salt spray (Carrow and Duncan 1998; Loch et al. 2006). Resorts are now being developed in arid, semiarid, and tropical areas where potable water is very limited or nonexistent, and saline sources are the only irrigation option for grasses and landscape plantings.

A fourth driving force is the environmental concern over protection of surface and subsurface waters and the sustainable protection of soil quality (Duncan et al. 2000, 2009; FAO 2008a, 2008b). Salinization of the ecosystem is a constant threat, and a whole-systems approach to managing the soil, water, and grass or landscape plants must be a primary focus. Since an ecosystem is a dynamic and constantly changing entity, introduction of salinity results in movement of salts upward and downward in the soil profile, impacting all plants grown in the ecosystem.

These forces driving the use of alternative poorer-quality irrigation water illustrate why salinity is an essential topic for any turfgrass water conservation book. Not only is use of saline irrigation water often one of the first water conservation best management practice (BMP) strategies that should be implemented, but once salts are consistently applied to a specific site, these salts must be managed to minimize soil accumulation (Carrow and Duncan 2008). The most important management practice to control salt levels in the plant root zone is a carefully controlled leaching program, while minimizing any adverse environmental effects. An exceptionally well-designed irrigation system in terms of efficiency of water distribution coupled with uniformity of coverage and the flexibility to apply water to small stress-challenged microclimate areas is essential for achieving acceptable grass density and performance standards. Also, site-specific irrigation applications to control salinity by leaching will require excellence in irrigation scheduling.

SALINITY: AN ISSUE NOT TO BE IGNORED

Salinity on a site cannot be ignored, especially when the source of salts is the irrigation water, since soils, plants, and water (surface and subsurface) are adversely affected (Oster 1994). Salinization of irrigated land occurs when dissolved salts accumulate in the upper soil layers and excessive salt loads come into contact with the waters. Plants soon respond to multiple salinity stresses.

Natural, or primary, salinization can occur from natural processes or secondarily as a result of human activities, including (Duncan et al. 2009):

- Accumulation of salts in the soil over long periods of time from weathering of salt-laden parent materials, especially in arid regions where natural leaching is limited by low and often sporadic precipitation.
- Oceanic salt carried by wind, rain, or flooding (storm surges, periodic high tides) onto adjacent land.
- Salt moving into the root zone from a naturally high saline water table, such as in coastal swamps or marshes. Coastal soils that are sandy in nature can be easily reclaimed by leaching. However, in coastal marine clays or more fine-textured soils, especially if the clay type is an expansive 2:1 clay, it can be very difficult to remove excess accumulated total soluble salts and high levels of accumulated sodium.
- Old ocean beds that have evaporated and left salt deposits at the surface or subsurface.
- Subsurface salt deposits that can salinize the groundwater.

Secondary salinization results from the activity of humans, including irrigation and drainage practices. Understanding the causes of secondary salinization is especially important since preventative measures can often minimize adverse effects. Types of secondary salinization include:

- Irrigation with saline irrigation water where leaching or drainage is insufficient to prevent salt accumulation in the plant root zone. The percentage of irrigated lands affected by salinization includes 20 to 25% in the United States, 13% in Israel, 30 to 40% in Egypt, 15% in China, and 15 to 20% in Australia (Gleick 1993).
- Irrigation with saline irrigation water where surface drainage results in salinization of groundwater.
- Salt-laden leachate waters intercepted by tile drains that deposit salts into surface water.
- Dryland salinity, which is a major problem in Western Australia (Pannell and Ewing 2006). Clearing native deep-rooted trees and shrubs from the land, coupled with the introduction of more shallow-rooted agricultural crops, can result in a rising water table that eventually leads to salinization and waterlogging of the surface. These changes in vegetation cause more water to drain past the root zone. The drainage water can raise the water table, which in turn mobilizes soluble salts that were located below the root zone but above the normal water table. If the salt-laden water table rises to the root zone or the capillary fringe is within reach of the plant root zone, rapid and serious soil salinization can occur, often resulting in plant death since the salinity tolerances of the plants are not adequate to withstand this surge. Moreover, the groundwater also becomes salinized.

Much of the research on salinization of lands by irrigation practices has focused on agricultural lands in rural areas (Rhoades et al. 1992; Ayers and Westcot 1994; Oster 1994; Grattan and Oster 2003; Qadir and Oster 2004). However, with more saline waters used on landscapes in urban areas, urban secondary salinization is receiving more attention (Wilson 2003). Another trend has been the increased interest in the potential effects of salinity on freshwater (drinking water) ecosystems (Hart et al. 1990; Nielsen et al. 2003).

A. F. Pillsbury, in "The Salinity of Rivers" (1981), notes the historical importance of salinization:

> Many ancient civilizations rose by diverting rivers and irrigating arid lands to grow crops. For such projects to succeed, human beings had to learn to work cooperatively toward a common objective. The most fruitful of the ancient systems was created at the southeastern end of the Fertile Crescent, the broad valley formed by the Tigris and the Euphrates in what is now Iraq. From there civilization spread eastward through present-day Iran, Afghanistan, Pakistan, India and thence into China, where ever rivers disgorged through valleys of recently deposited alluvial soil. At its peak of productivity, each irrigated region probably supported well over a million people. All these civilizations ultimately collapsed, and for the same reason: the land became so salty that crops could no longer be grown on it. The salts that were washed out of the soil at higher elevations became concentrated in the irrigated fields as the water evaporated from the surface and transpired through the leaves of the growing crops. Although floods, plagues and wars took their toll, in the end the civilizations based on irrigation faded away because of salination. (54)

Thus, history and current experience illustrate that the use of highly saline irrigation water greatly enhances the potential to degrade soil, plant, and water resources unless infrastructure improvements and skilled management practices are implemented. Management must target soils, plants, and water deposition on the site for holistic environmental protection (Rhoades et al. 1992; Duncan et al. 2000). Accumulation of excess total salts (salinization) and sodium (sodic soil formation) in the soil is more rapid as irrigation water quality declines unless salts are continuously managed.

Although saline irrigation water has the greatest impact on the site to which it is regularly applied, it can also impact the surrounding environment. Since the percentage of saline-irrigated turfgrass area is usually smaller than the total area of a community, there is a smaller potential for adverse environmental impacts on community surface and subsurface waters, as well as a smaller potential for the salinization of community landscapes and waters. However, in a location with numerous golf courses or other large irrigated turfgrass and landscape sites, salinity impacts on turfgrass and landscape areas can be significant if salinity is not properly managed. For example, in arid regions, golf courses or other landscape sites may be major users of reclaimed water from public water treatment facilities. If the water coming into the facility contains salts (such as from ion exchange salt-based water softeners or business-specific reverse osmosis units), the reclaimed water may contain excessive levels of salts. In these instances, public water treatment facilities and government entities must realize that the salts coming into the facilities are a public responsibility that should not be passed on to the user of reclaimed water. If excessive levels of salt are passed on to public or private landscape areas for irrigation, the applied salts soon become a community problem due to the deterioration of natural resources such as soils, surface waters, subsurface waters, and plants.

BEST MANAGEMENT PRACTICES FOR SALT-AFFECTED SITES

Sustainable turfgrass maintenance impacted by the issues associated with saline irrigation water requires a comprehensive, sustainable environmental management plan for salt-affected turfgrass sites. This plan must incorporate best management practices (BMPs). The BMP approach for salt-affected sites initially evolved out of the 1977 Clean Water Act protection of surface water and subsurface groundwater from pesticides, nutrients, and sediments (Carrow and Duncan 2008). However, the BMP approach can be successfully applied to all environmental issues, including salinity, since it is founded on principles that are

- science-based
- holistic or whole-systems in nature
- composed of strategies selected and applied on a site-specific basis
- considerate of all environmental (direct and indirect) impacts
- considerate of economic effects on the site and on society
- dedicated to educated long-term sustainable management
- dependent on continuous proactive (rather than reactive) monitoring and revisions

Key reference materials on managing salt-affected sites for general agriculture include USSL 1954; Abrol et al. 1988; Rhoades and Loveday 1990; Rengasamy and Olsson 1991; Rhoades et al. 1992; Ayers and Westcot 1994; Jayawardane and Chan 1994; Tanji 1996; Hanson et al. 1999; Qadir et al. 2000; and Grattan and Oster 2003. For a report on using a BMP approach on turfgrass sites with salinity issues, see Carrow and Duncan 1998; Duncan et al. 2009.

Table 8.1 suggests a planning process for developing a detailed BMP plan oriented toward salinity management for a facility such as a golf course. This process is based on the approach for developing a site-specific BMP plan for water use efficiency and conservation (Carrow et al. 2007a). The following sections discuss the twelve BMP strategies for sustainable management of salt-affected sites listed in section B of table 8.1.

A comparison of BMP strategies for salinity management with BMP strategies for water use efficiency and conservation reveals a number of similarities: for example, practices that enhance water use efficiency, such as irrigation system design for uniformity and flexibility, irrigation scheduling, cultivation and aeration, and using alternative irrigation water, can also enhance salt leaching. Managers can formulate a site-specific salinity management BMP-based plan by coupling elements of the BMPs for water conservation (Carrow et al. 2007a) with the discussion of BMPs for salinity management in this chapter. Given the many similarities, managers should consider developing both salinity and conservation BMP plans at the same time, because many infrastructure changes relate to both issues.

TABLE 8.1. ■ Planning process and components of golf course BMPs for salinity management

A. Initial planning and site assessment
1. Identify salinity management BMPs that have already been implemented by a course, including costs of implementation. This initial step aids in clarifying for the golf course management team and club members exactly what is entailed in BMPs for salinity control measures. Also, if the final document or program is shared with regulatory agencies, this information is valuable in pointing out that golf courses are not starting from zero in this area but have been implementing BMPs for many years.
2. Determine the purposes and scope of the site assessment. Site assessment is necessary to determine the best options for the specific course.
3. Conduct a site assessment and collect information:
    a. Determine current water use profile.
    b. Audit irrigation water and other water as needed.
    c. Evaluate alternative irrigation water sources; golf course design modifications; irrigation system design changes; microclimate soil, atmosphere, and plant conditions affecting irrigation system design, zoning, and scheduling; drainage needs for leaching of salts or any hydrological considerations that may arise from use of any particular irrigation water source.
4. Determine future water needs and identify an initial salinity management goal.

B. Identify, evaluate, and select BMPs strategies and options for salinity management.
1. Review information on salinity stresses.
2. Conduct a site assessment:
    a. Soil physical aspects.
    b. Soil chemical aspects.
    c. Irrigation water quality.
3. Select turfgrass and landscape plants.
4. Select irrigation water sources.
5. Maximize irrigation system design for uniformity and control.
6. Schedule irrigation for salinity leaching and efficient water use.
7. Select soil and water amendments and application methods.
8. Develop cultivation programs.
9. Design drainage.
10. Evaluate need for sand-capping.
11. Consider additional cultural programs as needed.
12. Establish monitoring and a process for revising the plan.

C. Assess the costs and benefits for all stakeholders associated with developing and implementing a long-term BMP salinity management plan. This is necessary not only for facility planning but also to demonstrate to regulatory agencies and possible critics of golf courses that the facility has invested substantial effort and cost in salinity management.
1. Benefits:
    a. Direct and indirect benefits to the owner or manager and site customers.
    b. Direct and indirect benefits to other stakeholders, including water savings, economic, environmental, recreational, etc.
2. Costs:
    a. Facilities for past and planned implementation of salinity BMPs: irrigation system changes, water storage, pumping, new maintenance equipment, water and soil treatments, course design alterations, etc.
    b. Labor.
    c. Changes in maintenance practices; use of different irrigation water sources (water treatment, soil treatment, storage, posting, etc.).
    d. Impact on community if salinity management strategies are implemented (especially mandated ones), such as revenue loss, job loss, etc.
    e. Permitting and treatment for properly regulated disposal of drainage and/or leachate.

D. The BMPs format can demonstrate to regulatory agencies the willingness of the facility to manage in a sustainable manner, while also pointing out the conflicts of interest or difficulties for a facility that occur when one agency requires the use of salt-laden recycled water while another agency imposes rigid regulations on salt and nutrient discharges that leave or leach from a site.

Source: After Carrow et al. 2007a.

1. Education about Salinity Stresses

Salinity management requires initial education and ongoing training to achieve effective decision making for the following reasons.

- There is no single salinity stress, but rather a complex of interacting stresses that are unique to each site.
- Soluble salts are spatially dynamic across a landscape and within a soil profile, while also being temporally dynamic in response to irrigation, rain, and variations in evapotranspiration (ET), soil properties, and plant conditions.
- Salinity that comes from irrigation water is a consistent secondary background stress that does not go away and must be continuously managed.
- Additional environmental stresses such as hot or cold temperatures, excess traffic or compaction, tree shade or reduced light intensity or quality, and high evapotranspiration caused by high winds and/or low humidity work in concert with salinity to escalate detrimental responses in grass or landscape plants.
- Salinity greatly impacts and complicates site management practices such as cultivation, fertilization, irrigation, and pesticide application, as well as the end use of the site (e.g., golf or other recreational activities).
- Salt-related corrosion increases the frequency and cost of maintaining and replacing equipment such as mowers, utility vehicles, electrical safety switches, and irrigation system components.

Since salinity stresses are site-specific and no single management practice resolves multiple salinity stresses, a turfgrass manager must develop a comprehensive, holistic, integrated, systems-oriented management plan that addresses the following four major site-specific salinity issues.

- **Total soluble salts.** Soluble salts induce water deficits or physiological drought stress in plants. Because the salts are soluble, if they do not react in the soil and precipitate as insoluble compounds or become attached to cation exchange capacity (CEC) sites, they can readily move with the soil water. Thus, soluble salts can affect the soil solution, surface water, and groundwater. Precipitated bicarbonate salts may cause or contribute to reduced internal drainage. Management of soluble salts, which involves cultivation and leaching, is the most important primary problem when dealing with saline irrigation water, whether from the perspective of grass and landscape management or that of environmental protection.
- **Sodium as a soil permeability hazard.** Excess sodium degrades soil by creating sodic or saline-sodic soils (Rengasamy and Olsson 1991; Oster and Schroer 1979). Sodic soils exhibit reduced water permeability (infiltration, percolation, and drainage), decreased gas exchange (low oxygen and reduced aeration, i.e., reduced oxygen flux into the soil profile), and a less favorable rooting media due to structural breakdown.
- **Ion toxicity or excess.** Ion toxicity from uptake of sodium, chlorine, and boron into roots and foliage, as well as ion contact on foliage by irrigation water spray, can affect plant selection and reduce vigor. Excessive levels of sulfate (SO_4) in irrigation water can contribute to black layer in the soil profile (see the section "Black Layer" in chapter 6).
- **Ion or nutrient imbalances.** Nutrient deficiencies (sodium, magnesium, potassium, phosphorus, nitrogen, sulfate, manganese, and others) can easily be induced in saline irrigated sites due to ion competition and imbalances. Soil fertility and plant nutrition problems arise not only when irrigation water constituents induce nutrient imbalances but also when leaching programs remove excess salts, when water and soil amendments are applied to prevent sodic conditions, and when soluble or relatively soluble nutrients and ions change their forms in the soil. Ion and nutrient imbalances can also occur when saline irrigation water drains into irrigation lakes and other surface waters.

2. Site Assessment

Site assessments are informational in nature. Two key, and related, challenges on salt-affected sites are getting adequate and accurate information about the site and assessing infrastructure changes. This information is critical in making educated decisions about costly infrastructure changes that may be necessary for effective salinity management. Also, salts are unforgiving, and unless excessive salts present in the root zone are actually moved elsewhere (hopefully downward), the stress does not abate. Thus, infrastructure alterations must be truly functional.

Except for the site assessment related to irrigation system design and scheduling (i.e., a water audit), which is discussed in later sections, important infrastructure site assessment information includes the following (Carrow and Duncan 1998; Duncan et al. 2009):

- Soil physical aspects
  - Construction and renovation considerations
    - impediments to infiltration, percolation, or drainage such as cemented caliche, clay, or rock layers that would impede salt leaching
    - deep-ripping or deep cultivation requirements prior to grass or landscape plant establishment
    - future cultivation equipment requirements
    - surface and subsurface drainage improvements
    - drainage outlets and salt disposal options
    - presence of fluctuating or high water tables
    - need for sand capping
    - preplant physical and chemical amendments to improve soil physical conditions
  - Identifying all salt additions
    - irrigation water
    - water table
    - capillary rise from salt-rich subsurface horizons
    - mixing of salt-laden soil during construction or dredging
    - fertilizing
    - drainage onto the site
  - Other
    - soil texture
    - clay type
    - soil physical analyses of root zone media, including water-holding capacity
    - organic or inorganic amendments such as sand substitutes
- Soil chemical aspects
  - routine soil test information on a standard soil test
  - Additional salt-related soil test information
    - saturated paste extract salinity test
    - SAR
    - ESP
    - EC_e
    - boron
    - free calcium carbonate content
  - Other
    - complete physical analysis (sand, silt, clay fractions)
    - saturated hydraulic conductivity rate, which is critical for leaching programs
    - capillary (water-filled) porosity versus non-capillary (air-filled) porosity
- Irrigation water quality
  - Complete agricultural irrigation suitability analyses
    - water quality aspects beyond the normal treatment facility emphasis on human exposure to biological organisms or chloride concentrations, and encompassing the comprehensive salinity impact
    - ammonia and ammonium nitrogen should also be requested since they are not normally included in most water quality test packages but are common in recycled water sources
  - Health aspects if needed
  - Multiple irrigation water sources
    - blending
    - drainage water reuse
    - reliability of each source
    - stability of each source in terms of constituents over time
    - potential for infusion into freshwater drinking reservoirs or aquifers

The primary focus of a site assessment is to obtain the information needed to make effective decisions about infrastructure changes, equipment needs, and management skills. The first step should be to assess how elements already on the site contribute to salinity management BMPs, especially if the site is a golf course or other extensive landscaping. This assessment of on-site elements is essential because it

- brings the management team at the site (e.g., golf course superintendent, club officials, pro, etc.) together with stakeholders (e.g., club members) to focus on salinity management
- assists in establishing and communicating a common understanding of what is involved in developing a BMP plan (i.e., scope, terminology, and components involved as noted in table 8.1)
- clarifies for the club the salinity management measures that are already instituted, which become a documented benchmark for further improvements in management practices and infrastructure (see Carrow et al. 2007a for a number of common BMP measures many golf courses currently use for water use efficiency and conservation; many of these apply to salinity management)
- creates documentation for regulatory agencies that the club is not starting at "ground zero" with respect to salinity management, and also documents that considerable time, effort, and resources have been expended toward water conservation in the past and are planned for the future

Since the salinity plan (or the combined salinity and water conservation plan) will likely be viewed by regulatory agencies, it is important to demonstrate that salinity practices (and water use efficiency and conservation practices) have already been implemented at the site. This educational information also establishes a benchmark for future actions.

3. Turfgrass and Landscape Plant Selection

Turfgrass species, and cultivars within a species, vary greatly in salinity tolerance levels (Carrow and Duncan 1998; Marcum 2001; Loch et al. 2003; Duncan et al. 2009). Selecting salt-tolerant turfgrass species and cultivars when using saline irrigation water

- prevents frequent salt-induced management problems, especially physiological (salt-induced) drought, nutritional disorders, wear injury, predisposition to insect and disease attack, and high- or low-temperature stress
- allows sufficient time to implement proactive preventative and corrective management practices before rapid onset of plant injuries
- allows a greater choice in irrigation water sources on many sites
- allows reuse of drainage water for irrigation on selected areas on a site
- minimizes salt-leaching requirements and enhances overall salt management
- aids the reclamation and protection of soil on salt-affected sites

Selecting salt-tolerant trees, shrubs, and other landscape plants must be a high-priority consideration on saline sites (see Duncan et al. 2009 for an extensive compilation of salinity tolerances for landscape plants). Tolerance to the contact of saline irrigation water on foliage is an important criterion; careful location of sprinklers or the use of drip irrigation can help avoid injuries caused by spray. Tolerance to the contact of soil-accumulated salts on roots, as well as tolerance to the uptake of salts into foliage, are also important criteria.

4. Selection of Irrigation Water Sources

Some sites may have more than one source of irrigation water, and each source may differ in quality. A feasibility study that analyzes water supply sources usually requires a qualified professional consultant who can evaluate the sources with respect to supply adequacy, economic viability, engineering considerations, time variables, and environmental impacts. Important considerations that may apply to sites using saline irrigation water include (Duncan et al. 2009)

- blending options and associated costs
- water quality variation over time and area for each water source
- pond or lake construction to prevent saline groundwater, runoff, or leakage from

entering underground reservoirs

- reliability and water volume of sources, both in the long term and over the course of a year
- quantification of the physical and chemical features of an aquifer that may influence groundwater or the potential for contamination from an alternative saline source
- specific requirements for salt-sensitive high-value plant materials such as golf greens where a dual irrigation distribution system would allow higher-quality water to be used on greens for routine irrigation or periodic leaching

5. Maximize Irrigation System Design for Uniformity and Control

On salt-affected sites, controlled salt leaching is the most important management practice, and effective leaching is very much a function of irrigation system design and operation (Carrow et al. 2000). Irrigation systems must be designed for uniformity of application (DU, or distribution uniformity) and flexibility to apply water in small, localized, site-specific areas. If leaching is ineffective, overirrigated sites will receive additional salt load, while underirrigated sites will accumulate salts, usually in the upper soil profile. Since excess salts induce physiological drought, deficiencies in the irrigation system's distribution and leaching become readily apparent; persistent windy conditions can enhance this problem.

Uniformity of water application is of prime importance in an irrigation system, but effective zoning (single-head control is the best) and flexibility in applying water (good controllers and enough water to allow adequate irrigation within a specified time) are also important. The system must apply enough water to allow infiltration into the soil with sufficient water volume for downward percolation to meet plant and leaching needs when water is needed and where it is needed. Efficient water use and conservation, as well as salinity management, require a substantial improvement over current practices in addressing these three irrigation questions.

Development of precision turfgrass management (PTM) programs based on the parallel concepts of precision agriculture (PA) is essential for progress toward more efficient application of inputs. A main premise of precision agriculture is site-specific management, where inputs (e.g., water, fertilizer, other chemical amendments, and pesticides) are applied only where, when, and in the quantity needed by the plant and for the specific soil conditions (Bouma et al. 1999; Corwin and Lesch 2005b; Bullock et al. 2007). However, optimal site-specific management decisions require more precise site-specific information than is currently available for turfgrass and landscape plant sites. Mobile sensor platforms for use at the field scale have been developed for precision agriculture applications to obtain the necessary site-specific information on soil and plant properties.

Two broad approaches for site-specific management have been to identify patterns within a field that are related to crop performance (e.g., yield data and plant stress) and to identify soil factors that affect yield (e.g., soil texture, soil moisture, and salinity) (King et al. 2005). The most widely used field approach has been to measure EC_a, especially by electrical magnetic devices, while zonal or microsite yield mapping provides crop performance information (Corwin and Lesch 2005a, 2005b; Rhoades et al. 1999). Electrical magnetic devices provide nonintrusive estimates of soil salinity in saline soils as well as estimates of spatial variability of soil moisture and bulk density in non-saline soils. The normal depth of the zone of determination is approximately 30 cm. The 4-wenner array method uses four equally spaced metal electrodes inserted about 2 cm deep into the soil to estimate the same soil properties through electrical resistivity, where the zone of determination is from 0 to 5 cm or greater at multiple depths (Rhoades et al. 1999).

Precision turfgrass management has not evolved in parallel with precision agriculture primarily due to the lack of mobile sensor platforms capable of mapping multiple critical soil and plant attributes in turfgrass landscapes. In 2005, the first experimental mobile platform unit developed for turfgrass to obtain spatial and temporal measurements of both soil and plant data over large landscape areas was the Toro Mobile Multi-Sensor, or TMM (Carrow et al. 2007b). The TMM can rapidly measure GPS-referenced soil volumetric water content (VWC) and penetrometer resistance in the soil surface 0 to 10 cm zone, and it can also measure turfgrass performance using the normalized differential vegetative index (NDVI). The TMM volumetric water content sampling incorporates approximately a 2.5-m grid composed of a 680 cm^3 sample soil volume, and it measures the normalized differential vegetative index at a continuous 60 ± 10 cm grass surface view while providing about three readings per 2.5 m. Intensive mapping of a typical golf course fairway can be done in 30 to 45 minutes on a 2.5-m grid. An electrical magnetic device coupled with a spectral sensor has been used to determine plant performance based on the normalized differential vegetative index for turfgrass sites with a weighted average soil resolution of about 30 cm depth (Stowell and Gelernter 2006).

As mobile devices capable of measuring important soil and plant attributes are developed, one of the first uses is for field mapping applications for improving irrigation system design and scheduling (Carrow et al. 2007b; Krum et al. 2008). This combination improves the ability to control salt applications and leach salts more effectively. In traditional agriculture, the primary field application is to define site-specific management units, subfield areas with similar soil properties and landscape attributes that result in similar plant responses, input use efficiency, and environmental impact (Boydell and McBratney 1999; Corwin and Lesch 2005a, 2005b; Corwin et al. 2006; Duffera et al. 2007; Yan et al. 2007).

Six field applications related to improving water use efficiency and salinity control on complex turfgrass sites have been evaluated (Carrow et al. 2007b; Krum et al. 2008). Specific protocols would be required to achieve the following field applications:

(a) use of initial mapping information to make immediate or relatively easy alterations in irrigation design and/or scheduling to improve water distribution uniformity, where problems may be associated with head alignment, wrong nozzles or nozzle sizing, incorrect scheduling, sprinkler wear, nozzle wear, or mismatched sprinklers and nozzles

(b) identification of site-specific management units on saline and non-saline sites, and make an assessment of the uniformity of volumetric water content on non-saline sites similar to the assessment of irrigation water distribution uniformity of the lower quarter (DU_{lq}) based on volumetric water content (rather than the current catch can method) (Mecham 2001; Dukes et al. 2006)

(c) evaluation of a landscape (e.g., a golf course fairway) for uniformity of soil volumetric water content using a volumetric water content–based DU_{lq} where uniformity may be influenced by system design, slope influences on effective infiltration of irrigation water and precipitation, and other factors

(d) determination of the best location for placement of soil moisture and salinity sensor arrays in a representative golf course fairway or other landscape site-specific measurement unit, with the ability to scale the placements for several fairways or measurement units

(e) evaluation of the design of a newly installed irrigation system for uniformity of water application and soil volumetric water content, allowing designers to improve initial designs and site managers to optimize use of the new system

(f) use of these technologies to monitor spatial and temporal salinity changes for salt management in salt-affected sites

Relative to direct salinity monitoring by soil depth, a mobile salinity monitoring platform has been evaluated in final testing that can monitor electrical resistivity in 10-cm soil zones to a depth of 30 cm and can also monitor normalized differential vegetative index (Carrow et al. 2008). Questions such as where to leach, how much water to apply, and whether leaching is effective could be addressed more efficiently from spatial and temporal salinity mapping information.

Field applications (a) through (d) above form the basis for a more robust, site-wide water audit for irrigation system uniformity than can be currently achieved using catch can testing. The basic concepts in these field applications can be applied to smaller landscape areas where hand-held sensor units can be used or larger turfgrass areas that would require mobile mapping platforms (Kieffer and O'Conner 2007). One practical outcome of determining the lower quarter distribution uniformity (DU_{lq}) and lower half distribution uniformity (DU_{lh}) using volumetric water content instead of catch-can data for each site-specific management unit is that the DU_{lh} can be used to determine a run time modifier (RTM) for efficient irrigation scheduling within the unit just as a catch-can DU_{lh} is currently used (Mecham 2001; Dukes et al. 2006).

6. Irrigation Scheduling for Salinity Leaching and Efficient Water Application

Irrigation scheduling influences both salt additions via the applied irrigation water and salt removal by leaching. Optimal irrigation scheduling will increasingly depend on integrating turfgrass and landscape manager experience and sensor-based irrigation scheduling using climatic, soil, plant, or combination approaches (Carrow et al. 2007b). As noted in the previous section, improved irrigation design using precision turfgrass management for site assessment to achieve efficient, uniform application of irrigation water is just as important for salinity control as it is for water use efficiency and conservation; but this strategy is only the first step toward efficient salinity management by leaching. Effective salinity leaching depends on

- identifying areas that need salt leaching
- targeting areas with high salt accumulation even when they are relatively small in size (i.e., subfield management versus whole field management)
- determining the least quantity of water needed to leach the salts
- preparing the site to enhance leaching through cultivation and chemical amendments
- developing a good irrigation scheduling program for salt leaching

Due to the detailed nature of these leaching-related topics, this section only summarizes the primary issues. For more information, see Duncan et al. (2009) and Carrow et al. (2000). In particular, a classic paper (Devitt et al. 2007) demonstrated the necessity of integrating knowledge of spatial and temporal salinity patterns, accurate estimates of ET, irrigation system uniformity, and timely adjustments of the LR for salinity control on golf course fairways and greens.

Salinity mapping can be applied to turfgrass situations (Carrow and Flitcroft 2005; Carrow and Duncan 2004), but spatial mapping must be performed quickly across large landscapes and within the soil profile (Krum et al. 2008). An experimental mobile unit based on the 4-wenner array method proved to be capable of monitoring electrical resistivity in 10-cm soil zones to a depth of 30 cm as well as the normalized differential vegetative index using GPS-referenced data (Krum et al. 2008). Mobile platforms will allow salinity-based site-specific measurement units to be developed (Yan et al. 2007). Site-specific measurement units defined on non-saline sites using volumetric water content and topography are stable, since volumetric water content is highly correlated to stable site attributes, especially soil texture and organic matter content (Krum et al. 2008; Corwin and Lesch 2005a). In contrast, site-specific management units on saline sites may change over time in response to salt accumulation or leaching and salt additions. Site-specific measurement units are dominant if salts are accumulated to the point of being the primary factor influencing plant performance (Yan et al. 2007). It is important to identify areas most prone to salt accumulation for site-specific leaching and placement of soil sensors to further refine leaching protocols. Once salts are leached to the point that they are not the dominant primary limiting factor influencing plant responses, the stable site-specific management units can be used for irrigation scheduling and other site-specific management decisions.

Site-specific leaching can be practiced once salinity levels are identified horizontally and vertically in the landscape (Devitt et al. 2007). However, the current state of turfgrass management depends on determining salinity status as outlined by using laboratory or hand-held field units (Carrow and Flitcroft 2005; Carrow and Duncan 2004).

The leaching requirement (LR) is the minimum amount of water that must pass through the root zone to control salts (i.e., keep salts moving) within an acceptable level. (For an in-depth discussion concerning both maintenance and reclamation leaching approaches to salinity control, see Carrow et al. 2000). The traditional leaching requirement approach is used for maintenance leaching where sufficient water is applied to maintain soil salinity at a currently acceptable level (Rhoades 1974; Carrow and Duncan 1998). The leaching requirement is intended to be applied with every irrigation event for maximum effectiveness and to obtain salt leaching with the minimum quantity of water.

Comments are often made that applying additional water for salt leaching will result in wet, soggy conditions, or that there is not sufficient time to apply all the extra water. These comments are not valid if a true maintenance leaching requirement program is followed, but they are valid when salt accumulation reaches a level requiring reclamation leaching. Reclamation leaching is required when salt accumulates above the acceptable level for the plant and salts must be leached to achieve an appropriate soil EC_e level. Since soil salinity levels are already excessive, reclamation leaching requires more water than does maintenance leaching to decrease salinity within the root zone to acceptable levels. Once this acceptable level is achieved, the leaching requirement irrigation approach (maintenance leaching) using less "extra" water can be effective.

To illustrate, as a general rule for the total quantity of irrigation water required for a specific irrigation event, 60 to 85% would go to replacement of ET losses, 10 to 30% would be consumed by nonuniformity of the irrigation system, and 5 to 15% would go to the leaching requirement. For example, if ET replacement is 1.0 inches, the quantity for nonuniformity of the system is 0.20 inches, and the leaching requirement is 7% (0.08 inches), the total quantity of irrigation water would be the sum of these, or 1.28 inches. The 0.08-inch leaching requirement does not cause wet conditions or require too much scheduling time. However, inaccurate estimates of replacement ET and nonuniformity of the irrigation system are major contributors to under- or overirrigation of specific problem areas (see Devitt et al. 2007).

Several methods have been or could be used to determine the leaching requirement (Corwin et al. 2007; Carrow and Duncan 1998). Various steady-state models and more complex transient models can be used to determine the leaching requirement (Corwin et al. 2007). However, the traditional method (Rhoades 1974) provides a good approximation and considers irrigation water salinity level (EC_w, in dS m^{-1}) and grass salinity tolerance level using the threshold EC_e (the soil salinity, EC_e, at which growth declines compared to growth under non-saline conditions):

$$LR = EC_w \div (5EC_e - EC_w)$$

where:

EC_w = electrical conductivity of irrigation water

EC_e = threshold EC, the electrical conductivity of saturated soil paste at which turfgrass growth starts to decline by at least 10%.

An example will illustrate the influence of irrigation water quality on the leaching requirement. For a turfgrass with a threshold EC_e of 10 dS m^{-1} and irrigation water quality whose EC_w is 2.0 dS m^{-1}, the leaching requirement by the above formula would be

$$LR = 2.0 \div [(5 \times 10) - 2.0]$$
$$= 0.042$$
$$= 4.2\%$$

As discussed above, the total irrigation amount would be the replacement ET plus the correction for nonuniformity of the irrigation system, plus the 4.2% leaching requirement. If the irrigation water has an EC_w of 4.0 dS m^{-1}, the leaching requirement becomes 8.7%.

Some of the models proposed to estimate leaching requirements (Corwin et al. 2007) include factors that are beyond the traditional leaching requirement, such as composition of irrigation water, salt precipitation processes, ET reduction under salinity, soil water content by rooting depth, preferential flow, and unsaturated flow affects. Which model should be used? In turfgrass situations with saline irrigation water and a perennial ground cover, salinity management by leaching is an ongoing process that must be proactively monitored and adjusted. The turfgrass system is not static or steady state: irrigation water quality may change over the year; high rainfall periods alter salinity of soil and irrigation lakes;

turfgrass growth changes with dormancy periods; and environmental stresses and traffic stresses may impact grass or landscape plant salinity tolerances among other factors. The steady state–based leaching requirement (Rhoades 1974) estimates a reasonable amount by accounting for two of the most important factors, namely, irrigation water quality and plant tolerance to salinity. It is a ballpark estimate that provides a good starting place for determining an effective site-specific leaching requirement.

The irrigation application method has a dramatic effect on the actual leaching requirement necessary for effective leaching. Heavy, continuous water application by sprinklers where the soil is essentially saturated or near saturation throughout the leaching period creates soil conditions similar to what may occur from heavy rainfall or continuous ponding or flooding on the soil surface. This heavy application requires the most water to achieve leaching, especially on fine-textured soils, since these soils foster saturated flow rather than unsaturated flow. Under saturated flow, or near saturated soil conditions, water flows primarily through the larger macropores and does not effectively leach between the macropores (i.e., within soil aggregates or between micropore areas). In unsaturated flow, water flows through the micropores and can leach salts more effectively.

Heavy applications of irrigation water that result in saturated surface soil moisture conditions foster greater runoff and uneven distribution of water over the landscape, with more pronounced wet and dry spots. Saturated flow also favors development of finger flow or preferential flow conditions in macropore channels. Runoff and preferential flow within a soil adversely affect salinity leaching across the landscape, and they also use water very inefficiently. Wetting agents would not have much effect in creating a more uniform wetting profile under saturated flow conditions, in contrast to unsaturated flow conditions, where they may be more beneficial.

Pulse irrigation is especially important for efficient salt leaching and water use (Carrow et al. 2000). With pulse irrigation (cycle and soak), relatively small amounts of water, generally from 0.20 to 0.33 inches (5 to 8 mm), are applied in increments, and time is allowed to pass before the next pulse is applied. This cycle is repeated until the desired total quantity of water for effective salt leaching is applied. Each cycle limits the quantity of water to avoid runoff and saturated surface conditions. This unsaturated condition allows the applied water to move as a more uniform wetting front across both macropore and micropore spaces. Thus, runoff from the soil surface is minimized and uniformity of application is maximized. Pulse irrigation simulates a light, continuous rainfall that applies water at less than the soil's saturated infiltration rate. Like these rainfall events, pulse irrigation leaches salt very effectively and efficiently, normally requiring only one-quarter to one-half of the water needed by heavy continuous irrigation. Pulse irrigation also conserves water efficiently on sites without salt issues. The irrigation cycles can be implemented over several nights and do not necessarily have to be accomplished in a single day for effective salt leaching.

7. Soil and Water Amendments and Application

Water and soil amendments can improve water infiltration and alleviate sodic conditions on sodic sites (Carrow et al. 1999; Carrow and Duncan 1998). Examples of situations where soil or water amendments may be necessary include

- sodic or sodic-saline soils
- acid sulfate soils, which are also often sodic
- irrigation water high in sodium (acidifying this water reduces bicarbonate reaction with calcium and magnesium, increasing the number of these ions available to counteract sodium)
- periods of high amounts of rain (timely seasonal application of calcium amendments before or during high rainfall dilutes the pure rainwater, improving infiltration, permeability, and ultimately sodium leaching)

Amendments must be selected properly and applied at the correct rates, especially if the soil is or may become sodic. To apply amendments, use the correct equipment, rates, labor, and schedule (see Carrow and Duncan 1998). If the irrigation water causes sodic soil conditions, aggressive treatment of the soil surface with gypsum is required in conjunction with cultivation. Penetrant wetting agents can often help improve salt leaching if they enhance infiltration of water and promote a more uniform wetting front under unsaturated flow conditions. However, treatment of irrigation water or the soil with amendments will not alleviate salt problems unless a good leaching program is followed. A whole-systems approach must be adopted when dealing with salt accumulation and salt movement.

8. Cultivation Programs

Infiltration, percolation, and drainage of applied water are essential requirements for effective salt leaching. The soil profile at each site on a golf course or other area should be assessed to delineate any barriers to water movement, starting with surface infiltration. Common soil physical problems on sandy and fine-textured soils that can impede water movement downward though the whole profile have been summarized by Carrow and Duncan (1998). Appropriate cultivation and timely soil modification can ensure that water and salts move with irrigation water or rainfall. On salt-effected sites, surface and subsurface cultivation programs are generally more intense than on similar non-saline sites since soil conditions must allow leaching of salts. Also, on sodic sites, the poor soil physical conditions and the shorter duration for effectiveness of cultivation requires very intense and well-designed cultivation to maintain adequate surface permeability. Cultivation coordinated with chemical amendment applications can avoid structural soil damage below the surface resulting from sodic irrigation water running to the bottom of aeration holes. With enhanced cultivation, equipment needs, scheduling, and costs also increase.

9. Drainage

Environmental impacts of saline irrigation water drainage can be diverse and serious, especially impacts on water resources (Dougherty and Hall 1995; Madramootoo et al. 1997; Tanji and Kielen 2002). Environmental impacts of drainage may occur beneath the surface if the drainage water goes into the underlying strata; or, impacts may occur at a disposal site if tile drains collect drainage water (or downstream if disposal is in a stream). Drainage and salt disposal should be considered as part of an overall water management plan (Carrow and Duncan 1998). Adequate salt movement and drainage in green cavities and bunkers on golf courses is particularly critical. Recycled irrigation water users may be faced with conflicting regulations from different state regulatory agencies: for example, one agency may require that recycled water be used if available without attention to salt load, while a different agency may regulate the salt load in water moving from the irrigation site. Since the owner or operator of the irrigation site does not have control over the salt load in the recycled water that must be used, this presents a real dilemma, especially since salts must be leached for landscape management.

10. Sand Capping

Soil conditions may be such that pulse irrigation is not effective, even with a good cultivation program. Very fine-textured soils may have low infiltration and percolation rates; if these soils are 2:1 expanding clays and have become sodic, infiltration rates are even lower, such as occurs with marine clays. Very shallow soils, such as a shallow layer of decomposed granite over an impervious caliche layer, may have good infiltration rates but little or no drainage.

In cases like these, sand capping may be necessary to improve infiltration and percolation. The sand cap may need to be 3 to 8 inches deep, depending on the severity of the problem and quality of the irrigation water. Sand capping may be done during construction or by renovation. Positive results may also be achieved by topdressing over a period of at least 3 years to build a sand layer 1 to 2 inches thick. A sand layer creates a soil zone that allows water to infiltrate and be held until it can percolate and drain under pulse irrigation. This sand layer is resistant to compacting forces and sodic-induced breakdown of soil structure, while being relatively easy to leach.

It is essential to develop a cultivation program that will penetrate the interface between the sand cap and the underlying soil. High levels of gypsum may be applied on top of fine-textured or native soil prior to sand-capping to help alleviate sodic conditions at this interface. For soil composed of crushed granite or volcanic pumice over a hard layer of uncrushed decomposed granite, volcanic rock, or caliche, any practices that can shatter this hard layer would help create channels for deeper water penetration and subsequent salt leaching.

11. Additional Cultural Programs

In addition to irrigation, cultivation, and drainage, the following key cultural programs must be adjusted for salt-affected sites (Duncan and Carrow 2005).

Fertilization

Soil fertility and plant nutrition become very dynamic relative to non-saline sites since they are affected by the constituents added from saline irrigation water, water treatment materials, and soil amendments, as well as by leaching programs that remove nutrients and elements. Soil and plant tissue concentrations of potassium, calcium, magnesium, iron, manganese, silicon, and zinc are particularly important, as are the ratios and balances among competing ions. While total soluble salts is the most common salinity problem, nutritional problems most commonly impact turfgrass or landscape plants. The dynamic nature of soil fertility and chemistry requires constant attention and adjustment by the site manager.

Climatic and traffic stresses

Salinity enhances stresses from drought, high and low temperature, and wear and traffic. These additional stresses must be carefully monitored and managed.

Cytokinin

Soil salinity suppresses cytokinin synthesis in the roots of plants. On saline-irrigated sites, grasses often increase root system redevelopment and hormone stabilization after application of this hormone, which is found in seaweed or kelp extract products.

Pest management

Pest stresses on salt-affected sites may differ from those on non-saline sites due to salinity stresses and alterations in management practices. Sodic soils are especially challenging due to the tendency for low oxygen and waterlogging problems to occur, creating a situation in which the grass is less aggressive than normal and the microclimate is conducive to rapid growth of pathogen populations. Salt-induced physiological drought stress can accentuate drought stress associated with root-feeding insects and root pathogens. Leaching programs should be timed to avoid high temperatures and humid conditions that may promote pathogens. If leaching is required, fungicides may be applied prior to leaching and possibly afterward.

12. Proactive Monitoring and Plan Revision

While initial site assessment is very important, an ongoing proactive, rather than reactive, monitoring program on salt-affected sites is essential for effective management of the ecosystem. Monitoring programs must be developed for plant, soil, and water in order to provide science-based information for infrastructure design and maintenance; soil, grass, and landscape plants management; and sustainable environmental decision making. Important aspects of proactive monitoring include the following.

- **Conduct soil tests and irrigation water quality tests.** Soil and water testing must be done frequently due to the dynamic nature of salt stresses. Irrigation water quality often varies over time and with multiple irrigation water sources, including dilution by rainwater. Variations in irrigation water quality coupled with climatic changes such as wet and dry seasons result in similar changes in soil constituents. Relatively inexpensive salt monitoring devices can be used onsite, or samples can be sent to laboratories for testing.
- **Monitor plant status.** Tissue testing can assist in defining potential nutritional issues. Visual observations of the rhizome, crown, and roots of plants under salinity stress can aid in identifying potential problems, especially when augmented by cores taken by a soil sampler that reveal issues such as black layer formation or layers impeding water movement or rooting. Observation of root tissues and rooting depth are important initial clues to impending salt stress limitations on grass and landscape plants.

CONCLUSION

Moderate to highly saline irrigation water cannot be applied without enhanced management skills, attention to potential environmental problems, increased costs for management inputs and infrastructure improvements, and a best management practices approach to whole-systems management. When considering the use of a saline irrigation water, the question of prime importance becomes “Is using this water sustainable and environmentally compatible?” This question can be answered in the affirmative only if science-based decisions are made concerning site selection, assessment, and development; irrigation system design and scheduling; drainage; water treatment; soil infiltration and percolation; soil amendments; plant selection; and other infrastructure decisions. Salinity is an unforgiving issue that can degrade water, soil, and plant resources if not properly addressed. Sustainable turfgrass and landscape plant management can be achieved only by using the best science-based best management practices for salt-affected sites.

REFERENCES

Abrol, I. P., J. S. P. Yadav, and F. I. Massoud. 1988. Salt-affected soils and their management. FAO Soils Bulletin 39. Rome: U.N. Food and Agriculture Organization.

Ayers, R. S., and D. W. Westcot. 1994. Water quality for agriculture. Rome: FAO Irrigation and Drainage Paper 29. Reprint 1994. FAO Web site, http://www.fao.org/documents/.

Bouma, J, J. Stoorvogel, B. J. van Alphen, and H. W. G. Booltink. 1999. Pedology, precision agriculture, and the changing paradigm of agricultural research. Soil Science 63:1763–1768.

Boydell, B., and A. B. McBratney. 1999. Identifying potential within-field management zones from cotton yield estimates. In J. V. Stafford, ed., Proceedings of the European Conference on Precision Agriculture. London: SCI. 331–341.

Bullock, D. S., N. Kitchen, and D. G. Bullock. 2007. Multidisciplinary teams: A necessity for research in precision agriculture systems. Crop Science 47:1765–1769.

Carrow, R. N., and R. R. Duncan. 1998. Salt-affected turfgrass sites: Assessment and management. Hoboken, NJ: Wiley.

———. 2004. Soil salinity monitoring: Current and future. Golf Course Management 72(11): 89–92.

———. 2008. Best management practices for turfgrass water resources: Holistic-systems approach. In M. Kenna and J. B. Beard, eds., Water quality and quantity issues for turfgrasses in urban landscapes. Ames, Iowa: Council for Agricultural Science and Technology. 273–294.

Carrow, R. N., and I. Flitcroft. 2005. Salinity monitoring of turfgrass sites. Recorded presentation, ASA-CSSA-SSSA 2005 International Annual Meetings Web site, http://crops.confex.com/crops/2005am/techprogram/P5117.HTM.

Carrow, R. N., R. R. Duncan, and M. Huck. 1999. Treating the cause, not the symptoms: Irrigation water treatment for better infiltration. USGA Green Section Record 37(6): 11–15.

———. 2000. Leaching for salinity management on turfgrass sites. USGA Green Section Record 38(6): 15–34.

Carrow, R. N., R. R. Duncan and C. Waltz. 2007a. BMPs and water-use efficiency/conservation plan for golf courses: Template and guidelines. University of Georgia, Georgia Turf Web site, http://www.commodities.caes.uga.edu/turfgrass/georgiaturf/Water/Articles/BMPs_Water_Cons_07.pdf.

Carrow, R. N., V. Cline, and J. Krum. 2007b. Monitoring spatial variability in soil properties and turfgrass stress: Applications and protocols. In Proceedings of the 2007 International Irrigation Show, San Diego, CA. Technical sessions CD-ROM. Falls Church, VA: Irrigation Association. 641–645.

Carrow, R. N., I. Flitcroft, and J. M. Krum. 2008. Development of a mobile 4-wenner array based salinity monitoring device for turfgrass situations. Proceedings of the American Society of Agronomy Annual Meeting, Oct. 5–9, Houston, TX.

Clean Water News. 2007. Regional water board adopts new salinity effluent limits for Delta dischargers. Clean Water News 1(3): 1. Central Valley Clean Water Association Web site, http://www.cvcwa.org/pdf%20files/Newsletter_V1_I3.pdf.

Corwin, D. L., and S. M. Lesch. 2005a. Characterizing soil spatial variability with apparent soil electrical conductivity. I: Survey protocols. Computers and Electronics in Agriculture 46:103–133.

———. 2005b. Characterizing soil spatial variability with apparent soil electrical conductivity. II: Case study. Computers and Electronics in Agriculture 46:135–152.

Corwin, D. L., S. M. Lesch, P. J. Shouse, R. W. Soppe, and J. E. Ayars. 2006. Delineating site-specific irrigation management units using geospatial EC_a measurements. In B. J. Allred, J. J. Daniels, and M. R. Ehsani, eds., Handbook of agricultural geophysics. Boca Raton: CRC Press. 247–254.

Corwin, D. L., J. D. Rhoades, and J. Simunek. 2007. Leaching requirement for soil salinity control: Steady-state versus transient models. Agricultural Water Management 90:165–180.

Devitt, D. A., M. Lockett, R. L. Morris, and B. M. Bird. 2007. Spatial and temporal distribution of salts on fairways and greens irrigated with reuse water. Agronomy Journal 99:692–700.

Dougherty, T. C., and A. W. Hall. 1995. Environmental impact assessment of irrigation and drainage projects. Rome: FAO Irrigation and Drainage Paper 53. FAO Web site, http://www.fao.org/documents/.

Duffera, M., J. G. White, and R. Weisz. 2007. Spatial variability of southeastern U.S. coastal plain soil physical properties: Implications for site-specific management. Geoderma 137:327–339.

Dukes, M. D., M. B. Haley, and S. A. Hank. 2006. Sprinkler irrigation and soil moisture uniformity. In Proceedings of the 2006 International Irrigation Show, San Antonio, TX. Technical sessions CD-ROM. Falls Church, VA: Irrigation Association. 446–460.

Duncan, R. R., and R. N. Carrow. 2000. Seashore paspalum: The environmental turfgrass. Hoboken, NJ: Wiley.

———. 2005. Just a grain of salt: As salinity increases, turf management will need to increase too. Turfgrass Trends (July): 70–75.

Duncan, R. R., R. N. Carrow, and M. Huck. 2000. Effective use of seawater irrigation on turfgrass. USGA Green Section Record 38(1): 11–17.

———. 2009. Turfgrass and landscape irrigation water quality: Assessment and management. Boca Raton: Taylor and Francis.

FAO (Food and Agriculture Organization of the United Nations). 2008a. Global network on integrated soil management for sustainable use of salt-affected sites. FAO Web site, http://www.fao.org/landandwater/agll/spush/degrad.htm.

———. 2008b. Salt-affected soils. ProSoil: Problem soils database. FAO Web site, http://www.fao.org/ag/aGL/agll/prosoil/salt.htm.

Gleick, P. H. 1993. Water in crisis: A guide to the world's fresh water resources. New York: Oxford University Press.

Grattan, S. R., and J. D. Oster. 2003. Use and reuse of saline-sodic waters for irrigation of crops. In. S. S. Goyal, S. K. Sharma, and D. W. Rains, eds., Crop production in saline environments: Global and integrative perspectives. New York: Food Products Press/ Haworth.

Hanson, B., S. R. Grattan, and A. Fulton. 1999. Agricultural salinity and drainage. Oakland: University of California Division of Agriculture and Natural Resources Publication 3375.

Hart, B. T., P. Bailey, R. Edwards, K. Hortle, K. James, A. McMahon, C. Meredith, and K. Swadling. 1990. Effects of salinity on river, stream, and wetland ecosystems in Victoria, Australia. Water Research 24(9): 1103–1117.

Jayawardane, N. S., and K. Y. Chan. 1994. The management of soil physical properties limiting crop production in Australian sodic soils: A review. Australian Journal of Soil Research 32:13–44.

Kieffer, D. L., and T. S. O'Conner. 2007. Managing soil moisture on golf greens using a portable wave reflectometer. In Proceedings of the 2007 International Irrigation Show, San Diego, CA. Technical sessions CD-ROM. Falls Church, VA: Irrigation Association.

King, J. A., P. M. R. Dampney, R. M. Lark, H. C. Wheeler, R. I. Bradley, and T. R. Mayr. 2005. Mapping potential crop management zones within fields: Use of yield-map series and patterns of soil physical properties identified by electromagnetic induction sensing. Precision Agriculture 6:167–181.

Krum, J., R. N. Carrow, I. Flitcroft, and V. Cline. 2008. Mobile mapping of spatial soil properties and turfgrass stress: Applications and protocols. In Proceedings of the 9th International Conference on Precision Agriculture, Denver, CO. 236–251.

Loch, D. S., E. Barrett-Lennard, and P. Truong. 2003. Role of salt tolerant plants for production, prevention of salinity and amenity values. In Salinity under the sun: Investing in prevention and rehabilitation of salinity in Australia. Proceedings of the 9th National Conference on Productive Use and Rehabilitation of Saline Land, Rydges Capricorn Resort.

Loch, D. S., R. E. Poulter, M. B. Roche, C. J. Carson, T. W. Lees, L. O'Brien, and C. R. Durant. 2006. Amenity grasses for salt-affected parks in coastal Australia. Final Project Report, Horticulture Australia. http://www.dpi.qld.gov.au/26_11948.htm.

Madramootoo, C. A., W. R. Johnston, and L. S. Willardson. 1997. Management of agricultural drainage water quality. Rome: FAO Water Reports 13.

Marcum, K. B. 2001. Growth and physiological adaptations of grasses to salinity stress. In M. Pessarakli, ed., Handbook of plant and crop physiology. 2nd ed. New York: Marcel Dekker. 623–636.

———. 2006. Use of saline and non-potable water in the turfgrass industry: Constraints and developments. Agricultural Water Management 80:132–146.

Mecham, B. Q. 2001. Distribution uniformity results comparing catch-can tests and soil moisture sensor measurements in turfgrass irrigation. In Proceedings of the 2001 International Irrigation Show, San Antonio, TX. Technical sessions CD-ROM. Falls Church, VA: Irrigation Association. 133–139.

Miyamoto, S., and A. Chacon. 2006 Soil salinity of urban turf areas irrigated with saline water. II: Soil factors. Landscape and Urban Planning 77:28–36.

Miyamoto, S., A. Chacon, M. Hossain, and I. Martinez. 2005. Soil salinity of urban turf areas irrigated with saline water. I: Spatial variability. Landscape and Urban Planning 71:233–241.

Nielsen, D. L., M. A. Brock, G. N. Rees, and D. S. Baldwin. 2003. Effects of increasing salinity on freshwater ecosystems in Australia. Australian Journal of Botany 51:655–665.

Oster, J. D. 1994. Irrigation with poor quality water. Agricultural Water Management 25:271–297.

Oster, J. D., and F. W. Schroer. 1979. Infiltration as influenced by irrigation water quality. Soil Science Society of America Journal 43:444–447.

Pannell, D. J., and M. A. Ewing. 2006. Managing secondary dryland salinity: Options and challenges. Agricultural Water Management 80:41–56.

Pillsbury, A. F. 1981. The salinity of rivers. Scientific American 245(1): 54–65.

Qadir, M., and J. D. Oster. 2004. Crop and irrigation management strategies for saline-sodic soils and waters aimed at environmentally sustainable agriculture. Science of the Total Environment 323:1–19.

Qadir, M., A Ghafoor, and G. Murtaza. 2000. Amelioration strategies for saline soils: A review. Land Degradation and Development 11:501–521.

Rengasamy, P., and K. A. Olsson. 1991. Sodicity and soil structure. Australian Journal of Soil Research 29:935–952.

Rhoades, J. D. 1974. Drainage for salinity control. In J. van Schilfgaarde, ed., Drainage for agriculture. Agronomy Monograph 17. Madison, WI: American Society of Agronomy. 433–461.

Rhoades, J. D., and J. Loveday. 1990. Salinity in irrigated agriculture. In B. A. Stewart and D. R. Nielson, eds., Irrigation of agricultural crops. Agronomy Monograph 30. Madison, WI: Soil Science Society of America. 1091–1142.

Rhoades, J. D., A. Kandiah, and A. M. Mashali. 1992. The use of saline waters for crop production. Rome: FAO Irrigation and Drainage Paper 48. FAO Web site, http://www.fao.org/documents/.

Rhoades, J. D., F. Chanduvi, and S. Lesch. 1999. Soil salinity assessment: Methods and interpretation of electrical conductivity measurements. Rome: FAO Irrigation and Drainage Paper 57. FAO Web site, http://www.fao.org/documents/.

Stowell, L., and W. Gelernter. 2006. Sensing the future. Golf Course Management 74(3): 107–110.

Tanji, K. K. 1996. Agricultural salinity assessment and management. New York: American Society of Civil Engineers.

Tanji, K. K., and N. C. Kielen. 2002. Agricultural drainage water management in arid and semi-arid regions. Rome: FAO Irrigation and Drainage Paper 61. FAO Web site, http://www.fao.org/documents/.

USSL (U.S. Salinity Laboratory). 1954. Diagnosis and improvement of saline and alkali soils. Washington, DC: Agriculture Handbook 60. USDA Agricultural Research Service Web site, http://www.ussl.ars.usda.gov.

Wilson, S. M. 2003. Understanding and preventing impacts of salinity on infrastructure in rural and urban landscapes. In Proceedings of the 9th National Conference on Productive Use of Saline Lands, Yappon, Queensland.

Yan, L., S. Zhou, L. Feng, and L. Hong-Yi. 2007. Delineation of site-specific management zones using fuzzy clustering analysis in a coastal saline land. Computers and Electronics in Agriculture 56:174–186.

9

Water Management Technologies

Bernd Leinauer and Robert Green

HIGH TEMPERATURES, LIMITED PRECIPITATION, AND uneven annual rainfall distribution in many parts of the world limit the sustainability of adequate turfgrass growth and quality unless frequent and abundant irrigation is applied. In addition, human population growth and urban development are sources of increasing stress on water supplies that range, depending on precipitation, from almost adequate to scarce. Consequently, strategies aimed at conserving potable water use for turf irrigation are encouraged. These strategies include the use of more efficient irrigation systems and the application of irrigation scheduling techniques to maximize irrigation efficiency. Irrigation is defined as efficient when the proportion of water delivered to the turf stand is beneficially used by the plant (Rogers et al. 1997). In order to achieve high efficiency, losses such as droplet evaporation, runoff, leaching, and wind drift must be minimized. Improving efficiency of traditional above-ground sprinkler systems often requires installing new types of sprinklers and nozzles. Alternatively, irrigation can be applied efficiently from the subsurface through microirrigation systems.

Strategies to reduce unnecessary irrigation water use should include the application of efficient irrigation systems and scheduling based on the actual water requirement of turf needed to maintain a desired quality level. Irrigation amounts can be estimated based on climatic factors, calculated from the plants' water status by monitoring soil moisture, or obtained from remote sensing technologies that detect and quantify drought stress.

IRRIGATION SYSTEMS

Sprinkler Irrigation

Sprinkler irrigation has been the accepted practice for irrigating lawns since Joseph Smith patented the first swiveling lawn sprinkler in 1894 (Connolly 2001) for areas where supplemental watering is required because natural precipitation is insufficient. In order to achieve efficient irrigation, a system must be properly designed and installed. For uniform irrigation, correct sprinkler head selection and spacing must create water spray patterns that match the shape of the landscape and avoid over- or underirrigation. In addition, larger irrigated areas should be "hydrozoned" (Huck and Zoldoske 2008). Hydrozones are areas of similar species, microclimates, soil types, and slopes that have similar watering requirements (Carrow et al. 2002). Overall, improving a sprinkler irrigation system's efficiency can help conserve water by reducing unnecessary losses due to wind drift, surface runoff, deep percolation, and evaporation from standing water when application rates do not match infiltration rates or the soil water-holding capacity (Carrow et al. 2002).

Irrigation uniformity

Determining how uniformly water is applied by sprinkler irrigation systems is an important step in achieving high irrigation efficiency. Nonuniform distribution can deprive some turf areas of required water and overirrigate other areas. The term "distribution uniformity" (DU) has been introduced to describe irrigation uniformity (Christiansen 1942). A catch can test is usually performed to calculate the low-quarter distribution uniformity (DU_{lq}) and to evaluate water delivery and distribution of the irrigation system. DU and DU_{lq} do not describe water use efficiency. Turf areas can be irrigated uniformly based on high DU_{lq}, but excess water can still be applied, which can lead to unnecessary runoff or deep percolation. It is therefore recommended that DU_{lq} be presented as a ratio and not as a percentage (Burt et al. 1997). Table 9.1 lists the rating of selected sprinkler types used in landscape and turf irrigation based on DU_{lq} (Mecham 2004).

The quality and uniformity of a sprinkler system has a significant impact on the amount of water required to irrigate a landscape. If 50 inches of irrigation water is deemed necessary to maintain a cool-season turf stand in the U.S. Southwest, improving the irrigation uniformity from a DU_{lq} of 0.55 (which is considered good for spray heads) to 0.75 will decrease the water amount required from 91 inches to 67 inches. Uniformity data summarized from over 6,800 irrigation audits across all types of residential and commercial lawns in Utah, Nevada, Colorado,

TABLE 9.1. Rating of low-quarter distribution uniformity (DU_{lq}) for sprinkler types used in turf irrigation

	Rating				
Sprinkler type	Excellent	Very good	Good	Fair	Poor
fixed spray	0.75	0.65	0.55	0.50	0.40
rotor	0.80	0.70	0.65	0.60	0.50
impact	0.80	0.70	0.65	0.60	0.50

Source: Mecham 2004.

Arizona, Texas, Oregon, and Florida show an average DU_{lq} of 0.5, regardless of the type of sprinkler head being used (Mecham 2004). In order to irrigate all areas of a lawn adequately with an irrigation system that has a DU_{lq} of 0.5, the amount of irrigation water is twice what the grass plant needs to maintain an adequate quality level. New technology in sprinklers may alleviate some of the performance problems due to evaporation and wind drift by providing a streaming spray pattern. The streams rotate and discharge large droplets, resulting in less evaporation and drift than the typical sprinkler mist with microdroplets (Lorenzini 2004).

Subsurface Irrigation

An alternative to sprinkler systems in turfgrass irrigation is subsurface irrigation. This includes subirrigation (also known as subground irrigation), which irrigates and drains through connected perforated pipes (tiles) or trays below the depth of root penetration (Leinauer 1998), and drip irrigation, which applies water from emitters just below the soil surface (fig. 9.1) (for a complete review of subsurface irrigation terminology, including trickle irrigation, drip irrigation, and subirrigation, see Camp 1998). Advantages of subsurface irrigation systems include the uninterrupted use of the turf area during irrigation, energy savings due to a lower operating water pressure, and potential water savings because irrigation is applied directly in the root zone and is not affected by wind drift or evaporation. Although the benefits of subsurface irrigation on water consumption and crop yield have been extensively studied in agriculture (Camp 1998), subsurface irrigation has only recently received attention for turf irrigation. Few studies have investigated the effects of tray-type or tile-type subsurface irrigation systems on water use by established turf, and the majority of the studies report significant water savings at no loss in turf quality when subirrigation systems are used. Water savings of up to 50% can be obtained when using subsurface irrigation (Stroud 1987; Chevallier et al. 1981), and irrigation on tile-type subirrigated turf plots was shown to use 90% less water than sprinkler-irrigated plots (Leinauer 1998; Leinauer et al. 2004). Despite the data demonstrating the water conservation potential of subsurface irrigation systems, they have not achieved full market acceptance. One argument against the use of subsurface irrigation is that spacing and depth of trays, pipes, or emitters are difficult to determine, especially in sloping areas. Other reasons for the limited use of subsurface irrigation are the relatively high cost of installation, difficulty in monitoring and troubleshooting damaged emitters, potential interference with maintenance practices such as aerification or pesticide applications, and the inability to establish turf from seed when irrigated below the surface.

FIGURE. 9.1. ■ Subsurface drip line with emitter in a turfgrass root zone. *Photo:* B. Leinauer.

Turf establishment under subsurface irrigation

Studies investigating turfgrass establishment using subsurface irrigation systems have given conflicting results. Successful establishment appears to depend on the type of subsurface irrigation system, depth of emitters, and soil type. When emitters are placed at a depth lower than capillary rise, subirrigation systems may not provide enough moisture to seedlings that have no established root system to access water in deeper profiles. Establishment was delayed on subsurface-drip-irrigated creeping bentgrass with drip lines installed 8 inches below the surface in a sandy, USGA-type root zone when compared with sprinkler irrigation (Leinauer and Mack 2007). However, when establishment was compared between a sprinkler system and a tray-type subirrigation system (the Evaporative Control System), the subirrigated bentgrass established significantly faster (Leinauer and Mack 2007). Another study (Johnson 2007) compared the establishment of several cool-season grasses in a sandy soil under subsurface drip and sprinkler irrigation when drip lines were installed only 4 inches below the surface; successful establishment with drip irrigation depended on the cultivar and species used. The tall fescue variety Southeast established better under drip irrigation than under sprinkler irrigation, while results were reversed for Tar Heel II tall fescue, which established faster with sprinkler irrigation. Perennial ryegrasses Brightstar SLT and Catalina, alkaligrasses Dawson and Salty, and hybrid bluegrass Thermal Blue showed no establishment differences between irrigation systems.

Turf performance and irrigation water savings under subsurface irrigation

No studies are available on the long-term performance of turfgrasses under subsurface irrigation. Most of the available published studies report turf quality over only 1 or 2 growing periods. Root intrusion into drip emitters is one problem that could affect water distribution and consequently turf quality when subsurface drip irrigation (SDI) is applied. The performance of three cool-season grasses (Kentucky bluegrass, perennial ryegrass, and tall fescue) and three warm-season grasses (bermudagrass, seashore paspalum, and zoysiagrass) has been compared under both subsurface and sprinkler irrigation (Gibeault et al. 1985). Of all six grasses tested, the turf quality of only Santa Ana bermudagrss was not affected by irrigation type during the 2-year test period. All other grasses showed a significant reduction in turf quality when irrigated from the subsurface. A 1-year study reported similar quality between subsurface drip irrigation and sprinkler irrigation on Midiron bermudagrass and no difference in water requirements between the two treatments (Suarez-Rey 1999). In the first of a 4-year study conducted at New Mexico State University, subsurface-drip-irrigated creeping bentgrass in a USGA-type green required 15% less water than sprinkler-irrigated bentgrass (Leinauer 2005). During the subsequent 3 years, the turf quality of drip-irrigated bentgrass was lower than that of the sprinkler-irrigated because of increased hydrophobicity in the root zone (Leinauer, unpublished data). When sprinkler-irrigated bentgrass was compared to tray-type subirrigated bentgrass, results were different: subirrigation yielded significant water savings during the entire test period, and subirrigated bentgrass had higher turf quality in 3 of the 4 years (Leinauer, unpublished data).

Outlook for subsurface irrigation

Irrigation water savings have been documented when tray- and tile-type subirrigated turf was compared to sprinkler-irrigated turf. However, more research is needed to determine whether similar water savings can be achieved when using subsurface drip. Most studies that have compared subsurface drip to sprinkler irrigation were conducted on level surfaces and on square or rectangular turf plots, which are easy to irrigate with sprinklers, with almost no runoff or overspray from sprinklers. These scenarios do not necessarily represent real-world situations. Slopes and irregularly shaped landscapes in particular are difficult to irrigate uniformly, and surface application from sprinklers can result in runoff and significant overspray. Therefore, applying water directly to the root zone can result in fewer losses and in more efficient irrigation (Moore 2006) (fig. 9.2).

FIGURE 9.2. Home lawn in subsurface drip irrigation. *Photo:* B. Leinauer.

IRRIGATION SCHEDULING

Reference Evapotranspiration (ET_o)

The amount of irrigation water applied to a turf stand should be based on its water requirement: the amount of water required for growth, the amount lost through transpiration, and the amount lost through evaporation from the soil surface (Huang 2008). With only 1 to 3% of the water taken up by the turfgrass plant used in the metabolic process (Beard 1973), evapotranspiration (ET) losses from a turfgrass stand provide an accurate measure of irrigation water requirements. Several methods are available to determine evapotranspiration. These include

- eddy covariance techniques
- atmometers such as Bellani plates (Livingston 1935)
- open pan ET (water loss from an open water surface, ET_{pan})
- actual ET (calculated from a weight reduction of lysimeters, ET_a)
- potential ET (ET_p)
- reference ET (ET_o)

ET_p and ET_o estimates are most commonly used when turfgrass irrigation scheduling is based on ET losses. Climate parameters such as solar radiation, air temperature, humidity, and wind speed are entered into mathematical models to calculate a "theoretical potential evapotranspiration." This term is somewhat general, as it describes water loss on a theoretical basis only and is not related to a specific crop. The Penman model (Penman 1948) was one of the first empirical models to estimate water loss based on climate data alone. More recently, ET models have been developed that describe water loss in two standard reference crops, alfalfa (ET_r) and a clipped cool-season grass (ET_o) (Allen et al. 1998).

Estimating turfgrass evapotranspiration

Evapotranspiration of different turfgrasses has been closely correlated with atmometer evaporation, open pan ET, and potential (model) ET estimates. For example, a strong correlation ($r^2 = 0.73$) has been documented between a Bellani plate evaporation and the measured ET of tall fescue, bermudagrass, buffalograss, and zoysiagrass (Qian et al. 1996). In the same experiment, the correlation between turfgrass actual ET (determined by means of weighing lysimeters) and open pan and potential ET was less precise, resulting in r^2 values of 0.67 and 0.60, respectively. To match actual turfgrass ET, most ET estimates require adjustments in the form of multipliers or coefficients to meet local climatic conditions and specific maintenance situations (Kneebone et al. 1992).

These crop coefficients (K_c), defined as the ratio of ET_a to ET_o, therefore represent a percentage of the reference value (Kneebone et al. 1992), and they can depend on parameters such as ET reference, quality expectations, season, grass type, maintenance level, and micro- and macroclimate. A summer K_c of 0.98 was reported for a Providence creeping bentgrass green in Minnesota (Sass and Horgan 2006) when ET_o (Allen et al. 1998) was compared with ET_a. When a Nebraska modified Penman equation was compared with ET_a, K_c values ranged from 0.7 to 1.3 for creeping bentgrass varieties, depending on cultivar and growing month (Salaiz et al. 1991). K_c values have been reported to be between 0.4 and 0.8 for ET_{pan} compared with ET_a of bermudagrass, zoysiagrass, and St. Augustinegrass, and tall fescue (Kneebone and Pepper 1982). Summer K_c values have been estimated to be in the range of 0.8 when Tifway bermudagrass ET_a was compared with ET_o (Brown et al. 2001).

Turfgrass evapotranspiration for irrigation scheduling

Crop coefficients not only adjust ET_o to ET_a but can also be used to calculate irrigation requirements. Numerous researchers have demonstrated that applying irrigation below 100% ET replacement does not necessarily result in a significant loss of turfgrass quality and function (Shearman 2008). The practice of irrigating below maximum water loss of turfgrass stands is defined as deficit irrigation (Feldhake et al. 1984) and is most effective as a water conservation strategy in areas that receive sufficient occasional rainfall to recharge the soil profile (Shearman 2008). Thus, accurate ET_o estimates in conjunction with specific crop coefficients can be used for irrigation scheduling and offer the opportunity for significant irrigation water savings. Crop coefficients based on

ET_{pan} and ET_o for estimating irrigation requirements for turfgrasses in California have been published for warm- and cool-season grasses (Meyer et al. 1985). A summer K_c of 0.8 has been suggested when ET_o is used to irrigate creeping bentgrass greens in Minnesota (Sass and Horgan 2006). Several states offer automated, Web-based potential and reference ET values for irrigation scheduling purposes. A Penman-Monteith equation (Monteith 1965) is commonly used to model ET and has been generally accepted as the most stable form of ET calculation worldwide (Howell 1996).

In California, the most commonly accepted source of ET_o data is the California Irrigation Management Information System (CIMIS), an integrated network of over 120 automated weather stations located at key agricultural and municipal sites throughout the state (fig. 9.3). CIMIS uses the modified Penman equation with a wind function, also called CIMIS Penman equation, to estimate ET_o. In addition to CIMIS ET_o, CIMIS also provides ET_o values estimated using the Penman-Monteith equation. Studies have shown that there are no significant differences between Penman-Monteith and CIMIS ET_o. The reference crop at most CIMIS stations is a 4.7-inch-tall cool-season grass (tall fescue) that is transpiring near the maximum rate. Currently, there are efforts to increase the ability to accurately estimate CIMIS ET_o in municipal areas and microclimates.

FIGURE 9.3. ■ Weather station no. 44 of the California Irrigation Management Information System (CIMIS), in Riverside. *Photo:* R. Green.

The irrigation industry has introduced irrigation controllers (smart controllers) that automatically adjust to daily changes in ET (Huck and Zoldoske 2008). Turf irrigation in residential and industrial areas in particular has been identified as a major source of high water use during the summer months, as water is applied in excess of ET demand (Barnes 1977; Haley et al. 2007; Kjelgren et al. 2000). These areas would greatly benefit from smart irrigation scheduling technologies, as they adjust watering to local climate conditions. A 30% reduction of irrigation water applied to home lawns has been documented in Florida when an ET controller was used for irrigation scheduling compared with homeowner-controlled scheduling (Haley et al. 2007). The U.S. Department of the Interior, Bureau of Reclamation, has published a 2008 summary of 14 publicly available reports and articles evaluating water savings of weather-based irrigation controllers. Despite differences in study methods, irrigation system performance, and installation and programming of the various controllers, all studies reported reductions in irrigation water applied when smart controllers were used, with water savings as high as 80% compared with traditional irrigation scheduling. In order to provide incentives to conserve irrigation water use on home lawns and landscapes, municipal water authorities and utilities (such as the Metropolitan Water District of southern California) have introduced rebate programs for the installation of smart irrigation controllers (MWD 2008).

ET-based irrigation scheduling: Outlook

Using ET rates to schedule irrigation for maximum efficiency depends on correctly estimating the climatic parameters at the site to be irrigated. In 1998, evaporation was measured over 2 years at numerous locations on a golf course using Bellani plates, and the collected evaporation data was compared with weather station ET estimates (Jiang et al. 1998). Weather station ET exceeded evaporation on golf tees by more than 22%, and evaporation varied by more than 20% among golf tees. Because weather station locations do not always accurately represent microclimate conditions on all irrigated areas, site-specific adjustments by means of different crop coefficients become important to avoid over- or underirrigation. Crop coefficients differ with species, season, microclimate, maintenance level, and quality expectations. Furthermore, ET_0-driven irrigation estimates do not account for different soil conditions (e.g., soil moisture levels) and plant conditions (depth of root system or stress level) (Carrow et al. 2002). Therefore, climate-based irrigation scheduling is the least site-specific scheduling approach.

Soil Moisture

An alternative to using climate parameters to estimate irrigation amounts needed to replace water losses is to measure changes in soil moisture. Irrigation scheduling based on soil moisture aims at keeping the root zone within a target moisture range by replenishing ET and drainage losses (Muñoz-Carpena 2004). It is considered the most intuitive way of determining how much and when to irrigate.

Methods to determine soil moisture

The numerous methods available to measure soil water status can be classified as either direct or indirect. Direct measurement involves removal of water from the soil pores by means of heating (oven drying) and is known as the gravimetric method (Topp and Ferré 2002). This is the most commonly used method in scientific and laboratory soil analyses, but results are not immediately available and the sampling technique is destructive. Because of the time and labor associated with direct measurement, determination of soil moisture for irrigation scheduling purposes relies entirely on indirect methods of measurement.

The indirect methods for measuring soil water can be divided into two groups: the first group measures the amount of water present in the pore space (soil water content), and the second group determines the energy status of water present (soil water potential). Soil moisture sensor technologies currently used to schedule landscape and turf irrigation include dielectric sensors and heat-dissipating sensors for the measurement of soil water content, and tensiometers and granular matrix sensors (or gypsum blocks) to measure soil water potential (Huck and Zoldoske 2008). Both types of sensors have advantages and disadvantages; when selecting a type, consideration must be given to the soil type, range of moisture measured, and expected soil salinity (for a detailed review of field-based soil moisture sensors, see Muñoz-Carpena 2004).

Sensors for measuring soil water potential

Tensiometers estimate soil matric potential and do not require soil-specific calibration, but they must have regular maintenance. Because the water that is drawn from the plastic tube into the root zone through the ceramic porous tip needs to be replaced on a regular basis, the sensor must be accessible when installed in the landscape. Granular matrix sensors (GMS) measure the electrical resistance between two electrodes embedded in quartz material, which is correlated with the matric potential of the root zone. GMS can show an inability to rewet when the root zone changes from very dry to moist, and therefore they work best for values close to saturation (Muñoz-Carpena 2004). In order to calculate irrigation requirements based on volume, soil moisture tension or suction values must be converted to volumetric soil moisture content by means of a moisture release curve. Determining this soil-specific curve requires laboratory equipment. Therefore, for the purpose of irrigation scheduling, sensors that measure soil water content directly might offer an advantage over devices that measure moisture potential.

Sensors That Measure Soil Water Content

Dielectric sensors measure volumetric soil moisture by using a correlation between the dielectric constant (K_a) of soil, air, and water and the volumetric soil moisture content (Θ_v) at electromagnetic frequencies (Paltineanu and Starr 1997). Two methods, time domain reflectometry (TDR) and frequency domain reflectometry (FDR, or capacitance), use the dielectric-permettivity-sensitive relationship between mineral soil particles and water to measure K_a, which is used to determine Θ_v. Consequently, the accuracy of measuring soil moisture content by determining the dielectric constant depends on the travel time analysis (TDR) or phase shift analysis (FDR) of an electromagnetic impulse and the algorithm correlating K_a and Θ_v (Lin 2003). A third-degree polynomial function of $K_a(\Theta_v)$ works well for mineral soils up to field capacity (Topp et al. 1980; Muñoz-Carpena 2004). Factors generally affecting the reflection of a TDR or FDR waveform through signal attenuation, such as length of the rods, soil texture, soil density, and soil electrical conductivity, influence the accuracy of measurements and can limit the applicability of dielectric soil moisture measurement systems.

Several models of dielectric soil moisture sensors are available. They differ in ease of handling, measurement depth, and cost. Some are portable, simple to use, provide data instantly on a digital display, and allow for soil moisture measurements in relatively short time periods. Others are stationary, require a defined setup, can include the use of several probes on one signal generator and data-logging capability, and can be connected directly to an irrigation controller. More recently, units that transmit soil moisture readings wirelessly have been introduced (Leinauer 2006). The combination of dielectric soil moisture measurements with wireless technology allows for long distances between the location of measurement and that of data processing without the use of cables.

Accuracy of soil moisture sensors and their application for irrigation scheduling

In a study conducted at New Mexico State University, TDR and FDR sensors were examined for accuracy in a USGA-type sandy root zone across salinity levels ranging from 1 to 8 dS m^{-2} (Leinauer, unpublished data). At soil salinities lower than 4 dS m^{-2} all sensors determined volumetric soil moisture accurately and sensor values correlated strongly with volumetric moisture measured gravimetrically ($0.88 < r^2 > 0.98$). At soil salinities greater than 4 dS m^{-2} only sensors with a rod length of 10 cm or shorter remained accurate ($r^2 > 0.80$). Accuracy of sensors with rods of 20 or 30 cm in length dropped to r^2 values between 0.69 and 0.40.

Soil moisture sensing to determine irrigation requirements has been successfully used for decades in agriculture, but it has only recently gained acceptance in turfgrass and landscape application (Huck and Zoldoske 2008). Perceived limitations were cost, increased maintenance, reliability concerns, and errors due to soil or root zone heterogeneity. Single-point moisture measurements in soils were considered nonrepresentative, and replication of moisture sensors or a combination of different types of sensors was deemed necessary (Jones 2007; Huck and Zoldoske 2008). One study suggests that although absolute moisture values may vary considerably over an entire landscape, sensors are not necessary in multiple locations to schedule irrigation; sensors should be installed in a location representative of the area and the difference in soil moisture between the beginning and the end of a dry-down be used to schedule irrigation (Carrow et al. 2002). The approach of using moisture extraction over time within the range of soil moisture contents is more consistent for irrigation scheduling than using absolute values.

Water savings through soil moisture-based irrigation

Several studies have investigated the effect of soil moisture–based scheduling on irrigation water savings. Tensiometer-based irrigation of bermudagrass has been found to yield monthly savings of 42% and 95% compared with irrigation based on automatic clock settings (Augustin and Snyder 1984). A 50% reduction in irrigation water required on creeping bentgrass has been observed when soil moisture–based irrigation systems were changed from 12% volumetric water content to 10% (Miller 2006). A study conducted at New Mexico State University in 2006 recorded a 66% (July) and 50% (August) reduction in water use on a perennial ryegrass stand when irrigation was scheduled based on wireless FDR moisture readings as opposed to 80% ET_o irrigation (Leinauer, unpublished data). The U.S. Department of the Interior's Bureau of Reclamation (2008) reported that soil moisture–based controllers used between 0% and 82% less irrigation water than either traditional or ET-based irrigation scheduling.

REMOTE SENSING

The use of remote sensing technology has been suggested as a potential tool to quantitatively and objectively monitor turf areas and to detect drought stress. Early work in the 1980s and 1990s measured leaf surface temperature of plants in the 10.5 to 12.5 micrometer (μm) waveband by means of an infrared thermometer to quantify drought stress level (Idso et al. 1981; Everest 1984). A crop water stress index calculated from remotely measured leaf surface temperatures has been suggested for irrigation scheduling of cool- and warm-season turfgrasses (Throssell et al. 1987; Jalali-Farahani et al. 1993). More recently, interest has shifted, and multispectrum radiometry and calculated reflectance ratios from visible wavelengths (400 to 700 nm) and from the near-infrared region (NIR) (700 to 2500 nm) have been used to determine plant stress (Carter 1993). Many turfgrass studies have used a normalized difference vegetation index (NDVI), which is calculated from the reflectance at two wavelengths in the red (R) range (600 to 700 nm) and the NIR range, to determine plant coverage, turf quality, and measure stresses. While these technologies have helped researchers detect and quantify stress caused by drought, saline conditions, and many other biotic and abiotic factors, to date no automated remote sensing irrigation scheduling technology is commercially available.

CONCLUSION

Efforts to conserve water used for recreational and ornamental turf have focused mainly on plant selection or the complete elimination of turf because of a perceived high irrigation water requirement. Improving the uniformity of irrigation systems or using irrigation scheduling technologies based on ET estimates or soil moisture offer additional approaches for reducing irrigation water needs. Very often the potential for significant water conservation through applying new irrigation technologies remains untapped.

REFERENCES

Allen, R. G., L. S. Pereira, D. Raes, and M. Smith. 1998. Crop evapotranspiration (Guidelines for computing crop water requirements). FAO Irrigation and Drainage Paper 56. Rome, Italy: FAO.

Augustin, B. J., and G. H. Snyder. 1984. Moisture sensor-controlled irrigation for maintaining bermudagrass turf. Agronomy Journal 76(5): 848–850.

Barnes, J. R. 1977. Analysis of residential lawn water use. MS thesis, Department of Civil and Architectural Engineering, University of Wyoming.

Beard, J. B. 1973. Turfgrass: Science and culture. Englewood Cliffs: Prentice Hall.

Bonachela, S., F. Orgaz, F. J. Villalobos, and E. Fereres. 2001. Soil evaporation from drip-irrigated olive orchards. Irrigation Science 20:65–71.

Brown, P. W., C. F. Mancino, M. H. Young, T. L. Thompson, P. J. Wierenga, and D. M. Kopec. 2001. Penman Monteith crop coefficients for use with desert turf systems. Crop Science 41(4): 1197–1206.

Burt, C. M., A. J. Clemmens, T. S. Strelkoff, K. H. Solomon, R. D. Bliesner, L. A. Hardy, T. A. Howell, and D. E. Eisenhower. 1997. Irrigation performance measures: Efficiency and uniformity. Journal of Irrigation and Drainage Engineering 123 (6)(Nov./Dec.): 423–442.

Camp, C. R. 1998. Subsurface drip irrigation: A review. Transactions of the ASAE 41(5): 1353–1367.

Carrow, R. N., P. Broomhall, R. R. Duncan, and C. Waltz. 2002. Turfgrass water conservation: 1: Primary strategies: Water conservation should be the first priority of golf courses and other recreational turf venues. Golf Course Management 70(5): 49–53.

Carter, G. A. 1993. Responses of leaf spectral reflectance to plant stress. American Journal of Botany 80:239–243.

Chevallier, C., M. Corbet, and J. P. Guérin, 1981. Use of low-density materials as substratum for concrete platform with subirrigation. In R. W. Sheard, ed., Proceedings of the 4th International Turfgrass Research Conference, Guelph, Ontario. 233–240.

Christiansen, J. E. 1942. Irrigation by sprinkling. Berkeley: University of California Agricultural Experiment Station Bulletin 670.

CIMIS (California Irrigation Management Information System). CIMIS Web site, http://wwwcimis.water.ca.gov.

Connolly, J. 2001. Turning irrigation upside down. Turf West (July): 6–15.

Everest, M. M. 1984. Agricultural research utilizing infrared thermometry. ASAE Paper 84-2076. St. Joseph, MI: American Society of Agricultural Engineers.

Feldhake, C. M., R. E. Danielson, and J. D. Butler. 1984. Turfgrass evapotranspiration: II: Responses to deficit irrigation. Agronomy Journal 76(1): 85–89.

Gibeault, V. A., J. L. Meyer, V. B. Youngner, and S. T. Cockerham. 1985. Irrigation of turfgrass below replacement of evapotranspiration as a means of water conservation: Performance of commonly used turfgrasses. In F. Lemaire, ed., Proceedings of the fifth international turfgrass research conference. Paris, France: Institut National de la Recherche Agronomique. 347–355.

Haley, M. B., M. D. Dukes, and G. L. Miller. 2007. Residential irrigation water use in Central Florida. Journal of Irrigation and Drainage Engineering 133: 427–434.

Howell, T. A. 1996. Irrigation scheduling research and its impact on water use. In C. R. Camp, E. J. Sadler, and R. E. Yoder, eds., Evapotranspiration and irrigation scheduling. St. Joseph, MI: American Society of Agricultural Engineers. 21–33.

Huang, B. 2008. Turfgrass water requirements and factors affecting water usage. In J. B. Beard and M. P. Kenna, eds., Water quality and quantity issues for turfgrasses in urban landscapes. Ames, IA: Council for Agricultural Science and Technology. 193–203.

Huck, M. T. and D. F. Zoldoske. 2008. Achieving high efficiency in water application via overhead sprinkler irrigation. In J. B. Beard and M. P. Kenna, eds., Water quality and quantity issues for turfgrasses in urban landscapes. Ames, IA: Council for Agricultural Science and Technology. 223–241.

Idso, S. B., R. D. Jackson, P. J. Pinter Jr., R. J. Reginato, and J. L. Hatfield. 1981. Normalizing the stress-degree-day parameter for environmental variability. Agricultural Meteorology 24:45–55.

Jalali-Farahani, H. R., D. C. Slack, D. M. Kopec, and A. D. Matthias. 1993. Crop water stress index models for bermudagrass turf: A comparison. Agronomy Journal 85:1210–1217.

Jiang H., J. D. Fry, and S. C. Wiest. 1998. Variability in turfgrass water requirements on a golf course. HortScience 33(4): 689–691.

Johnson, C. 2007. Establishing cool- and warm-season turfgrasses using saline irrigation in combination with subsurface drip irrigation. Master's thesis, Department of Plant and Environmental Sciences, New Mexico State University.

Jones, H. G. 2007. Monitoring plant and soil water status: Established and novel methods revisited and their relevance to studies of drought tolerance. Journal of Experimental Botany 58(2): 119–130.

Kjelgren, R., L. Rupp, and D. Kjelgren. 2000. Water conservation in urban landscapes. HortScience 35:1037–1040.

Kneebone, W. R., and I. L. Pepper. 1982. Consumptive water use by sub-irrigated turfgrasses under desert conditions. Agronomy Journal 74(3): 419–423.

Kneebone, W. R., D. M. Kopec, and C. F. Mancino. 1992. Water requirements and irrigation. In D. V. Waddington, R. N. Carrow, and R. C. Shearman, eds., Turfgrass. Agronomy Monograph 32. Madison, WI: Agronomy Society of America. 441–472.

Leinauer, B. 1998. Water savings through subirrigation. Golf Course Management 66(10): 65–69.

———. 2005. Effect of greens type, irrigation type, and root zone material on irrigation efficiency, turfgrass quality, and water use on putting greens in the Southwest. In J. L. Nus, ed., 2004 USGA Turfgrass and Environmental Research Summary. Far Hills, NJ: USGA Green Section.

———. 2006. Precision irrigation: Prolonged water shortages require innovative measures. TurfNews 30(2): 66, 68.

Leinauer, B., and J. Makk. 2007. Establishment of golf greens under different construction types, irrigation systems, and rootzones. USGA Turfgrass Environmental Research Online 6(7): 1–7.

Leinauer, B., R. Sallenave, D. VanLeeuwen, and H. Schulz. 2004. A comparison of construction types and their associated irrigation systems: Effect on turfgrass quality, drought avoidance, and irrigation water use. Acta Horticulturae 661:123–129.

Lin, C. 2003. Frequency domain versus travel time analyses of TDR waveforms for soil moisture measurements. Soil Science Society of America Journal 67:720–729.

Livingston, B. E. 1935. Atmometers of porous porcelain and paper, their use in physiological ecology. Ecology 16:444–472.

Lorenzini, G. 2004. Simplified modeling of sprinkler droplet dynamics. Biosystems Engineering 87:1–11.

Mecham, B. 2004. A summary report of performance evaluations on lawn sprinkler systems. Northern Colorado Water Conservancy District Web site, http://www.ncwcd.org/ims/ims_info/SummaryEvaluationSprinklerSystems.pdf.

Meyer, J. L., V. A. Gibeault, and V. B. Youngner. 1985. Irrigation of turfgrass below replacement of evapotranspiration as a means of water conservation: Determining crop coefficient of turfgrasses. In F. Lemaire, ed., Proceedings of the fifth international turfgrass research conference. Paris, France: Institut National de la Recherche Agronomique. 357–364.

Miller, J. P. 2006. Sensor based irrigation and wetting agent application effects on a sand based putting green. Master's thesis, University of Arkansas Department of Horticulture.

Monteith, J. L. 1965. Evaporation and the environment. In G. E. Fogg, ed., The state and movement of water in living organism. Vol. 19. New York: Academic Press. 205–234.

Moore, J. 2006. Does this stuff work or not? USGA Green Section Record 44(3): 14–16.

Muñoz-Carpena, R. 2004. Field devices for monitoring soil water content. Gainesville: University of Florida IFAS Bulletin 343.

MWD (Metropolitan Water District of Southern California). 2008. Tips and rebates. MWDSC Web site, http://www.mwdh2o.com.

Qian, Y. L., J. D. Fry, S. C. Wiest, and W. S. Upham. 1996. Estimating turfgrass evapotranspiration using atmometers and the Penman-Monteith model. Crop Science 36(3): 699–704.

Paltineanu, I. C., and J. L. Starr. 1997. Real-time soil water dynamics using multisensor capacitance probes: Laboratory calibration. Soil Science Society of America Journal 61:1576–1585.

Penman, H. L. 1948. Natural evaporation from open water, bare soil, and grass. In Proceedings of the Royal Society of London, Series A 193:120–146.

Rogers, D. H., F. R. Lamm, M. Alam, T. P. Trooien, G. A. Clark, P. L. Barnes, and K. Mankin. 1997. Efficiencies and water losses of irrigation systems. Manhattan: Kansas State Research and Extension Irrigation Management Series MF-2243.

Salaiz, T. A., E. J. Kinbacher, T. P. Riordan, and R. C. Shearman. 1991. Creeping bentgrass cultivar water use and rooting responses. Crop Science 31(5): 1331–1334.

Sass, J. F., and B. P. Horgan. 2006. Irrigation scheduling on sand-based creeping bentgrass: Evaluating evapotranspiration estimation, capacitance sensors, and deficit irrigation in the Upper Midwest. Applied Turfgrass Science Online, http://www.plantmanagementnetwork.org/ats/, doi:10.1094/ATS-2006-0330-01-RS.

Shearman, R. C. 2008. Turfgrass cultural practices for water conservation. In J. B. Beard and M. P. Kenna, eds., Water quality and quantity issues for turfgrasses in urban landscapes. Ames, IA: Council for Agricultural Science and Technology. 205–222.

Stroud, T. 1987. Subsoil irrigation systems. Grounds Maintenance (Feb.): 80–83.

Suarez-Rey, E. M. 1999. Subsurface drip irrigation on bermudagrass in arid climates. Master's thesis, Department of Agricultural and Biosystems Engineering, University of Arizona.

Throssell, C. S., R. N. Carrow, and G. A. Milliken. 1987. Canopy-temperature-based irrigation scheduling indices for Kentucky bluegrass turf. Crop Science 27:126–131.

Topp, G. C., and P. A. Ferré. 2002. Water content. In J. H. Dane and G. C. Topp, eds., Methods of soil analysis: Part 4, Physical methods. Madison, WI: Soil Science Society of America. 417–547.

Topp, G. C., J. L. Davis, and A. P. Annan. 1980. Electromagnetic determination of soil water content: measurements in coaxial transmission lines. Water Resources Research 16:574–582.

U.S. Department of the Interior, Bureau of Reclamation. 2008. Summary of smart controller water savings studies. Final Technical Memorandum 86-68210-SCAO-01. Bureau of Reclamation Web site, http://www.usbr.gov/waterconservation/docs/WaterSavingsRpt.pdf.

10

Water Conservation in the Urban Landscape

Dale A. Devitt and Robert L. Morris

JOHN STEINBECK, IN HIS NOVEL *EAST OF EDEN*, WROTE OF THE Salinas Valley in the early twentieth century, "And it never failed that during the dry years the people forgot about the rich years and during the wet years they lost all memory of the dry years. It was always that way." In the twenty-first century, such a loss of memory of the dry years must not occur. However, with the looming effects of global warming this may not be an issue, as wet years may very well become fewer and fewer, and spaced at greater intervals. How we manage water must be based on the premise that every drop wasted will affect not only our ability to maintain an acceptable quality of life but also the ability of future generations to do so.

Water conservation, especially conservation associated with the use of water in the urban landscape, can and should occur in every region of the United States. However, in communities located in the southwestern United States, which have arid to semiarid climates, a higher percentage of the water is used outdoors. For example, in Las Vegas, Nevada, the residential sector uses approximately 60% of all the water, with approximately 70% of that water used for the irrigation of residential landscapes (Devitt and Morris 2008). To make matters worse, many communities, including Las Vegas, continue to grow at a rapid pace while facing an uncertain future with regards to water resource availability.

In the Colorado River Basin, the amount of water entering the system varies on a yearly basis. From 2002 to 2007, the basin received below-average recharge, which led to a hydrologic drought for downstream users. A glaring visualization of this drought can be seen in the water level in Lake Mead, which dropped over 90 feet during this time period (fig. 10.1). In a recent article in *Science*, the authors indicate that water systems have been historically designed under the assumption of stationarity, which infers that resources fluctuate in a predictable range (Milly et al. 2008). Unfortunately, the impact of the current drought condition has already demonstrated this premise to be incorrect. As such, water managers must look to an uncertain future.

FIGURE 10.1. Lake Mead, Nevada, has dropped over 90 feet during the past 8 years, exposing foundations from the community of St. Thomas, abandoned after completion of Hoover Dam and submerged for over 70 years. *Photo:* D. Devitt.

Water managers must plan for a future where more people exist, less water is available, and some of the water available for use is of poorer quality. In light of this, are cities located in arid and semiarid regions sustainable? In particular, are urban landscapes sustainable with regards to water? Sustainable water use can be defined as "the use of water that supports the ability of human society to endure and flourish into the indefinite future without undermining the integrity of the hydrological cycle or the ecological systems that depend on it" (Gleick et al. 1995). Based on this definition, many communities in the southwest may find it difficult to accomplish water sustainability in the twenty-first century. Whether we as a culture have "evolved to the point where we are no longer bound by biophysical limits of nature" may be answered by a severe drought that is "the tipping point that will test the resilience of desert cities" (Baker et al. 2004). Many cities in the Southwest have begun implementing comprehensive conservation programs that will hopefully prevent such a tipping point from being exceeded. However, population growth in many regions continues to erode water savings obtained through conservation.

In the purest sense, landscapes are sustainable only if they do not require any additional resources —if they achieve a certain level of self-sufficiency. Although this is a water use goal that communities in wetter regions can strive to attain, arid and semiarid regions can hope only to move toward a greater level of sustainability. It is therefore appropriate and critical that cities, especially those in arid environments, implement conservation programs that significantly reduce per capita water use, with special emphasis on urban landscapes.

A significant reduction in urban landscape water use must occur. This does not mean that all landscapes have to follow the same steps toward conservation. However, it is critical that the reductions occur soon and that they be permanent. This chapter addresses the attitudes and perceptions people have toward water conservation, the planning and design of low-water-use landscapes, and specific aspects that need to be addressed to achieve more sustainable, low-water-use landscapes.

ATTITUDES AND PERCEPTIONS

A number of studies and surveys have been conducted in the United States to assess attitudes and perceptions people have toward water conservation (Lohr and Bummer 1992; Lant and Sims 1993; Baumann and Opitz 1993; St. Hilaire et al. 2003; CUWCC 2007). The majority of these studies have indicated that acceptance of conservation measures increases as residents realize the reality of water shortages. However, there is also a tendency to want conservation measures to weigh more heavily on new growth and on the nonresidential sectors. One of the reasons people gave for not conserving was that "conservation encourages new growth" (Baumann and Opitz 1993). Although growth can account for a significant part of a community's economy, such growth does not have to be linked to high water use. In Las Vegas, more high-density and high-rise residential housing is being built. If such a paradigm shift in community growth truly occurs, more people can be sustained with less water.

If water resources become less reliable in the future and population continues to grow, communities will be forced to continually reduce water demands. Such a demand-side management approach (Vickers 1991) will rely on conservation and planned growth to play a greater and greater role. The savings associated with conservation measures will need to become permanent so that water planners can rely on these estimates in assessing available water resources. Residential water users generally have a distorted idea of how much water they actually use and how they use it (Lant and Sims 1993; CUWCC 2007). This would suggest that conservation must be founded on educating water users on the current status of water resources, rationale for conservation measures imposed, water savings realized, and the associated costs. However, education may play a significantly less-effective role than passing ordinances, metering water use, and imposition of fines for water waste (Morris et al. 1996). Communities are more apt to accept water conservation if lifestyle infringement is minimized and conservation efforts are both effective and economically sound (Lant and Sims 1993).

Conservation must first start with behavioral changes, followed by structural changes (Baumann and Opitz 1993). Behavioral changes do not require the installation of pipes and pumps, just a shift in how we use water. Although water savings can and should take place indoors, the greatest challenge is to significantly reduce outdoor water use in urban landscapes. Much can be done on an individual basis, and it starts with understanding the range of values held by individuals and groups, followed by the changing of attitudes toward low-water-use landscapes. People's attitudes toward water-conserving landscapes are not deeply held and can be changed (Lohr and Bummer 1992). The challenge is to move people into action and begin the process of lowering water use in each and every landscape setting. In one study, the majority of respondents indicated that they would use desert plants in their landscape, but the respondents who actually had desert landscaping was significantly lower (80% versus 51% for front yards) (St. Hilaire et al. 2003).

Outdoor water use must be reduced significantly. If a goal were set to reduce outdoor water use by half over the next decade, what would the urban landscape have to look like?

PLANNING AND DESIGN

Low-water-use landscapes just don't occur, they need to be properly designed based on careful consideration of plant species, plant density, exposure, and how the plants are irrigated. The design must take into account not only the landscape but the entire residential or urban setting.

People have been impacting their surrounding landscape through design for thousands of years (Butzer 1993). Societies have experimented with medicinal, architectural, food, and forage aspects of desert landscaping during this time (Wescoat 1990). Most of the early history of garden design centered on symbolism. Examples include the gardens recorded in Egyptian tomb paintings thought to be as early as 3500 BC, Persian gardens designed to reflect heaven on earth, and the hanging gardens of Babylon situated somewhere in present-day Iraq. Gardens during this era were enclosed designs that were usually meant to provide privacy. The classical European concept of the garden is as an extension of the house into the natural environment (Jellicoe 1966). Some of the earliest discussions concerning gardens and their place in urban planning were written by Vitruvius, a Roman writer, architect, and engineer, sometime in the first century BC when he began laying the foundation for landscape design in the context of municipalities (Turner 2010).

It was not until the end of the twentieth century that scholars brought the topic of landscape architecture into the theoretical realm. In his approach toward landscape architecture, J. D. Hunt (2000) divided the world into three physical natures based on the ideas of the Italian humanist Jacopo Bonafadio: wilderness, places of habitation (middle landscape), and the garden. Four years later, a study investigating plant use in desert designs modified Hunt's concepts when relating it to design trends such as xeriscape, hydrozoning, and minioasis (Kotzen 2004).

The contemporary aim of garden design, landscape design, and landscape architecture is to make "good outdoor space" (Turner 2010). Both garden design and landscape architecture are concerned with the design of outdoor space using five compositional elements: vegetation, landforms, water, paving, and structures. However, in water-limiting arid environments the use of water features in the landscape must be appropriately scaled for desert climates or eliminated altogether.

With increased settlement and urbanization in arid regions during the twentieth century, landscape architecture and other allied professions were forced to address unique challenges associated with immigrants moving into these arid and desert locations. Immigrants moving into these often harsh desert environments brought with them their own sense of place. In landscape design "sense of place" is a nontechnical way of summing up the totality of a place and the processes that shape it: water, soil, and vegetation (Franklin 1997). Since most of these immigrants came from wetter climates, that sense of place included turfgrass, high plant densities and large trees and shrubs common to mesic climates, all driving forces in high-water-use landscapes.

Until late in the twentieth century, ornamentals derived from mesic environments dominated the commercial nursery trades throughout the United States. Many of the plants imported to dry regions were not suited to the extreme climate and soils found in arid environments, and because of this, the effective plant palette available for landscape design was limited. Desert or native plant materials were typically unavailable, and the few landscape architects and designers who were designing with native plants frequently had to collect their own seed and have them custom grown.

For many years urban landscapes designed for the desert Southwest had no sense of place or regionalism because the designs used mesic concepts combined with mesic plants. These designs were transported from wetter climates that used turfgrass to fill negative space, large trees to frame buildings, and plants to soften architectural lines or act as foundation plants. The imposition of landscape designs and plant materials from mesic climates into xeric climates created urban landscapes that used large amounts of water due to the selection of plant species without regard to their mature size, potential water use, or total landscape biomass.

For a shift toward regional design to occur there needed to be acceptance of a change in landscape design and the commercial availability of regional or bioclimatic plant material. In the arid West it made sense that this change be centered around water and its role in design.

Four major forces merged in the latter half of the twentieth century and worked together to create a shift away from mesic landscapes: the rising cost of water, a growing environmental movement, increased availability of xeric plants, and the growing popularity of xeriscape and similar arid design philosophies. Environmental activism and scientific research have been effective in challenging modern development trends and impacts (Hester 1990). These groups have been instrumental in shaping desert landscape design to be sensitive to the need for reduced irrigation, an increased use of native and drought-adapted species, and the reuse of water for landscape irrigation (Wescoat 1990).

This new landscape philosophy advocated the use of native plants, a decrease in landscape plant biomass, and the adoption of a set of landscape design principles developed and marketed by the Denver water department in an attempt to conserve water. The xeriscape concept embodies seven sound principles: appropriate planning and design, soil analysis, practical turf areas, appropriate plant selection, efficient irrigation, use of mulches, and appropriate maintenance (Welch et al. 2008).

Xeriscape landscape designs focused on excluding turfgrass as a design element to fill negative space but rather encouraging its use, when needed, in practical turfgrass areas. Negative space in designs was filled with low-water-use ground covers or mulches, replacing a potentially high-water-use area with a low- or zero-water-use area. Rock mulches are now common in desert designs with a Sonoran Desert regional emphasis, while wood mulches are more common in landscape designs originating in the Great Basin and higher elevations of the Rocky Mountains. Numerous studies point out the benefit of both rock and organic mulches in water conservation (Li 2003; Boeken and Orenstein 2001). Using regional native plants or plants originating from a similar bioclimatic region are emphasized in xeriscape design. This emphasis typically reduces the chance of plant failure, lowers maintenance costs, and helps establish a bioclimatic sense of place. The most common view of xeriscape in desert regions currently correlates architectural planting with climate and not the local ecology. Unfortunately, this ignores issues of landscape character and landscape quality (Kotzen 2004), leading to the planting of xeric plants from various arid regions while in some cases ignoring the local landscape ecology.

Problems can arise with the introduction of native and bioclimatic species from other dry regions of the world. While mesic plants had little chance of surviving in arid and desert climates without irrigation, newly introduced species from arid parts of the world in some cases can thrive outside their adopted landscape. Species introduced from xeric areas in Africa and the Middle East, such as fountain grass (*Pennisetum setaceum* (Forsk.)), have escaped from dry urban landscapes into the native landscapes of nine U.S. states. (Arizona Sonora Desert Museum 2008; NRCS 2010). It is "not enough to ask whether a certain species will survive or not. We need to ask ourselves what effect or impact the planting will have for the future of the environment, ecology and landscape in an area" Kotzen (2004).

The xeriscape concept was further refined and termed "hydrozone irrigation" and "minioasis," which divided the urban desert landscape into three zones: a wet zone, a dry zone, and a zone between them of progressively lower water use called the transition zone (Jones and Sacamano 2000). The wet zone is the smallest of the landscape zones, where water is used intensively and would correlate with Hunt's "garden." The two driest zones equate to the "middle landscape" concept. In hydrozoning, individual irrigation stations would deliver water to all plants in the same zone at the same time. Water savings could be achieved through delivering precise irrigation amounts (minimizing waste) and lengthening the time between irrigations for more xeric plants. Care would need to be taken to make sure larger plants with more extensive root systems in adjacent zones do not exploit the water from other zones.

A natural consequence of this series of events was the emerging concept of sustainable landscape design. Sustainable design is "a process of raising consciousness and changing basic attitudes—attitudes so ingrained we are often unaware that they shape our design and management of the land" (Franklin 1997). By doing so, perhaps we come closer to appreciating and incorporating a "desert ethic" into landscape designs.

Numerous guidelines exist for designing and installing landscapes that have been reported to conserve water (see Bennett and Hazinski 1993; Borland et al. 1993; Chaplin 1994; EPA 1993). Most of these guidelines use or incorporate the seven xeriscape principles (Welch et al. 2008). Field-based research does not exist that demonstrates water savings (conservation) associated with mixed landscapes (fig. 10.2) over extended periods (greater than 5 years); however, several documents produced primarily by municipalities, water conservation agencies, or water purveyors report water conservation over time by homeowners using published landscape guidelines (Nelson 1987, 1994; Sovocool and Rosales 2005; Testa and Newton 1993). However, a turfgrass industry trade journal warned that savings gained through design and plant selection can be nullified by poor irrigation management (Golf Course News 2001). Another study found that irrigation management by homeowners in the desert Southwest did not change substantially after landscapes were converted from traditional to more xeric designs, and no decrease in total landscape water use was realized (Peterson et al. 1999). More research is needed to document the water-saving potential from using xeriscape landscape design and mixed landscapes to replace traditional landscapes.

THE PLANT FACTOR

Landscapes differ not only in size but also in species composition, planting density, canopy structure, microenvironments and soil types. It is therefore not surprising that water requirements vary tremendously

FIGURE 10.2. Mixed landscapes represent a challenge to water management. Such landscapes should be redesigned using the principles of hydrozoning. *Photo:* D. Devitt.

from landscape to landscape. Although much is known about the water requirements of turfgrass (Huang and Fry 1999; Beard 1973; Shearman 1985, 1989), much less is known about the water requirements of trees, shrubs, and ground cover (Wullschleger et al. 1998; Zajicek and Heilman 1991; Devitt et al. 1994; Levitt et al. 1995; Schuch and Burger 1997; Balok and St. Hilaire 2002). Many plant lists rank the water requirements of trees, shrubs, and groundcover (see Costello et al. 2000), but these rankings are rarely based on quantifiable water use numbers. Water requirements depend on how a plant is grown (fertilization, irrigation, pruning, mulch, etc.), which can shift a species from one water use category to another. Because all plants use water, removing any plant from a landscape can save water. Large trees can use significant amounts of water (Wullschleger et al. 1998) as can cool-season turfgrass species (Feldhake et al. 1983; Kopec et al. 1988; Brown et al. 2004). Similar water use in mixed landscape areas can be achieved by varying the species composition (plants of different sizes with different levels of water use), density of plantings, and the total landscape area planted. Individual homeowner preference may create a landscape design dominated in its water use by a large evergreen tree species, while another landscape is dominated by an equivalent water use area planted to a warm-season turfgrass species. Water savings can be achieved under many different landscape designs. Species composition can be quite varied among landscapes in arid climates and can be encouraged by appreciating the natural trade-offs that can occur among trees, shrubs, grasses, and flowering annuals with different rates of water use.

Too often, plant selection is not based on what the landscape will look like when it has fully matured. Water savings must be evaluated not only during the first year but also projected 5, 10, and even 20 years into the future (fig. 10.3). Homeowners must be willing to modify the landscape over time to maintain water savings and as their family needs change. Proper planning and design prior to installation of a landscape can minimize the need to make major alterations in future years.

Emphasis in plant selection should be given to native species that are suitable to the environment

FIGURE 10.3. ■ Quantifying water savings requires assessing water use over multiple years. Water savings during the first year almost always overestimate the long-term water savings. *Photos:* D. Devitt.

and known to be low water users. Selection must take landscape factors into account: skunkbush sumac (*Rhus trilobata* Nutt.), a native to arid habitats and considered drought tolerant, used more water under nonlimiting soil water conditions than did other less-drought-tolerant species (Montague et al. 1998). Landscapes should demonstrate a good ecological fit with the bioclimatic zone of the region. Plants that are smaller in stature and more prostrate should be given greater consideration in the design process. A reduction in canopy size and overall leaf surface area should lead to reduced evapotranspiration rates (de Wit 1958; Heilmeier et al. 2002).

Fertilizers should be applied only to meet the basic nutritional requirements of the plants and not at rates that would encourage rapid and luxurious growth. Unfortunately, this is opposite of the agricultural approach most homeowners take in trying to achieve plant size and maturity as quickly as possible. Applied nitrogen is a significant driving force in plant growth (biomass) and water use of turfgrass (Devitt et al. 1992). In Las Vegas, lowering the nitrogen input on 100 acres of bermudagrass from 0.60 to 0.12 lb per 1,000 ft^2 per month (which also would lower total biomass) would lead to a projected water savings of 148 ac-ft per year (Devitt, unpublished data). Nitrogen management should be viewed as an important tool in urban water conservation.

Judicious pruning to maintain smaller canopies can be of value in reducing water requirements. However, care must also be taken to not encourage rapid regrowth or to damage the canopy architecture. Correct timing of pruning can have a more dwarfing effect in some landscape plants and potentially lead to lower water use. Plants closer to the ground will have aerodynamic resistances significantly different from larger plants such as individual trees and will not be as prone to an "oasis effect" (Oke 1987). Whenever trees are used in the landscape, they should be well placed to create and enhance microenvironments. Although trees can provide cooling to residential structures, studies have demonstrated that water costs often outweigh energy savings (McPherson and Dougherty 1989; McPherson et al. 1988). As landscapes decrease in size and water loss via evapotranspiration goes down, microclimates of desert cities will become warmer, associated with what is called the "urban heat island" (Stabler et al. 2005). City planners, architects, and builders will need to address this issue in the twenty-first century.

As water resources become more limiting and water costs rise, the water allocated for urban landscapes will decrease. As water use decreases, plant quality will also diminish. When this occurs, user expectations must change. Using plant material that still looks acceptable at incipient water stress was suggested by Kjelgren et al. (2000). The new landscapes must be flexible, with removal of plants based on performance at low water levels: "Under water shortages, the objective of landscape maintenance is reduced from full growth and appearance of the plants to survival of the plants in acceptable condition" Ferguson (1987). Unlike agricultural crops, where evaluation of water efficiency is linked to a marketable yield, urban landscape water efficiency is linked to aesthetics and user acceptance. Recent studies have evaluated the plant water needs of ornamentals to achieve acceptable aesthetic appearance (Shaw and Pittenger 2004).

FIGURE 10.4. Any plant can be overwatered in the urban landscape. Is the inability to capture water savings because of a plant factor or a human factor? *Photo:* R. Morris.

Under California coastal conditions, many species were demonstrated to have minimal loss in aesthetic appearance at irrigation rates between 18 and 36% of ET_o. Additional studies are being conducted at other California locations to determine aesthetic appearance under more arid conditions.

In the Southwest, turfgrass often dominates the more mesic landscapes. Reducing turfgrass area has been strongly supported by water agencies. In one study, 81% of the variation in total outdoor water use could be described by the total turfgrass area (tall fescue) at each residential site by (Devitt and Morris 2008). Although such results provide merit for turfgrass limitations, it must be stressed that the results support the restriction of a cool-season grass growing in an arid environment. Removing turfgrass is of course much easier than removing trees and shrubs, but the reduction in irrigated landscape area is also important. A permanent size reduction should lead to significant water savings. In the study cited above, 62% of the variation in total outdoor water use could be accounted for based simply on the landscape area irrigated (Devitt and Morris 2008).

The emphasis on turfgrass in arid landscapes should be linked to recreational use. Only warm-season grasses should be grown in water-limiting arid environments such as the Mojave Desert, with no overseeding during the winter months. A survey in Albuquerque, Las Cruces, and Santa Fe, New Mexico, showed that nearly 85% of homeowners selected the most preferred landscape as having no more than 25% of the area in turfgrass, with almost 70% of homeowners in Santa Fe selecting no grass at all as the preferred landscape (Hurd 2006). It should be noted, however, that Santa Fe has more critical water supply issues and higher water rates (pricing) than the other two cities.

THE MANAGEMENT FACTOR

Maximizing water savings in urban landscapes requires not only the selection of plants that use less water but also the proper irrigation of those plants (fig. 10.4). Any plant can be over-watered. The goal is to apply just enough water to landscape plants to minimize stress and loss of aesthetic quality. Instead of adjusting irrigation timers once or twice per year, they should be adjusted on a weekly basis. Homeowners must embrace science-based solutions that incorporate the latest technology. Soil-based sensors can provide real-time data to assess the maximum allowable depletion (MAD) of soil moisture in the effective root zone. All plants have different soil moisture threshold values. The level that causes a plant to close stomata is different from the level that causes wilting, and these levels depend on soil texture (Fernandez-Illescas et al. 2001). However, plants that can tolerate greater depletion often have maximum allowable depletions greater than 50%.

Installing soil-based moisture sensors would allow irrigation timers to adjust the irrigation frequency and duration to meet the proper threshold value (Qualls et al. 2002). Although this may sound challenging to the typical homeowner, sensors would be placed in each hydrozone and would directly control the valve that delivers water to the specific zone. The irrigation timer would allow the user to define the critical soil moisture level (related to the MAD). This might require some fine-tuning, but eventually a proper setting could be reached based on plant performance.

Under extreme drought conditions, deficit irrigation may need to be imposed for prolonged periods of time. Not all plant species can survive under such conditions. Extended droughts can cause cavitation in the vascular tissue of trees, leading to canopy dieback and even death, at a significant cost to the homeowner fig. 10.5 (Tyree and Dixon 1986; Tyree and Cochard 1996). However, native desert species such as catclaw acacia *(Acacia greggii)*, which grows in the Mojave Desert, can survive under annual rainfalls of less than 4 inches concentrated in washes. Turfgrass species also vary widely in their tolerance to an extended drought (White et al. 2001). In one study, tall fescue was deficit-irrigated for a 119-day summer period in Las Vegas, followed by a 71-day recovery period (Brown et al. 2004). Water savings of over 60 cm (approximately 2 ft) were demonstrated under the greatest deficit treatment, yet all treatments returned to 100% cover and prestressed color ratings by day 28 of the recovery period.

Irrigation volumes should be set based on the assessment of environmental demand (Devitt et al. 1995a), soil moisture, and depth of rooting. California and Arizona both maintain a network of weather stations to assess potential evapotranspiration (CIMIS, AZMET), with information available via the Internet. Irrigations in the Southwest should track the typical bell-shaped curve of potential evapotranspiration. New irrigation timers for homeowners are now available based on this feedback approach. Satellite ET controllers have been reported to produce 20% savings in outdoor water use on residential landscapes (Devitt and Morris 2008). These savings were demonstrated to occur without creating soil moisture deficit conditions or loss in plant health. Such timers can and should have rain sensors to shut down the system when significant rainfall occurs. Irrigations should be timed to occur during late evening and early morning hours. However, care should be taken to observe wetting patterns to make sure water is being distributed as designed. In turfgrass areas, irrigation uniformities must be maximized. Christiansen uniformity (CU) coefficients on residential turfgrass areas are typically poor, usually less than 0.65 (Devitt et al. 2007). Sprinkler uniformities must be improved to values achieved on golf courses, typically greater 0.85 (Devitt et al. 2007). This may require moving sprinkler heads, replacing parts, replacing entire sprinkler heads, or perhaps even changing our current irrigation technology used for residential irrigation. Monthly checks of the system should be made to observe how the system is

FIGURE 10.5. ■ Canopy dieback (cavitation) of a mature ash tree associated primarily with turfgrass removal and inadequate irrigation. *Photo:* R. Morris.

operating. Cooperative Extension offices associated with land grant institutions in every state can provide assistance to homeowners wishing to evaluate their irrigation systems.

Residential landscapes in the future should be metered separately from the water that is delivered for indoor use, and this information can be used as a feedback tool in resetting landscape irrigation volume and run times. A tiered rate structure should be imposed that rewards individuals who, through design changes and proper management, reduce their outdoor water use. Block rate pricing has been found to drive higher consumer sensitivity and price elasticity (Dalhuisen et al. 2003). Based on pricing and information obtained from water meters, landscapes will begin to undergo a natural evolution toward lower water use, which will be attained under a wide range of landscape designs and plant composition. Incentive plans provided by local water districts that help offset the cost of purchasing smart irrigation controllers or help in the redesign of residential landscapes should continue and be expanded.

WATER QUALITY

As the population in a community goes up, so does the amount of reuse water generated for release. Every community values reuse water differently. However, as demand for potable water goes up, more communities will add reuse water to their water resource portfolios. Unfortunately, reuse water contains elevated levels of soluble salts. In the case of Las Vegas, reuse water released from the main treatment plants has an electrical conductivity that varies from 1.8 to 2.1 dS m^{-1}. This represents a doubling of the salt load found in Colorado River water (0.9 dS m^{-1}). At these higher levels, a greater risk of plant and structural damage exists: foliar damage to landscape ornamentals, loss in aesthetic appearance of water features, and salt buildup that can exceed salinity thresholds for many species have been well documented (Devitt et al. 2005a, 2005b, 2007; Tanji et al. 2008). Irrigation management must include a leaching fraction to maintain favorable levels of salinity in the soil profile. Proper plant selection is also critical, as is the application of water directed to the soil surface (drip or subsurface irrigation) away from the foliage. Because of these limitations, we currently have reservations about supporting any transition of the residential sector to reuse water. However, in the large urban landscapes under professional management such as golf courses, parks, and schools we fully embrace the transition. In a recent survey of golf course superintendents that assessed their attitudes and perceptions about using reuse water for irrigation, little opposition existed toward the use of reuse water for landscape irrigation (Devitt et al. 2004).

TRANSFER OF INFORMATION

A critical component to the successful transition to lower water use on urban landscapes, especially residential landscapes, is the transfer of information. Community-based educational programming will need to be expanded. Web-based dissemination of information must be increased. Cooperative Extension and conservation departments of local water districts will need to work closely together to achieve this goal. All of the previously mentioned changes outlined in this chapter require more educated and conscientious homeowners and professionals to maintain and adjust their landscapes to ensure permanent water savings. Implementing these water management options will have an impact only if water savings are captured by reducing the amount of water used for irrigation. Clearly, if drought management plans limit water use in the landscape or if prices increase to the point that homeowners reduce water consumption, water savings may occur at the expense of the landscape, which will affect the community's quality of life. If, however, homeowners use the preemptive resource management techniques outlined above, 50% water reductions can occur while still maintaining aesthetically pleasing landscapes. Some of this reduction can come from simply reducing the area of the irrigated landscape: as noted earlier, in a residential landscape study in Las Vegas, 62% of the variation in total outdoor water use could be accounted for based simply on the total landscape area irrigated. The other water savings must come through proper management (plant selection, irrigation management, etc.), since improved management could significantly reduce the need to decrease the size of the landscape.

AN UNCERTAIN FUTURE

Major water projects completed in the first half of the twentieth century in the Southwest were undertaken to control and manage water resources with the intent of further developing the region. Sixty years later, the result is a population that has increased 133% in California, 387% in Arizona, and 799% in Nevada (CensusScope, June 2008). Unfortunately, early estimates of water resources were associated with wet periods, and extended dry periods are now being predicted for much of this region in the twenty-first century (Milly et al. 2008). Water resources impact growth, economic development, and quality of life. Although it is difficult to predict what water resources will be available for a community like Las Vegas in 50 years, it is clear that current water use of 255 gallons per day (Doug Bennett, Southern Nevada Water Authority, pers. comm. 2008) on a per capita basis is too high. Much of the high per capita use is linked to landscapes in the residential sector. If we can achieve a 50% reduction in outdoor water use on a permanent basis, this would translate into a current annual water savings of over 100,000 ac-ft per year for the greater Las Vegas area. This reduction is a realistic goal and one that we believe can be achieved in urban-residential landscapes through a transformative process. However, it will require full participation. Voluntary participation would be ideal; but research has shown that savings ranged from 18 to 56% during periods of mandatory restrictions, but only 4 to 12% during periods of voluntary restrictions (Kenney et al. 2004). Key to convincing homeowners to participate on a voluntary level will be the ability of agencies, organizations, and universities to implement educational programs that inform and transfer user-friendly information and builds a "desert ethic" in the community to achieve these water conservation goals.

REFERENCES

Arizona Sonora Desert Museum. 2008. Museum Web site, http://www.desertmuseum.org.

Baker, L. A., A. T. Brazel, and P. Westerhoff. 2004. Environmental consequences of rapid urbanization in warm, arid lands: Case study of Phoenix, Arizona (USA). In N. Marchettini, C. Brebbia, E. Tiezzi, and L. C. Wadhwa, eds., The sustainable city III. Boston: WIT Press. 155–164.

Balok, C. A., and R. St. Hilaire. 2002. Drought responses among seven southwestern landscape tree taxa. Journal of the American Society for Horticultural Science 127:211–218.

Baumann, D. D., and E. M. Opitz. 1993. Measurement of conservation attitudes and behaviors: Trends in southern California. In Proceedings of CONSERV 93. Denver: American Water Works Association.

Beard, J. B. 1973. Turfgrass: Science and culture. Upper Saddle River, NJ: Prentice Hall.

Bennett, R. E., and M. S. Hazinski. 1993. Water efficient landscape guidelines. Denver: American Water Works Association.

Boeken, B., and D. Orenstein. 2001. The effect of plant litter on ecosystem properties in a Mediterranean semi-arid shrubland. Journal of Vegetation Science 12(6): 825–832.

Borland, D., L. Inman, J. Kotewicz, M. Leese, and M. Upshaw. 1993. Landscape design and maintenance guidelines for water conservation. In Proceedings of CONSERV 93. Denver: American Water Works Association.

Brown, C. A., D. A. Devitt, and R. L. Morris. 2004. Water use and physiological response of tall fescue turf to water deficit irrigation in an arid environment. HortScience 39(2): 388–393.

Butzer, K. 1993. The classical tradition of agronomic science: Perspectives on Carolingian agriculture and agronomy. In P. L. Butzer and D. Lohrmann, eds., Science in Western and Eastern civilization in Carolingian times. Basel: Birkhauser Verlag. 539–596.

CensusScope Web site, http://www.censusscope.org/. June 1, 2008.

Chaplin, S., 1994. Water-efficient landscaping: A guide for utilities and community planners. Snowmass, CO: Rocky Mountain Institute Water Program.

Costello, L. R., N. P. Matheny, and J. R. Clark. 2000. A guide to estimating irrigation water needs of landscape planting in California. University of California Cooperative Extension and California Department of Water Resources.

CUWCC (California Urban Water Conservation Council). 2007. Residential survey findings. CUWCC Web site, http://www.cuwcc.org/.

Dalhuisen, J. M., R. J. G. M. Florzs, H. L. F. de Groot, and P. Nijkamp. 2003. Price and income elasticities of residential water demand: A meta analysis. Land Economics 79:292–308.

Devitt, D. A., and R. L. Morris. 2008. Water savings associated with ET controllers on residential landscapes. Journal of Irrigation and Drainage Engineering 134:74–82.

Devitt, D. A., R. L. Morris, and D. C. Bowman. 1992. Evapotranspiration, crop coefficients, and leaching fractions of irrigated desert turfgrass systems. Agronomy Journal 84(4): 717–723.

Devitt, D. A., R. L. Morris, and D. S. Neuman. 1994. Evapotranspiration and growth response to three woody ornamental species placed under varying irrigation regimes. Journal of the American Society for Horticultural Science 119(3): 452–457.

Devitt, D. A., D. Kopec, M. J. Robey, R. L. Morris, P. Brown, V. Gibeault, and D. C. Bowman. 1995a. Climatic assessment of the arid southwestern United States for use in predicting evapotranspiration of turfgrass. Journal of Turfgrass Management 1:65–81.

Devitt, D. A., D. S. Neuman, D. C. Bowman, and R. L. Morris. 1995b. Comparative water use of turfgrasses and ornamental trees in an arid environment. Journal of Turfgrass Management 1(2): 48–62.

Devitt, D. A., R. L. Morris, D. Kopec, and M. Henry. 2004. Golf course superintendents' attitudes and perceptions toward using reused water for irrigation in the southwestern United States. HortTechnology 14(4): 1–7.

Devitt, D. A., R. L Morris, L. F. Fenstermaker, M. Baghzouz, and D. S. Neuman. 2005a. Foliar damage and flower production of landscape plants sprinkle-irrigated with reuse water. HortScience 40(6): 1871–1878.

Devitt, D. A., R. L. Morris, M. Baghzouz, M. Lockett. 2005b. Water quality changes in golf course irrigations ponds transitioning to reuse water. HortScience 40:2151–2156.

Devitt, D. A., M. Lockett, R. L. Morris, and B. M. Bird. 2007. Spatial and temporal distribution of salts in surface soils of fairways and greens irrigated with reuse water. Agronomy Journal 99:692–700.

de Wit, C. T. 1958. Transpiration and crop yields. Agricultural Research Reports [Wageningen, Netherlands] 64(6): 88.

Feldhake, C. M., R. E. Danielson, and J. D. Butler. 1983. Turfgrass evapotranspiration: 1: Factors influencing rate in urban environments. Agronomy Journal 75:824–830.

EPA (U.S. Environmental Protection Agency). 1993. Xeriscape landscaping: Preventing pollution and using resources efficiently. EPA/840/B/93/001. Washington, DC: Water Resource Center.

Ferguson, B. K. 1987. Water conservation methods in urban landscape irrigation: An exploratory overview. Water Resources Bulletin 23:147–152.

Fernandez-Illescas, C. P., A. Porporato, F. Laio, and I. Rogriguez-Iturbe. 2001. The ecohydrological role of soil texture in a water-limited ecosystem. Water Resources Research 37:2863–2872.

Franklin, C. 1997. Fostering living landscapes. In G. E. Thompson and F. R. Steiner, eds., Ecological design and planning. New York: Wiley. 262–293.

Gleick, P. H., P. Loh, S. V. Gomez, and J. Morrison. 1995. California water 2020: A sustainable vision. Oakland, CA: Pacific Institute.

Golf Course News. 2001. So-called "native" plants offer no guarantee of water conservation. Golf Course News (Nov.). BNET Web site, http://findarticles.com/p/articles/mi_qa4031/is_200111/ai_n9011792.

Heilmeier, H., A. Wartinger, M. Erhard, R. Zimmermann, R. Horn, and E. D. Schulze. 2002. Soil drought increases leaf and whole-plant water use of *Prunus dulcis* grown in the Negev Desert. Oecologia 130:329–336.

Hester, R. T. Jr. 1990. Garden of the world. In M. Francis and R. T. Hester Jr., eds., The meaning of gardens. Cambridge: MIT Press. 184–187.

Huang, B., and J. D. Fry. 1999. Turfgrass evapotranspiration. In M. B. Kirkham, ed., Water use in crop production. New York: Food Products Press. 317–334.

Hunt, J. D. 2000. Greater perfection: The practice of garden theory. New York: Thames and Hudson.

Hurd, B. H. 2006. Water conservation and residential landscapes: Household preferences, household choices. Journal of Agricultural and Resource Economics 31:173–192.

Jellicoe, G. A. 1966. Studies in landscape design. Vol. 2. London: Oxford University Press.

Jones, W., and C. Sacamano. 2000. Landscape plants for dry regions. Tucson: Fisher Books.

Kenney, D. S., R. A. Klein, and M. P. Clark. 2004. Use and effectiveness of municipal water restrictions during drought in Colorado. Journal of the American Water Resources Association 40(1): 77–86.

Kjelgren, R., L. Rupp, and D. Kjelgren. 2000. Water conservation in urban landscapes. HortScience 35(6): 1037–1040.

Kopec, D. M., R. C. Shearman, and T. P. Riordan. 1988. Evapotranspiration of tall fescue turf. HortScience 23(2): 300–301.

Kotzen, B. 2004. Plant use in desert climates: Looking forward to sustainable planting in the Negev and other world deserts. Acta Horticulturae 643:39–49.

Lant, C. L., and J. H. Sims. 1993. Social ideologies of urban water conservation. In Proceedings of CONSERV 93. Denver: American Water Works Association.

Levitt, D. G., J. R. Simpson, and J. L. Tipton. 1995. Water use of two landscape tree species in Tucson, Arizona. Journal of the American Society for Horticultural Science 120(3): 409–416.

Li, X.-Y. 2003. Gravel-sand mulch for soil and water conservation in the semiarid loess region of northwest China. Catena 52(2): 105–127.

Lohr, V. I., and L. H. Bummer. 1992. Assessing and influencing attitudes toward water-conserving landscapes. HortTechnology 2:253–256.

McPherson, E. G., and E. Dougherty. 1989. Selecting trees for shade in the southwest. Journal of Aboriculture 15:35–43.

McPherson, E. G., J. R. Simpson, and M. Livingston. 1988. Effects of three landscape treatments on residential energy and water use in Tucson, Arizona. Energy and Buildings 13:127–138.

Milly, P. C. D., J. Betancourt, M. Falkenmark, R. M. Hirsch, Z. W. Kundzewicz, D. P. Lettenmaier, and R. J. Stofffer. 2008. Stationarity is dead: Whither water management? Science 319:573–574.

Montague, T., R. Kjelgren, and L. Rupp. 1998. Surface energy balance affects gas exchange of three shrub species. Journal of Arboriculture 24(5): 254–262.

Morris, R. L., D. A. Devitt, A. M. Crites, G. Borden, and L. N. Allen. 1996. Urbanization and water conservation in Las Vegas Valley, Nevada. Journal of Water Resources Planning and Management 123:189–196.

Nelson, J. O. 1987. Water-conserving landscapes show impressive savings. Journal of the American Water Works Association 79(3): 35–42.

———. 1994. Water saved by single-family xeriscapes. In 1994 AWWA Annual Conference Proceedings. Novato, CA: North Marin Water District. 335–347.

NRCS (U.S. Department of Agriculture, Natural Resources Conservation Service). 2010. *Pennisetum setaceum* (Forssk.) Chiov., crimson fountaingrass. The PLANTS Database, http://plants.usda.gov/java/profile?symbol=PESE3.

Oke, T. R. 1987. Boundary climates. New York: Routledge Taylor and Francis.

Peterson K. A., L. B. McDowell, and C. A. Martin. 1999. Plant life form frequency, diversity and irrigation application in urban residential landscapes. HortScience 34:491.

Qualls, R. J., J. M. Scott, and W. B. DeOreo. 2002. Soil moisture sensors for urban landscape irrigation: Effectiveness and reliability. Journal of the American Water Resources Association 37(3): 547–559.

Schuch, U. K., and D. W. Burger. 1997. Water use and crop coefficients of woody ornamentals in containers. HortScience 122:727–734.

Shaw, D. A., and D. R. Pittenger. 2004. Performance of landscape ornamentals given irrigation treatments based on reference evapotranspiration. Acta Horticulturae 664:607–614.

Shearman, R. C. 1985. Turfgrass culture and water use. In V. A. Gibeault and S. T. Cockerham, eds. Turfgrass water conservation. Oakland: Division of Agriculture and Natural Resources Publication 21405. 61–70.

———. 1989. Perennial ryegrass cultivar evapotranspiration rates. HortScience 24:767–769.

Sovocool, K. A., and J. L. Rosales. 2005. A five-year investigation into the potential water and monetary savings of residential xeriscape in the Mojave Desert. Southern Nevada Water Authority Web site, http://www.snwa.com/html/cons_wsl_xeriscape.html.

Spinti, J. E., R. St. Hilaire, and D. VanLeeuwen. 2004. Balancing landscape preferences and water conservation in a desert community. HortTechnology 14:72–77.

Stabler, L. B., C. A. Martin, and A. J. Brazel. 2005. Microclimates in a desert city were related to land use and vegetation index. Urban Forestry and Urban Greening 3:137–147.

Steinbeck, J. 1952. East of Eden. New York: Viking.

St. Hilaire, R., J. E. Spinti, D. VanLeeuwen, and C. Smith. 2003. Landscape preferences and attitudes toward water conservation: A public opinion survey of homeowners in Las Cruces, New Mexico. Las Cruces: New Mexico State University Agricultural Experiment Station Research Report 750.

Tanji, K., B. Sheikh, S. Grattan, D. Shaw, A. Harivandi, C. Grieve, L. Wu, and L. Rollins. 2008. A comprehensive literature review on salt management guide for landscape irrigation with recycled water in coastal southern California. Alexandria, VA: National Water Research Institute.

Testa, A., and A. Newton. 1993. An evaluation of a landscape rebate program. In American Water Works Association Conserv'93 Proceedings. Mesa, AZ: AWWA. 1763–1775.

Turner, T. 2010. Hyper-landscapes: The garden and landscape guide. Gardenvisit.com Web site, http://www.gardenvisit.com/.

Tyree, M. T., and H. Cochard. 1996. Summer and winter embolism in oak: Impact on water relations. Annals of Forest Science 53:173–180.

Tyree, M. T., and M. A. Dixon. 1986. Water stress induced cavitation and embolism in some woody plants. Physiologia Plantarium 66:397–405

Vickers, A. 1991. The emerging demand-side era in water management. Journal of the American Water Resource Association 83:38–43.

Welch, D., W. Welch, and R. Duble. 2008. Landscape water conservation: Xeriscape. Texas A&M University Aggie Horticulture Web site, http://aggie-horticulture.tamu.edu/extension/xeriscape/xeriscape.html.

Wescoat, J. L. Jr. 1990. Challenging the desert. In M. P. Conzen, ed., The making of the American Landscape. London: Allen and Unwin. 186–203.

White, R. H., M. C. Engelke, S. J. Anderson, B. A. Ruemmele, K. B. Marcum, and G. R. Taylor II. 2001. Zoysiagrass water relations. Crop Science 41:133–138.

Willens, A. 1977. Planting in hot, arid climates. In B. Clouston, ed., Landscape design with plants. London: Heinemann.

Wullschleger, S. D., F. C. Meinzer, and R. A. Vertessy. 1998. A review of whole-plant water use studies in trees. Tree Physiology 18:499–512.

Zajicek, J. M., and J. L. Heilman. 1991. Transpiration by crape myrtle cultivars surrounded by mulch, soil, and turfgrass surfaces. HortScience 26:1207–1210.

11 Turfgrass Water Conservation: Summary

David M. Kopec

OVER THE LAST COUPLE OF DECADES, THE COMPETITION for water sources has been becoming increasingly intense among diverse facets of the general population. The documented benefits of irrigated turfs are many, but the visible aspect of turfgrass irrigation often draws public attention whenever below-average rainfall, drought, or water restriction occurs (Devitt and Morris 2006). Considerable data about turfgrass water use has been collected, and many facts are known about turfgrass water use, which can be expressed as an irrigation requirement when one takes into account irrigation system design, delivery, control, efficiency, and scheduling techniques. Despite the availability of an abundance of technical information, the public's first response to conserve water is often to reduce or eliminate supplemental turfgrass irrigation. In addition to water-related issues, other public concerns regarding turf and green spaces now include concern over the use of pesticides in public spaces, which includes golf courses, parks, and undeveloped areas.

There are over 16,000 golf courses in the United States, which accounts for nearly 10% of the total green space in urban environments. Irrigated turf on golf courses, commercial landscapes, public properties, and residences generally show that irrigation of landscape plants and turf can be 50 to 70% of the overall composite water use. Most water use information (in terms of outdoor watering) is directed at turfgrass water use, irrespective of the fact that trees and shrubs are irrigated as well.

This chapter provides an overview of the paradigms of public perception and policy of landscape water use, advances in turfgrass stress physiology, new germplasm manipulation techniques for improvement of plant drought and salinity stress, advances in soil systems, best management practices for water application efficiency, and advances in irrigation technology. For a more detailed discussion of these topics, please refer to the chapters indicated, as well as chapter 12, "Practicum."

PEOPLE, WATER, AND SPACE

Water Use and Public Perceptions

While communities require a large amount of water for health and sanitary reasons, landscape irrigation often uses the same amount or greater. In areas with low rainfall, all forms of landscape irrigation at some point are subjected to some kind of water conservation strategy. This may include requiring low-water-use plants, restrictions on the amount of total landscaped surface area, limits on the total turf area, or a combination of these. Implementing strategies to conserve water can be a formal or informal process (see chapter 10, "Water Conservation in the Urban Landscape"). In mesic areas of the United States in which relatively large amounts of rainfall are the main source of potable water replenishment, periodic droughts can cause water shortages because of the lack of systematic rainwater storage. When drought occurs, the lack of water is reflected not only in the landscape, but also by the water level in reservoirs.

Planning for the future population density and geographic location must consider how much water is available and how long society can depend on that water. Thus, the debate over conservation versus a linear increase in water demand as population increases usually involves both curative and preventive processes, often which occur at the same time (see chapter 10).

Attitudes and perceptions of people toward water conservation and the use and acceptance of a low-water-use landscape are often dynamic. The intent of water conservation programs is to avoid crisis response as the major effort in landscape water conservation. The premise of these conservation programs is thus twofold. First, they provide educational programs to promote behavioral changes. Here the motive is to get the public to realize that water savings can be achieved by selection of suitable plant materials, by using new irrigation technologies, and other conservation practices. Second, structured changes follow (tiered water-rate structures, mandated plant lists, and placing limits on plantings by size or surface area.). However, data show that when water resources become less reliable or less available as the population grows, increases in the price of water have a greater role in conservation than that of educational programs. Homeowners should be aware that the single largest water savings in xeriscape designs is due to the fact that the majority of the landscape area is not set to plants at all, but instead to hardscapes. Not all the plant material included in local or regional xeriscape plant lists uses less water on a ground area basis than do turfgrasses.

In order for landscape water conservation to be a just and equitable measure, water should be metered separately between indoor and outdoor use. This would allow for rewards for low water users when a tiered-rate billing structure is used, which would thus promote conservation. Likewise, new residential construction should include at a minimum stub plumbing for gray water reuse. In the explosion of new housing construction in Nevada and Arizona from 1990 to 2008, less than 1% of all new houses include gray water or rainwater harvesting features. This is a simple water-harvesting technology that unfortunately has largely been ignored in new housing construction.

Educational programs are paramount for promoting changes in attitudes and rewarding those who embrace new plant products, design concepts, and more sustainable ways to irrigate landscapes in a given environment. Not only are water use amounts important in the public view, water quality issues are becoming increasingly important (see chapter 7, "Irrigation Water Quality, Management, and Policy Issues"). Many water conservation and quality programs are provided by cooperative extension services (part of the land grant university system) in conjunction with water providers and other conservation groups. Individual programs are tailored for turfgrass management professionals as well as for the general public (see chapter 10).

Public Space and Wildlife

In the last 25 years, wildlife conservation was mainly associated with the conservation of habitat in undeveloped areas. Since then, the rapid development of "urban wildlife" as a science has generated movements for urban wildlife protection, including species diversity as well as species introduction and maintenance. Golf courses can serve as spaces for direct habitat use, food sources, and migration paths, all of which are key elements in urban and suburban wildlife locations. Various organizations are involved with these issues, and many offer services for developing conservation and wildlife habitat protocols. When obtaining information for using large turf areas (e.g., golf courses) for wildlife enhancement, it is suggested that the turf facility determine whether the site would provide a food source, migration path, or direct habitat for specific wildlife, and whether nominal changes to water features could be incorporated into the facility that minimize chemical and fertilizer movement off-site. Examples include mixed vegetation buffer strips of tall grasses and multistemmed shrubs, meandering flow patterns, and undisturbed slopes.

The environmental organization Audubon International has been actively collaborating with golf courses at many levels to enhance bird population and migratory resting places and biological diversity but also to provide educational and environmental stewardship programs. An abundance of literature is now available that describes practices to minimize environmental damage during design, construction, and grow-in phases of golf courses; management practices to reduce pesticide and nutrient runoff; using best management practices for long-term success; and strategies and approaches aimed at increasing wildlife habitat and environmental stewardship programs. Over 2,000 golf courses are collaborating with Audubon International in its Cooperative Sanctuary program. More recently, the Wildlife Links Program (a collaboration of the USGA and the National Fish and Wildlife Foundation) has developed joint funding collaborations for studying the role of golf courses in providing surrogate riparian habitats and adequate habitat and nesting sites for a number of endangered bird species, including burrowing owls (see chapter 3, "Environmental Issues Surrounding Turf-Dominated Urban Landscapes").

TURF FACTORS

Turf Water Use

Evapotranspiration (ET) is the sum of water lost from the soil and thatch surface (evaporation) and water lost from the green vegetation (transpiration) and is thus a measure of water used by the grass system over time. ET rates typically vary from 3 to 8 mm per day for cool-season (C_3) grasses, and from 2 to 5 mm per day for warm-season (C_4) grasses and are often environmentally specific (see chapter 3, "Environmental Issues Surrounding Turf-Dominated Urban Landscapes," and chapter 5, "Water Use Physiology in Turfgrasses"). When comparing the ET rates of grasses, it is important to consider the environment and season under which the ET measurements were made, as climatic differences have a major effect on ET between warm- and cool-season turfgrasses. ET summed over a specific period of days, weeks, months, seasons, or a calendar year is referred to as consumptive water use (CWU). Many experiments have been conducted in the last three decades that have generated consumptive water use values for various warm- and cool-season turfgrasses. When ET is measured for comparison purposes, soil moisture levels are not limiting, and the turf is free to respond to evaporative demand (the drying power of the air). This is generally regarded as the maximum water use (maximum grass ET). ET values are very valuable for irrigation scheduling purposes since the "target amount" of water (the volume of water to apply via irrigation) is based on the water use of grass that has no soil moisture stress. Maintaining turf at irrigation target amounts that are lower than ET is called deficit irrigation. Factors contributing to successful deficit irrigation are multiple and complex and include the length of irrigation cycles, soil properties, turfgrass species, soil salinity, and irrigation uniformity components.

When soil moisture is limiting, turfgrass water use decreases because water movement into the roots is reduced. In response, the leaf temperature increases due to a decrease in evaporative cooling at the leaf surface, exposing the turf to heat stress as well as drought stress. While tolerance to heat can be investigated in controlled environmental conditions, the separation of heat tolerance and drought when soil moisture limits water uptake is difficult to delineate in the field. Nonetheless, evidence of turfgrass heat stress can often be seen in summer even when adequate irrigation or rainfall is provided. Field studies have identified grass species or cultivars exhibiting direct heat tolerance that could be useful to turf managers and other turf users, especially in humid environments where rainfall is adequate and occasional irrigation may be required.

Other trials have measured turfgrass ET over time starting with a well-watered root zone without further application of water, then measuring ET on a daily basis afterward until the turf responded to self-imposed drought stress (determined by visible wilt, leaf temperature increase, leaf blade firing, loss of turfgrass quality, etc). Although turf in these cases can be monitored for water use, of greater value is knowing how long the turf can keep pace with daily reductions in root zone moisture and cumulative atmospheric demand for water at the same time. Grasses that maintain a higher realized crop coefficient (K_c) value across a wide range of plant-available soil moisture should require less irrigation between rainfalls, since a greater fraction of the plant-available water is being extracted (Garrot and Mancino 1994).

When soil moisture measurements are included in these tests, information is generated on drought avoidance capabilities based on the rate of soil moisture depletion and soil moisture status alone. These tests do not produce data suitable for irrigation scheduling purposes, but they can be of importance when using soils sensors for irrigation scheduling (see chapter 8, "Salinity in Soils," and chapter 9, "Water Management Technologies").

Physiological Plant Responses to Drought

Physiological responses by turfgrasses to dry-down cycles have been extensively studied (see chapters 3 and 5). Responses may include changes in rates of photosynthesis, as well as the induction of specific enzymes that help the plant cope with water stress or take up more water. Common responses include cellular osmotic adjustment, stomatal control, and carbohydrate allocations to roots. These responses can be used by scientists to identify plants that maintain a higher level of normal plant processes under drought conditions and heat stress. Direct measurements of plant parameters, such as plant water potential, relative water content (RWC), and transpiration rates, are used to measure the response to plant stress or become selection criteria themselves. These measurements are often time consuming and are usually employed on turf as a response to physical or chemical treatment, as opposed to performing measurements on large numbers of individual plants for selection and breeding purposes. These measurements promote a better understanding of plant responses to heat and drought stress, of how well plants convey attributes of whole-plant avoidance or tolerance to heat and drought stress, and of the plants' general physiological thrift prior to and during atmospheric and soil drought (see chapter 5). These responses may have practical applications in management schemes. The ultimate goal is for breeders to use these physiological characteristics to select for plants with superior drought resistance and avoidance abilities (see chapter 4, "Developing Turfgrasses with Drought Resistance and Heat and Salinity Stress Tolerance").

Rooting and Drought Stress

The physiology of roots and turf rooting patterns has been extensively studied over the past 25 years. Root viability has as great a function in water uptake as does root density (the concentration of roots in a specified soil volume) and root depth. As noted earlier, different species of turfgrasses react differently to deficit irrigation and prolonged soil drought (see chapter 2). For deep rooting to occur, carbohydrates must be diverted from shoots, stems, stolons, and rhizomes before or during the period of stress itself (see chapters 3 and 5). The previously accepted practice of mowing cool-season grasses low in the fall and spring and then raising the mowing height during the summer has been recently challenged. Even during the early summer, cool-season grasses typically do not produce substantial carbohydrate reserves. Rather than waiting until early summer to raise the mowing height, it would be better to raise the mowing height in the spring to allow the development of a deeper or more concentrated root system at a time when carbohydrates are still being produced.

Estimating Turfgrass Water Use

Measuring the water use of turf relative to the atmospheric demand for water has traditionally been achieved through the use of Class A pan evaporation data. More recently, this evaporation data has been replaced by the use of weather stations that use near-real-time estimates of wind speed, temperature, wind run, relative humidity, and solar energy to simulate the water use of a defined transpiring ground cover. These estimates are then compared to lysimeter water use data and used to model turfgrass water use. The actual amount of water that the turf consumes compared with the atmospheric estimate for water demand is expressed as a decimal value, which then can be used for irrigation purposes. This decimal adjustment factor, called a crop coefficient (K_c), represents the derived percentage of actual turf water use compared with the atmospheric estimation of the drying power of the air. Since both the actual water use of the grass (pan data) and the estimated drying power of the air are in the same units (inch or mm) they cancel each other, providing a unitless value (K_c). The K_c values for nonstressed turfs vary from roughly 0.65 to 0.90. Cool-season grasses tend to have higher K_c values than warm-season grasses under the same environmental conditions.

The normally accepted reference ET (or ET_o) model for turf is the modified Penman equation, which approximates the water use of a 6-inch-tall cool-season grass completely covering the ground without any soil moisture stress. This equation is now the standard for measuring ET_o for turfgrass studies (Brown et al. 2001). Differences in wind function assumptions, computational indices, and data averaging processes vary among ET_o equations. Thus, different ET_o values result when using the same data set of environmental measurements. Likewise, these different equations may require different K_c values as well. For more information, see chapter 9.

Applying Crop Coefficients for Irrigation Purposes

Irrigation software either computes on site ET_o values from a local weather station or collects the information from a companion weather network. The ET_o value is subsequently multiplied by the K_c. The result is the estimate of the grass water use for the previous 24-hour period. The central controller unit (often a standard office computer with commercial software) uses the grass water use estimate as the target irrigation amount for the next irrigation event. The software then divides the target irrigation amount by the precipitation rate of the sprinkler irrigation system and sends sprinkler run times to each field station or satellite. The commercial employment of this concept is a major industry-wide improvement in turfgrass irrigation and water conservation, since irrigation target amounts are based on dynamic near-real-time ET. With this information, the irrigation software calculates sprinkler run times for each irrigation event (see chapters 8 and 9). Since water use estimates are calculated using local environmental conditions, ET_o values can change as quickly as the weather. Instead of manually adjusting the run times on the field clocks to apply the irrigation replacement value every night, the computer does this automatically in a few seconds.

WATER QUALITY

The use of alternative irrigation water sources, such as reclaimed water and other nonpotable water, is considered a conservation strategy for potable water. However, water quality changes can affect maintenance practices that further affect turfgrass quality (e.g., fertility, salinity, and sodium hazard management). These impacts are dynamic in nature and should be examined on a composite water source evaluation basis, not just by a standard hazard or "classification" level interpretation (see chapter 8).

Nonpotable Water Sources

The main source of nonpotable water for turfgrass irrigation is reclaimed municipal waste water (RWW), also known as treated effluent. Recycled water is not necessarily reclaimed waste water, but can be any form of reuse that is independent of the original use as well. Previously labeled as and often referred to as sewer water, RWW will become a major irrigation source since large volumes are produced in urban areas for use on turf sites located close by. Using RWW keeps delivery costs low, and turf is viewed in a better light for using a nonpotable water source. Other nonpotable sources include saline or brackish groundwater, surface storm water, and irrigation return water.

Water Quality Parameters

The water quality parameters assessed for agricultural water use apply to turf irrigation water quality (salinity, sodium hazard, toxic ion levels, and pH) as well. Special considerations when using nonpotable sources may include physical, chemical, and biological quality concerns (see chapters 7, 8, and 10). Some of the quality parameters are of agronomic importance, while others are of environmental and human health importance (see chapter 7). This section describes standard water quality parameters that are measured when assessing the suitability of waters used for irrigation.

Salinity

Two common ways to measure salinity in irrigation water are to measure how much electricity moves through a solution (electrical conductivity, EC) and to measure how much salt is in a solution of soil or water (total dissolved solids, TDS). The EC is often expressed in the more common units of mmhos/cm or dS m (decisiemen per meter). TDS is expressed in units of mg/l (milligram per liter), which is equal to ppm (parts per million). For both methods, higher readings indicate that more salt is present in the solution. Classification values are given in chapter 7. Most water of acceptable quality for turfgrass irrigation contains from 200 to 800 ppm soluble salts. Soluble salt levels above 2,000 ppm may injure some turfgrass species. Irrigation water with salt levels up to 2,000 ppm may still be tolerated by some turfgrass species, but only on soils with high permeability and subsoil drainage. A few other species can tolerate excessively high levels of salts, such as alkaligrass, seashore paspalum, and inland saltgrass (Pessarakli and Kopec 2008).

From a management standpoint, the only way to remove salts from root zones when using salty irrigation water is to try to leach the salts out of the root zone by applying more water. This critical exercise can prevent excessive amounts of salts from accumulating in the soil solution. The amount of extra irrigation water to apply is defined as the leaching requirement, which is the percentage of water needed to travel past the root zone to wash away the existing salty water. Other management options include blending two or more water sources and promoting aggressive root zone drainage through mechanical means (see chapters 7, 8, and 9). New techniques to quickly map soil salinity levels will most likely be commercially available in the future (see chapter 8).

Sodium hazard

Sodium, often a major component of the total salinity load, is often misunderstood and mismanaged, both from an irrigation and a soils perspective. In addition to being a component of soluble salts, sodium is more often a soils problem (see chapters 7 and 8). This is because sodium tends to destroy desirable soil structure or aggregation. High sodium content in soils often results in an unstructured (deflocculated) soil that in essence seals itself, causing poor oxygenation and promoting standing water. The result is often a high water content at the soil surface, which is prone to compaction. Sodium management begins by estimating the percentage of the total soil cation exchange capacity (CEC) that is occupied by actual sodium. This is referred to as the exchangeable sodium percentage (ESP), which can be obtained from a standard soils lab test. If the ESP value is 15% or greater, infiltration problems occur on most soil types, except for pure sands.

Based on the soil texture class and soil ESP values obtained from a soil test, the required amount of gypsum is often recommended as a remediation amendment. The addition of gypsum is not a one-time event but usually a regular management practice, since sodium is still being added with each irrigation event. Gypsum is available in low-cost powders and granulated formulations as well.

Bicarbonates

Bicarbonates (and sometimes carbonates) in the irrigation water are often misinterpreted and mismanaged. Bicarbonates in the soil solution can bind to calcium and magnesium by forming insoluble limestone and dolomite, respectively. The result makes more cation exchange sites available for sodium ions and consequently increases the ESP to undesirable levels. Bicarbonates are often mismanaged because they are used as a criterion for adding acid to the irrigation water, without knowledge of the residual sodium carbonate value (RSC), The RSC represents the amount of carbonate and bicarbonate versus the desirable cations of calcium and magnesium on a charge per charge basis (meq/L). Water sources with negative RSC values are highly desirable, and those with positive values up to 1.5 are generally safe for irrigating turf. Waters with RSC values of 1.5 or higher are likely to cause a soil with an undesirable ESP if sufficient sodium is present (the RSC formula does not include Na). Acid injection systems are often sold and implemented based on water pH and not the RSC value, which is of greater importance than simply water pH alone.

Water pH

The pH of most irrigation water ranges from 6.5 to 8.4, although the desirable soil pH for most turfgrasses is 5.5 to 7.0. The pH of water is influenced by compounds dissolved in it. The pH of irrigation water in itself is not a limiting factor for acceptable use or not; rather, extremes in pH are indicators of high absolute or relative concentrations of certain compounds. Water pH values of 8.0 or above usually indicate a high bicarbonate content, a high sodium content, or both. Low pH values in water, which rarely occurs in the western United States, are usually associated with high sulfides or sources associated with elemental sulfur, which produces sulfuric acid. Lowering the pH of irrigation water will not appreciably lower the soil pH on calcareous-based soils that have a high free calcium carbonate classification. On silica sand root zones, low-pH water may slowly lower the soil pH (see chapters 7 and 8).

Boron

As a trace element, boron can sometimes occur at high levels in western irrigation water sources. It is more of a potential problem on ornamental trees and shrubs than on turf, since boron accumulates in leaf tips and can cause leaf tip burn. When necessary, boron levels are managed by leaching (see chapter 7).

BREEDING AND GENETIC TECHNIQUES FOR IMPROVING STRESS TOLERANCE

Turfgrass species, and to some extent cultivars, vary in their standard ET water use as well as their relative responses to drought tolerance or avoidance, heat tolerance, salinity tolerance, root growth, and maintenance under stress. The selection of species and cultivars that have improved performance for major or multiple stress factors should contribute to improved water use efficiency. Selection and breeding for the improvement of these desirable parameters is a realistic goal as part of improving water use efficiency in turfgrass management.

Standard Turfgrass Breeding Approaches

Over the last 50 years, turfgrass breeding and cultivar development have created the practical understanding and employment of specialized applied breeding techniques for genetic advancement in turfgrass quality. Most perennial grass species are cross-pollinated, producing heterogeneous populations of highly heterozygous plants. This has led to moderately easy detection and selection for enhancement of single and multiple traits, as well as successful gains in selection through either phenotypic or genotypic recurrent selection schemes.

These traditional breeding methods have been successful, starting with early breeding programs that practiced the selection of low-growing plants that survived biotic and abiotic stresses. From there, selecting for specific traits (mostly for disease resistance) and production characteristics was incorporated. Selecting for drought resistance almost always selects to some extent for heat tolerance, particularly among cool-season grasses. Similarly, selection for drought tolerance has often been based on plant appearance, without knowing the mechanisms involved in either drought tolerance or avoidance (see chapters 3 and 5).

Certain genera of grass species used for turf are closely related and can sometimes directly produce terminal hybrids or can be used as crossing bridges between the donor and receptor species. Interspecific hybrids have already been made using traditional techniques. Examples include *Agrostis* spp., perennial and annual ryegrass *(Lolium hybridum)*, Texas-Kentucky bluegrass (*Poa* spp.) hybrids, and *Cynodon* spp. (improved turf-type seeded cultivars), as well as sterile vegetative hybrids, *Zoysia* crosses, *Cynodon* crosses, and fertile *Festuca-Lolium* hybrids. Some of these hybrids have been devised to increase either heat tolerance *(Agrostis, Poa)* or drought tolerance *(Festulolium)*.

Molecular Approach

Many physiological studies have been conducted in the last 25 years that defined morphological criteria physiological responses. Results from these studies are sometimes intended for use as selection criteria for the improvement of tolerance to drought and heat (see chapter 5). To complement the findings, some of these physical traits and physiological responses have been identified by using new molecular techniques that allow for the elucidation of qualitative gene groupings, which aid in selection for and understanding of linkages among and between species for stress tolerant genes. Likewise, the revolution of gene splicing, mapping, sequencing, and informatics is rapidly changing the potential for overcoming traditional bottlenecks that often occur in traditional plant breeding (see chapter 4). Molecular manipulation includes the beneficial use of gene markers, marker-assisted selection techniques, and direct transformation. These techniques have allowed for marker selection for heat tolerance in wild species of *Agrostis*, in which gene sequences detected in *A. scabrus* have also been demonstrated to exist in commercially available heat-tolerant cultivars of creeping bentgrass *(A. palustris)* that were originally screened using a heat bench method.

While species crosses can serve as a bridging mechanism for gene flow or as a new varietal product, specific bottlenecks are often associated with them. These include terminal sterility, endosperm blockage, and loss of gene expression related to ploidy level conflicts. Introgression by using transformed gene products shows promise in this regard for traits that are controlled by one or two genes. Novel genes from unrelated species have some potential to be introduced into the desirable turfgrass host species to bolster the stress-related effect in question (see chapter 4).

Selecting Plants and Genes for Drought and Salinity Stress

When grasses undergo drought stress, they can produce hormones that control water loss, such as abscisic acid (ABA). Researchers have identified a gene for ABA that can be inserted into plants. ABA regulates the activity of water loss cells (stomates) on the surface of the leaf. It has been applied to turf in field conditions with mixed results for alleviating internal plant drought stress responses. Scientists found that ABA can help grasses survive drought. ABA is more effective in stomatal control when applied before drought occurs; it has less effect once the plant has been stressed. Hopefully in the near future, a commercial product will be available that could be economically applied to turfs to assist in managed drought stress periods (see chapter 5).

Opportunities may arise to improve nonhalophytic species or to improve the turf-type attributes of existing grass halophytes by using more in-depth molecular approaches (see chapter 4). Development of species and cultivars of turfgrasses with improved salt tolerance is under way. Research programs have objectives that range from improving the salinity tolerance of existing nonhalophytic germplasm (seedling germination and whole plant tolerance) to releasing new halophyte species that have unique management requirements whether they are used in saline environments or not (e.g., seashore paspalum). Likewise, true halophyte species that already exist, such as *Distichlis* spp., are undergoing screening for turf-type growth habits, since salinity tolerance is inherent (Christensen and Qian 2008).

CONSTRUCTED SOILS AND ROOT ZONE MANAGEMENT

The physical properties of soils are inherently important in turfgrass water use efficiency, since the soil is the reservoir and the release agent for water. Certain soil properties and soil types conserve water more than others, and their limits call for new management techniques or a constructed soil.

Natural Soil Systems

In natural soil systems, the lack of uniformity in soil properties can cause irrigation management problems. This is due to innate large-scale variation in infiltration, water-holding capacity, subsurface drainage, and other issues such as fertility, pH, and accelerated organic matter content formation. Thus a best management practices (BMP) approach is often recommended for managing the soil water complex in turf. Water relations in soils are a function of retention and transmission, with the matrix portion of water potential having the greatest single affect on a non-saline and nonsodic soil.

Constructed Root Zones

Constructed artificial soil profiles were essentially adopted for turfgrass used in highly specialized situations such as golf courses and sports fields. They were originally used to enhance surface drainage and minimize and alleviate compaction. The improved drainage, soil moisture retention, and capillary rise in a perched water table (i.e., a hanging water column) have been the main reason for constructing root zones. Another benefit is high infiltration rates, which allow for the capture of rainfall with less runoff losses. Little research has been reported on water use issues and conservation efficiency on constructed root zone systems.

While we still take advantage of perched water root zone systems, there has been a substantial body of work accomplished in the last 25 years that addresses slopes, layered soils, and the depth of root zone across slopes in relation to infiltration, water movement, collection, redistribution, retention, and plant-available water (see chapter 6). A summary of the research has demonstrated that better surface turf performance has been observed on sand root zones that retain more water (with associated reduced rooting) than with root zones retaining less water (and associated greater rooting). Moreover, ET appears not to be affected by root zones that differ in saturated hydraulic conductivity and water retention, even when turf is maintained under well-watered conditions. For sand-based root zones, greater rooting depth has not been related to better turf performance or water use efficiency when root growth and root health status are not factors (see chapter 6). Still, the cultural practices that have more than a nominal effect on turfgrass performance related to soil water relationships are not to be ignored. Slicing, grooving, spiking, and aerification with and without root zone medium replacement can alleviate organic matter accumulation, black layer formation, low oxygen content, and subsurface siltation layering (see chapter 6). These management practices are beneficial on natural soil systems, since overall infiltration and percolation characteristics improve water efficiency through improved rainfall and irrigation capture.

Water quality also affects constructed root zones. When saline water is used for irrigation and leaching fractions must be applied, water retention is much less of a concern, as are macropore and micropore drainage. Repeated flushes of water past the root zone (leaching) are needed to remove salt from the small and large soil voids. Water movement through the root zone profile, coupled with root zone system drainage (full removal of water with successive irrigations or soil profile flushing) is paramount. Likewise, irrigation water sources with a high RSC value, assuming high sodium levels are present, warrant the use of a constructed root zone with a high infiltration and percolation rate and low CEC capacity. This practice should assist in minimizing soil surface sealing and formation of layers as the root zone ages.

Soil Cultivation

Along with the concept of constructed root zones, the advent of new aerification machines has enabled managers to make specific aerification requirements for turfgrass. Some machines allow for incorporating sand or other suitable root zone materials during aerification. In response to industry requests, deep tine equipment is available with different tine sizes, types, spacing, and lengths, which can promote improved infiltration and percolation rates, particularly in soils with poor water uptake due to high levels of sodium. The machines also help remove salts from the root zone by enhancing steady-state percolation rates and internal drainage, and by mitigating soil compaction.

IRRIGATION TECHNOLOGY AND IMPLEMENTATION

Irrigation Uniformity

Water conservation in turfgrass irrigation is achieved using two major strategies: efficient systems and controls, and applying advanced irrigation scheduling techniques. New commercially available designs in sprinkler nozzles and combinations of trajectory and spacing can improve water conservation by increasing system uniformity. Irrigation uniformity, once benchmarked by Christiansen's coefficient of uniformity (CCU), is now replaced by the distribution uniformity (DU). The DU value considers a certain portion (25% or 50%) of the drier areas in relation to the overall application output. This information can be used to calculate run time modifiers that can be liberal or conservative in the application of water based on the mean application rate. Software exists that can use individual sprinkler profile performance values to determine sprinkler spacing distances for improving irrigation DU (Oliphant 1999). Turf managers should make every effort to correct deficiencies determined by a field audit and then calculate the mean application rate for base run times according to actual field data.

Soil Moisture and Salinity Sensors

Soil moisture sensors for controlling irrigation include tensiometers, gypsum blocks, time domain reflectometers (TDR), and frequency domain reflectometers (FDR). Tensiometers and gypsum blocks can accurately measure water content in only a limited range and can also be affected by salinity. Commercially available TDR and FDR units are used in combination with irrigation systems. FDR measures a phase shift of an electromagnetic pulse as affected by water content, rather than attenuation of a signal affected by moisture in time (TDR).

Technical advances in the development of soil moisture and salinity measuring devices may soon assist turfgrass maintenance personnel in measuring salinity loads and soil moisture contents (see chapter 9). Units can be integrated into the irrigation system, which provides the necessary data to automatically determine leaching fraction amounts along with the required run times to leach the current salt load to an acceptable level. However, soil density, texture, salinity, and range of moisture content to be expected as well as the length of the sensor rods must be considered (see chapter 9).

Soil sensors must be properly placed to ensure uniformity of irrigation amounts across the entire turf. Sensors do not have to be placed in multiple locations on a site if they are used to measure soil moisture content within a range of usable water or if the sensors are used in an indicator site. In the latter case, the location would gather data (critical soil moisture or salinity information) that applies to a widely applicable representative area of the total site. Thus, the data gathered is maximized using a minimal number of sensors. Another strategy is to place one soil moisture sensor in each area that qualifies as a dissimilar soil type. Areas that differ in soil water-holding capacity, texture, and horizon must be monitored separately. Care must be taken upon installation regarding potential lateral movement of water over the sensor area (see chapters 8 and 9).

Just as with soil moisture, the uniformity of irrigation application becomes critical when soil salinity increases. Areas that receive less than the mean target irrigation amount will quickly increase in soil salinity and develop associated agronomic problems (see chapters 8 and 9). Salinity sensors are key to the field performance of the irrigation system. As a general rule, dry spots will develop into salty spots because such areas receive insufficient water for leaching, allowing salts to build up quickly and cause salt stress. This is especially true in arid regions, where annual rainfall amounts are low and irrigation water sources often have elevated salinity levels. The importance of achieving the highest sprinkler uniformity as reasonably possible cannot be overstated when salinity is an issue in areas of low rainfall.

Subsurface Irrigation

Subsurface irrigation has demonstrated mixed results for water savings when compared with sprinkler irrigation. Establishment and long-term performance of the turf and the irrigation components must be considered when using non-overhead irrigation designs. Over the last 25 years, new products have been developed that use wicking and lateral movement of subsurface applied water. These systems are slope and soil specific, perhaps even more so than traditional drip lines. The use of subsurface irrigation systems may find a commercial use on high-profile turfs of limited surface area, where water is priced quite high (see chapter 9).

Reference ET_0 (Reference Models)

Previous sections in this chapter have addressed the derivations and the application of reference ET (ET_0) when used with the K_c values to generate an irrigation replacement value. Various forms of calculating ET_0 exist, such as the Penman equation, the modified Penman, and the Penman-Monteith model. Many state agencies have developed modifications of these atmospheric models largely due to climate differences among states. Since 2001, the Penman-Monteith equation has become the scientific standard for turfgrass ET computations (Brown et al. 2001). This was done in an effort to eliminate biases that inflate or decrease ET_0 values seasonally and regionally. Other methods available for estimating ET_0 from on-site atmospheric water demand include the use of atmometers (also called Bellani plates). Low-cost atmometers are available to measure ET_0 values directly as a measure of water loss from the instrument itself. Atmometers are relatively easy to use, and like on-site weather stations, they must be installed in specific locations in order to provide the best estimates of ET_0. Several atmometers can be used on a large area like a golf course, which can experience a wide range of microenvironments (see chapters 8 and 9).

CONCLUSION

The science and technology of turfgrass irrigation has greatly advanced in the past two decades. Using the combination of weather-based irrigation scheduling and a valve-in-head sprinkler system operated by a personal computer is perhaps the single biggest water conservation improvement in the last 25 years. This is especially true for low-rainfall areas where regular irrigation is essential to keep turf alive. In the not-too-distant future, soil moisture sensors and turf stress sensors may be able to pinpoint to the nearest square yard when and how much water needs to be applied on an area of turf, activating only the sprinkler heads that wet that location. Soil-placed salinity sensors and a personal computer will determine how much water is needed in addition to that required for turfgrass ET in order to leach salts. The use of nonpotable irrigation water is already established as a water conservation strategy. However, management must address the quality of nonpotable water, for example, with more complex and dynamic fertility programs, accounting for nutrients in reclaimed water to avoid overfertilization, salinity control, and sodium management. Turf managers are now better able to select soil cultivation equipment that can help remove salts from the root zone. And last but not least, grasses will become available that take longer to wilt, tolerate higher salinity levels in the soil, and recover more quickly from drought.

REFERENCES

Brown, P. W., C. F. Mancino, M. H. Young, T. L. Thompson, P. W. Wierenga, and D. M. Kopec. 2001. Penman Monteith crop coefficients for use with desert turf systems. Crop Science 41:1197–1206.

Christensen, D., and Y. Qian. 2008. Response to selection for turf traits in *Distichlis spicata.* 2008 Turfgrass and Environmental Research Summary: 27.

Christensen, D., Y. Qian, S. Wilhelm, T. Koski, and H. Hughes. 2006. Salt tolerance of inland saltgrass. USGA Turfgrass and Environmental Research Online 5(24).

Devitt, D. A., and R. L. Morris. 2006. Urban landscape water conservation and the species effect. In J. B. Beard and M. P. Kenna, eds., Water quality and quantity issues for turfgrass in urban landscapes. Ames, IA: Council for Agricultural Science and Technology. 1–17.

Garrot, D. J., and C. F. Mancino. 1994. Consumptive water use of three intensively managed bermudagrasses growing under arid conditions. Crop Science 34:215–221.

Oliphant, J. C. 1999. SPACE Pro: Sprinkler profile and coverage evaluation. Software and documentation. Fresno: California State University Center For Irrigation Technology Publication 991003.

Pessarakli, M., and D. M. Kopec. 2008. Establishment of three warm-season grasses under salinity stress. Acta Horticulturae Science 783:29–37.

12

Practicum: Applying the Science of Turfgrass Water Conservation

Stephen T. Cockerham and Bernd Leinauer

THE FOLLOWING SECTIONS HAVE BEEN COMPILED WITH information from each chapter. They are intended to summarize the chapters' scientific information in an applied manner.

CHAPTER 3: ENVIRONMENTAL ISSUES SURROUNDING TURF-DOMINATED URBAN LANDSCAPES

- A number of potential environmental problems are associated with the construction and management of urban green spaces, particularly golf courses, including water depletion, excessive runoff and soil erosion, contamination of surface water and groundwater with pesticides and nutrients, and loss of habitat and biodiversity.
- In a world of increasing urban growth and decreasing natural resources, a philosophy of environmental stewardship and best management practices (BMPs) is being increasingly promoted and adopted by the turfgrass industry. The following is a summary of strategies that address these environmental issues; for more information, see the other chapters in the book.

Strategies to address water depletion issues

- Develop and use grass varieties that use less water or can tolerate water of poorer quality.
- Adopt improved, more efficient irrigation technology.
- Use nonpotable water for irrigation purposes.
- Implement BMPs for water conservation. These BMPs combine proper plant selection and cultural maintenance practices that minimize water use while still maintaining adequate turf quality.

Practices to avoid environmental damage during design and construction of new courses

- Unique natural ecosystems should be preserved. Organizations such as the Nature Conservancy should be consulted to better assess the ecological characteristics and uniqueness of the site. If preservation is not possible, consider designing an ecologically naturalistic course that would allow some of the environmental integrity of the site to be saved.
- Avoid disturbing or damaging sensitive wildlife areas and wetlands during initial design and construction.
- Select plant species that are adapted to local conditions and require minimum inputs of pesticides and fertilizers.
- Take all necessary steps during construction to prevent soil erosion and manage storm water runoff on disturbed areas.
- When developing a golf course on reclaimed land, use the natural (predevelopment) environment of the region as a template to encourage the reestablishment of native species that may have been extirpated through urbanization.

BMPs to reduce losses of pesticide and nutrient applications in runoff from turf

- Grow a solid turf stand that reduces off-site transport of sediments and applied chemicals.
- Control the rate, method, timing, and type of chemicals being applied.
- Establish and maintain vegetated buffer strips between treated areas and receiving surface waters.
- Avoid applying pesticides and fertilizers when soil moisture is high.
- Develop management programs that use pesticide and fertilizer formulations that have low runoff potential.
- Adopt an integrated pest management (IPM) approach that uses monitoring along with the least amount and least toxic pesticides possible to achieve acceptable pest control.
- Avoid excessive application rates of nutrients, particularly nitrogen and phosphorus.
- Locate mixing, loading, and rinsing sites the required distance from surface waters or wells with links to groundwater.

Practices to increase wildlife habitat and maintain a healthy environment

- When designing a naturalistic golf course, strive for a balance between the needs of golfers and the needs of other living organisms sharing the course. To this end, cooperation is needed between golf course architects and ecologists familiar with ecosystems and the game of golf. Take steps to preserve as much natural habitat as possible when designing golf holes.
  - Elevate tee areas so golfers hit shots over natural areas such as wetlands and prairies onto target areas of managed turf.
  - Build raised walkways and cart paths through wetlands and other sensitive habitats so golfers do not disturb the habitat.
- With 70% of the total area of an average golf course considered to be rough or out-of-play, courses have the potential for incorporating substantial wildlife habitat into these areas.
  - Retain dead limbs and snags to create cover and increase habitat diversity.
  - Set up food and water sources.
  - Provide nesting boxes to attract cavity-nesting species of birds.
  - Maintain natural areas with limited human contact.
  - Plant native species that offer berries, seeds, and nuts as food sources.
  - Create vegetation corridors to link isolated habitats throughout the golf course and provide travel corridors for wildlife in the landscape.
  - Leave buffer strips of vegetation along streams and receiving waters to reduce surface runoff of chemicals and sediments and to increase habitat diversity and wildlife species distribution.
  - Compost organic debris such as turf clippings, tree branches, etc.
  - Consult a wildlife biologist during design.

CHAPTER 4: DEVELOPING TURFGRASSES WITH DROUGHT RESISTANCE AND HEAT AND SALINITY STRESS TOLERANCE

- Breeding and improving turfgrasses is a long-term program. It can take 15 to 20 years to develop a new cultivar.
- Turfgrass industry concerns over water quality and quantity, reduced inputs, and energy conservation are trends that turfgrass plant breeders are addressing.
- Conventional breeding methods continue to be important in improving turfgrasses to develop improved tolerance to drought, heat, and salinity stress. Technologies such as molecular markers, marker-assisted selection, transgenic techniques, and interspecific hybridization also play a role in turfgrass improvement.
- Much of the early improvements with turfgrasses took advantage of the natural selection process, and many of the existing cultivars are the result of natural selection.
- Breeders interested in developing turfgrasses with improved drought resistance, heat tolerance, and salinity tolerance generally develop germplasm with these characteristics by selecting genotypes from naturally occurring populations that evolved under these abiotic stresses.
- Breeders select plants from the original population and develop crosses among the individuals expressing the desired traits.
- Seed collected from these crosses are planted and evaluated in turfgrass trials, and plants are further screened through exposure to drought, heat, or salinity stress under controlled environment and field conditions. The recurrent selection process is repeated to develop cultivars.
- Water conservation and potential drought stress go hand-in-hand with the need to improve drought resistance in turfgrass species. Identifying drought-resistant germplasm is an integral part of a program to develop cultivars with improved performance under drought stress.

- Drought resistance mechanisms include escape, avoidance, and tolerance. The escape mechanism is of limited or little interest to turfgrass breeders, since plants complete their life cycle prior to the onset of drought stress and start anew from seed sources with the onset of favorable growing conditions.
- Drought-avoidant grasses maintain high internal water potential, show no signs of wilt, and continue to grow and develop when exposed to drought stress conditions. Drought-tolerant genotypes withstand low internal water potential and tissue dehydration and can recover growth after exposure to long periods of drought stress when moisture stress is no longer a limiting factor.
- Buffalograss (*Buchloe dactyloides* (Nutt.) Engelm.) is an excellent example of a drought-tolerant turfgrass species that also has drought-avoidant attributes, while tall fescue (*Festuca arundinacea* Schreb.) exhibits excellent drought avoidance characteristics.
- Turfgrass breeding using selection from naturally occurring populations regularly exposed to drought stress is typically slow to show improvement due to the low heritability of drought stress mechanisms, spatial variation in field studies, and the limitation of cycles in a growing season.
- Cool-season turfgrasses are often exposed to heat and drought stress simultaneously, making it important to screen them for heat tolerance as well as drought resistance.
- High-temperature stress can occur with warm-season as well as cool-season species.
- Cool-season turfgrass top and root growth decline as soil temperatures rise above the optimum for the species. Rooting depth, plasticity, and health are critical to drought resistance. Any decline in root production associated with heat stress can be used as a selection criterion.
- Water conservation strategies include use of nonpotable water and marginal-quality sources based on salinity hazards. Improvement in salinity tolerance has been achieved through selection of salt-tolerant genotypes from naturally occurring populations exposed to salt stress. Criteria used for salinity tolerance assessment in agronomic and horticultural crops include biomass production and crop yield reduction. Turfgrass assessment includes salinity impacts on shoot and root growth, turfgrass color and quality, and overall stress tolerance.
- Screening methods for turfgrass salt tolerance are often expensive and time consuming. Techniques such as salt gland density may be useful to breeders, since this is a trait that can easily be determined.
- Plant biotechnology uses cellular and molecular levels of plant biology to better understand turfgrass genetics, and it is a tool to supplement traditional plant breeding with molecular markers, marker-assisted selection, gene transfer, and similar approaches to speed up breeding and genetic improvements.
- Traditional plant breeding and wide hybridization coupled with manipulation of chromosome pairing is important in producing superior cultivars. Wide hybridization is an effective approach, and opportunities exist for improved turfgrass performance through interspecific hybridization.
- Molecular approaches, such as marker-assisted selection and breeding, as well as gene transfer, have been a successful part of efforts to improve crops for biotic and abiotic stresses. The use of molecular approaches to improve stress tolerances in turfgrass is not as readily apparent due to the complexity of perennial turfgrass systems. Biotechnology provides feasible opportunities to develop improved turfgrass cultivars with enhanced drought resistance and heat and salt tolerance.

CHAPTER 5: WATER USE PHYSIOLOGY OF TURFGRASSES

- Plant water relations are a dynamic process that includes the absorption of water from the soil, its translocation throughout the plant, and its loss to the environment, mainly through transpiration for individual plants or through evapotranspiration from a turfgrass canopy.
- Transpiration is the process whereby water is lost from leaves into the atmosphere as water vapor, mainly through the leaf's surface. Transpiration is a beneficial mechanism plants use to cool themselves, and it pulls the water stream up the plant for nutrient transport.
- Plant water status is controlled by the amount of water taken up through root systems and the amount of water lost through transpiration from the turfgrass canopy.
- Maintaining a balance between water absorption and water loss or use is critical for cellular hydration, which controls cell growth and elongation.
- Developing efficient irrigation management programs and improving drought tolerance of turfgrasses through breeding or genetic engineering has become extremely important in order to maintain functional turfgrass with limited water resources.
- Water uptake from the soil depends on root morphological characteristics (e.g., size of a root system, root length density, and root distribution) and physiological properties (e.g., viability and hydraulic conductivity).
- An extensive root system is critical for turfgrasses growing in non-water-limiting environments in order to explore a large volume of soil and efficiently use available water. Turfgrass species or cultivars with root systems of high viability in combination with extensive root size and distribution will increase water uptake capacity as well as water use efficiency.
- Deep rooting is considered an important drought resistance trait and contributes positively to increased water uptake under stress in various turfgrass species. Water will be conserved if the plant has a sparse but deep root system with high hydraulic resistance and slow growth rate with a slow rate of extension.
- The pathway for water movement in a single root is from bulk soil across the rhizosphere, the cortex, and the endodermis, and then into the lumen of the xylem and on to stems and leaves.
- Root resistance represents a limitation on water movement within a plant, and it influences leaf water status and plant growth in moist and dry soil.
- Hydraulic conductivity describes a coefficient relating the gradient of water potential to water flow rate, and it varies with root age from the root tip to the base.
- In an environment where drought is temporary or soil water often is supplied by irrigation, high root hydraulic conductivity is advantageous for rapid water uptake and plant growth in dry soils.
- The continued response to increased water availability is made possible by the production of new roots.
- Of the total amount of water absorbed into a plant and transported to leaves, over 90% is transpired from the leaves. Some water is also lost through evaporation from the soil, and only 1 to 3% is actually used for metabolic processes. Turfgrass water use rates are typically measured by evapotranspiration (ET) values.
- Species and cultivar variations in water use rate are largely controlled by genetic variability in growth and metabolic activities. They range from 3 to 8 mm per day for cool-season turfgrasses and 2 to 5 mm per day for warm-season grasses under nonlimiting soil moisture conditions.

- Water use of turfgrasses is associated with growth characteristics and physiological activities. Growth characteristics include leaf morphological and anatomical characteristics, canopy configuration, growth rate, tiller or shoot density, and growth habit; physiological activities include hormone synthesis and osmotic adjustment.
- Turfgrasses with a rapid vertical shoot extension rate tend to have higher water use rates than slower-growing or dwarf-type grasses because of increasing leaf area from which transpiration occurs. Dense, compact turfgrass canopies have lower water loss from soil evaporation than thin, open canopies.
- Better turfgrass performance under drought stress is also positively related to leaf thickness, epicuticular wax content, and tissue density, but it is negatively associated with stomatal density and leaf width.
- Stomatal closure is a key factor regulating plant water use. Abscisic acid (ABA), a plant hormone, has been shown to regulate stomatal closure, and foliar application of ABA in drought-stressed turf resulted in increased plant water use efficiency and maintenance of more turgid and greener leaves.
- Cellular hydration status is largely controlled by the level of osmotic adjustment, which facilitates movement of water into the cells and reduces water flow out of the cells.
- Osmotic adjustment is achieved through accumulation of nonprotein amino acids, ammonium compounds, sugars, polyols, inorganic ions, organic acids, and hydrophilic proteins.
- Species vary in the magnitude of osmotic adjustment, with buffalograss being equal to zoysiagrass, bermudagrass greater than zoysiagrass, and tall fescue greatest of all. The recuperative ability of turfgrasses following rewatering was positively correlated with the magnitude of osmotic adjustment.
- Osmotic adjustment is one of the most widely used selection criteria in breeding for drought tolerance in various crops, but breeding efforts using this trait in turfgrasses are limited in drought tolerance improvement.
- Plant growth regulators (PGRs) that contribute to the development of a short, compact turf have been shown to reduce ET rates in turfgrass. These regulators include trinexapac-ethyl (TE), flurprimidol, and mefluidide.

CHAPTER 6: MODIFIED ROOT ZONES FOR EFFICIENT TURFGRASS WATER USE

- Uniform soil conditions make it easier to provide uniform turf and more efficient irrigation. However, lawns are frequently grown on nonuniform modified soils (anthropogenic soils) where topsoil has been removed or mixed with subsoil. Furthermore, sod is often laid on compacted subsoils, with the result that rooting into the underlying soil is limited.
- Soil variability increases the need for site-specific management in irrigation programming, using the knowledge of soil properties such as texture, structure, organic matter content, compaction, drainage, slope, fertility, and pH, as well as shade and air movement.
- Water relations in soils depend on retention and transmission. Soluble salts can control how much water is available to roots in salt-affected soils. As a soil dries or as soluble salt content increases, less water becomes available for plant uptake.
- Sand-based profiles that have relatively narrow particle size distribution are widely used with or without amendment for highly trafficked turf areas such as golf putting greens and other sports turfs to ensure adequate water infiltration, percolation, and drainage, and to prevent excessive soil water content.

- Profile designs that encourage the development of a water table can conserve water. Such designs on limited slope and when drained to field capacity can have a water content distribution ranging from unsaturated and well aerated at surface depths to nearly saturated (satiated) at the lowest depths.
- Placing a finer-textured sand over coarser material (gravel) creates a zone of greater water retention (perched or suspended water table) within the sand above the interface with the gravel layer. The USGA Green Section specifications for putting greens use a 2-layer or 3-layer profile. The 2-layer profile is most widely used and has a 300-mm sand root zone mix of a specific particle size distribution placed over appropriately sized gravel. Drain tiles are installed in the gravel layer. During construction, these specifications are sometimes followed carefully, sometimes not; if not, undesired conditions may occur in plant-available water or drainage patterns.
- The California design is a 1-layer system consisting of a well-draining sand of particular particle size distribution that is placed over compacted (impermeable) native soil. Drain tiles are installed in trenches in the native soil. Water retained at the bottom of the root zone is more typical of a perched water table if there is very limited or no drainage into the underlying soil.
- Drainage from the 2-layer (USGA) putting green profile tends to be independent of the sand mix, while the 1-layer (California) green profile drains slower, with finer sand mixes. Thus, the 1-layer profile tends to hold more water for turf use than does the 2-layer profile. The 2-layer profile has only a short-term perched water table effect due to the downslope subsurface movement of water. When the root zone mix is too deep, water stress increases, leading to localized dry spots, especially in the highest elevations of a putting green. If the top mix is too shallow on putting greens, it may be difficult to place the hole liner and wet areas may occur, which can enhance development of black layer.
- Subirrigation can significantly reduce irrigation requirements (70 to 90%) compared with surface irrigation. Drainage tiles placed on top of plastic liners in subirrigation systems can be closed to prevent leaching. These tiles can be attached to pumps to draw water out or pump water into the sand profile. The water table can be raised or lowered as needed, depending on root depth. The particle size range and depth of sand dictate the degree of capillary rise of water. Problems with subirrigation include managing high levels of soluble salts and sodium, and uniform root zone water content in sloping putting greens.
- Repeated sand topdressing enhances infiltration on native soil putting greens and other sports fields. Water that had previously run off sloping putting greens tends to be held in the sand layer. When dry, topdressed sports fields have a lower surface hardness.
- Hydrophobic soil conditions, as found in localized dry spots (LDS) or dry patches, frequently develop in sand media. These spots often occur in areas where irrigation coverage is inadequate, on slopes where water tends to run off rather than infiltrate, and on slopes facing the sun. Fully developed localized dry spots are difficult to rewet. Application of wetting agents, cultivation (aerification), thatch control, and careful monitoring of soil water levels and syringing are the most common corrective practices applied.
- Sand putting greens grown with aggressive, high-density cultivars of creeping bentgrass and bermudagrass are susceptible to accumulation of excess organic matter, which can seal the surface, resulting in loss of roots, turf stress, and the formation of black layer.

- Management practices to prevent or remove black layer include providing more oxygen to the affected zone through reduced irrigation (with emphasis on syringing), cultivation, a topdressing program that prevents layer formation, improving drainage, controlling organic matter, and monitoring fertility practices.
- Better turf performance has been observed on root zones that retain more water with reduced rooting compared with root zones that retain less water with greater rooting. In sand-based root zones, greater rooting depth has not been related to better turf performance or greater efficiency in water use. There is evidence to suggest that greater water conservation can be achieved with the more-water-retentive sand-based root zones.

CHAPTER 7: IRRIGATION WATER QUALITY, MANAGEMENT, AND POLICY ISSUES

- Waters of impaired quality include saline or brackish groundwater, drainage water, irrigation return water, and reclaimed wastewater (recycled water). In most cases, these sources can be used for turfgrass irrigation, with modified management practices.
- Water salinity is reported quantitatively as total dissolved solids (TDS) in parts per million (ppm) or as electrical conductivity (EC_w) in decisiemens per meter (dS m^{-1}). Electrical conductivity is directly related to the salt content of the water; EC_w above 0.7 dS m^{-1} indicates potential salinity problems for sensitive turfgrass species. Irrigation water with salt levels up to 3 dS m^{-1} may be tolerated by some turfgrass species but only on soils with high permeability and adequate subsoil drainage.
- The salt tolerance of turfgrass and other plants is expressed in terms of electrical conductivity of saturation extract (EC_e) of the root zone soil. Soils with an EC_e below 3 dS m^{-1} are considered satisfactory for growing most turfgrass species. Only a few salt-tolerant turfgrass species can survive in soils with EC_e above 10 dS m^{-1}.
- Plant roots absorb sodium and transport it to leaves, where it can accumulate and cause injury resembling salt burn. Irrigation water with high levels of sodium can be particularly toxic if applied by overheard sprinklers since salts can be absorbed directly by leaves.
- Water with high sodium content can also cause soil physical and hydrological problems due to clay and aggregate dispersion. A value that indicates whether sodium affects soil properties is the sodium adsorption ratio (SAR) of the soil water.
- High bicarbonate levels in irrigation water can increase soil pH and may affect soil permeability. Bicarbonates may cause white lime deposits to appear on leaves of plants irrigated by overhead sprinklers during hot, dry periods.
- Turfgrasses are relatively more tolerant of boron and chloride than are other plants in a landscape.
- Reclaimed or recycled water has been used for irrigation for decades, and no report has found that the use of this irrigation water has contributed to human illness, if properly managed.
- Residues from over-the-counter and prescription drugs, including antiphlogistics (such as ibuprofen and naproxen), lipid regulators, and beta-blockers, have been found in treated wastewater.
- Reclaimed water can serve as a source of nitrogen, phosphorus, and potassium. If the water is poorly managed, nutrient imbalances, eutrophication of surface waters, and contamination of groundwater may occur. Adjust fertilization practices for the added nutrient inputs to avoid overapplication that may impact surface water or groundwater quality.
- Leaching is a strategy to control salinity in irrigated soils. With conventional irrigation systems, the leaching requirement (LR) is the minimum leaching fraction (LF) that a plant can endure without salinity stress.

- Saline irrigation water can be improved through blending or cycling with non-saline water. Cycling substitutes saline water for the non-saline water when irrigating salt-tolerant turfgrasses at their nonsensitive growth stage and uses the non-saline water at other times. Blending mixes the saline and non-saline waters to obtain a composite that is suitable for irrigation.
- Soil and water amendments are often used to facilitate infiltration and leaching. A common amendment for sodic soils is gypsum to lower the sodium adsorption ratio (SAR). Common acidifying amendments used for reclaiming sodic-calcareous soils include sulfuric acid and elemental sulfur.
- Societal and climatic changes will continue to make good quality water less available for turfgrass irrigation. As a result, the turf industry will increasingly be required to use alternative water sources (e.g., reclaimed wastewater) for irrigation. Although alternative waters usually contain one or more constituents in an undesirably high concentration, through proper management these waters can be successfully and safely used for turfgrass irrigation.

CHAPTER 8: SALINITY IN SOILS

- Salinity management is complex, since salinity stresses are site specific and no single management practice can address the multiple problems associated with them.
- A best management practices (BMPs) approach for salinity management should be used that involves management of the whole system on a site-specific basis and implements BMPs to achieve a sustainable ecosystem.
- For irrigated turf, the management of soluble salts, which involves cultivation and leaching, becomes the main issue when using saline irrigation waters.
- The presence of sodium in irrigation water and in the root zone increases a soil's permeability hazard. Sodic soils exhibit reduced water permeability, provide a less favorable rooting medium, and limit water infiltration and percolation.
- Certain ions, such as sodium, chlorine, and boron, can reach toxic levels for plants, and excessive levels of sulfate (SO_4) in irrigation water can contribute to black layer. Other ions, such as calcium, magnesium, potassium, phosphorus, nitrogen, and manganese, are nutrients, but in saline-irrigated areas nutrient imbalances are to be expected and must be routinely managed to avoid excesses or deficiencies.
- Due to the complexity of salinity management, turfgrass managers must continuously educate themselves to adapt to new technologies, products, and concepts.
- Salt-tolerant grasses and landscape plants should be used for long-term environmental sustainability.
- To make informed decisions, a comprehensive site assessment is necessary, which entails collecting soil physical, drainage, and chemical data and assessing irrigation water quality.
- If multiple irrigation water sources are available, evaluate blending options, water quality variation over time, pond or lake construction, reliability and water volume, and the underlying aquifer of the site.
- On salt-affected sites, controlled leaching is the most effective management practice. This requires an irrigation system with a high uniformity of water application and considerable flexibility to apply leaching fractions only where required using pulse irrigation.
- Water and soil amendments to aid water infiltration and improve sodic sites are an important component of salinity management, but they are ineffective without a good leaching program to remove excess salts.

- The leaching requirement (LR) is the minimum amount of water needed to control salts. The LR is normally determined by combining the irrigation water salinity value with the turfgrass or landscape plant salinity tolerance level. Maintenance leaching refers to the application of sufficient water with every irrigation event to maintain soil salinity at an acceptable level.
- Reclamation leaching is required when salt accumulation is above the acceptable electrical conductivity (EC_e) level. Reclamation leaching requires a higher quantity of water to decrease salinity than does maintenance leaching.
- Leaching is traditionally done by heavy, continuous sprinkler applications, saturating the soil throughout the leaching period. Leaching by pulse irrigation (cycle and soak) is more efficient. With pulse irrigation, relatively small amounts of water are applied in increments, and time is allowed to pass before the next pulse is applied. The cycle is repeated until the quantity of water needed for effective salt leaching is applied. Pulse irrigation normally requires only one-quarter to one-half of the water used by heavy, continuous irrigation to perform adequate leaching.
- Recent developments in mobile salinity monitoring technology and soil sensors can enhance leaching efficiency by identifying localized sites that require leaching and by monitoring leaching effectiveness.
- On salt-affected sites, surface and subsurface cultivation programs must be more intense than similar practices on non-saline sites since the soil must allow for the leaching of salts. Salt disposal options should be a part of an overall water management plan. The environmental impacts of drainage may occur beneath the site if the drainage water is not intercepted. When tile drains collect drainage water, an appropriate disposal site must be available.
- Sand-capping fine-textured or sodic soils that have low infiltration and percolation rates or shallow soils that lie on an impervious layer can help water infiltrate, be retained, and drain. Cultivation must penetrate the interface between the sand-cap layer and the underlying soil in order for water to drain after saturation.
- Saline irrigation water affects soil fertility and plant nutrition by adding constituents such as salts, nutrients, water treatment materials, and soil amendments and by removing nutrients and elements through leaching. Soil salinity suppresses plant cytokinin synthesis; grasses often respond positively to the application of this hormone. Fertilization must stress not only normal nutritional needs but also maximizing the salinity tolerance of grasses, especially on managing potassium, calcium, manganese, and zinc.
- Proactive monitoring programs that include frequent plant, soil, and irrigation water quality analysis provide science-based information for managing turf areas and making environmentally sustainable decisions.

CHAPTER 9: WATER MANAGEMENT TECHNOLOGIES

- Strategies to reduce unnecessary irrigation water use should include using efficient irrigation systems and scheduling irrigation based on the actual water requirement of turf needed to maintain a desired quality level.
- In order to achieve high irrigation efficiency, losses such as droplet evaporation, surface runoff, leaching, and wind drift must be minimized. Furthermore, correct sprinkler head selection and spacing can match water spray patterns with the shape of the landscape, which helps avoid areas that are over- or underirrigated. Subsurface irrigation systems should be considered.
- Larger irrigated areas should be divided into hydrozones, areas of similar watering requirements.

- Distribution uniformity (DU) and low-quarter distribution uniformity (DU_{lq}) describe the water delivery and distribution of the irrigation system. An irrigation system with a DU_{lq} of 0.5 requires twice as much water as the grass plant needs to maintain an adequate quality level.
- Subsurface irrigation systems have shown great potential for water conservation, despite difficulties associated with determining spacing and depth of trays, pipes, or emitters; higher cost of installation; difficulty in monitoring and/or troubleshooting damaged parts; potential interference with maintenance practices; and the inability to establish turf from seed when irrigated below the surface.
- Irrigation amounts can be estimated based on climatic factors or calculated from the plants' water status by monitoring soil moisture or by using remote sensing technologies that detect and quantify drought stress.
- Evapotranspiration (ET) losses from a turfgrass stand provide an accurate measure of irrigation water requirements and have been closely correlated with atmometer evaporation, open pan ET, and potential (model) ET estimates (ET_p and ET_o).
- ET_p and ET_o estimates are most commonly used when turfgrass irrigation scheduling is based on ET losses. To match actual turfgrass ET, most ET estimates require adjustments in the form of multipliers or crop coefficients (K_c) to meet local climatic conditions and specific maintenance situations.
- K_c can vary from 0.4 to 1.1 depending on ET reference, quality expectations, season, grass type, maintenance level, and micro- and macroclimate.
- Crop coefficients can also be used to calculate irrigation amounts. Irrigation below 100% ET replacement (deficit irrigation) does not necessarily result in a significant loss of turfgrass quality and function.
- Several states offer automated, Web-based potential and reference ET values for irrigation scheduling. In California, the most commonly accepted source of ET data is the California Irrigation Management Information System (CIMIS).
- Smart controllers that automatically adjust to daily changes in ET have been introduced by the irrigation industry.
- The use of smart controllers can result in water savings as high as 80% compared with traditional irrigation scheduling.
- Municipal water authorities and utilities have introduced rebate programs for the installation of smart irrigation controllers.
- Irrigation scheduling based on soil moisture aims at keeping the root zone within a target moisture range by replenishing ET and drainage losses. This is considered to be the most intuitive way of determining how much and when to irrigate.
- Soil moisture sensor technologies currently used to schedule landscape and turf irrigation include dielectric sensors and heat-dissipating sensors for the measurement of soil water content, and tensiometers and granular matrix sensors (gypsum blocks) to measure soil water potential. Both types have advantages and disadvantages, and consideration must be given to the soil type, range of moisture measured, and expected soil salinity.
- Tensiometers estimate soil matric potential and do not require soil-specific calibration, but they do need regular maintenance. Granular matrix sensors measure the electrical resistance between two electrodes embedded in quartz material and correlate the resistance with the matric potential of the root zone.
- To calculate irrigation requirements based on volume, soil moisture tension or suction values must be converted to volumetric soil moisture content using a moisture release curve.

- Dielectric sensors record volumetric soil moisture directly; measurements can be affected by the length of the rods, soil texture, soil density, and soil electrical conductivity.
- Absolute moisture values can vary considerably over a landscape. If a sensor is installed in a location representative of an irrigated area, and if it records moisture extraction between maximum and minimum over time, using this data can lead to more consistent irrigation scheduling than using absolute values alone.
- Reported reductions in irrigation water applied range from 0% to 82% when soil moisture–based controllers were used for scheduling compared with either traditional or ET-based irrigation scheduling.
- Crop water stress indices and normalized difference vegetation indices (NDVI) calculated from remotely measured reflectance of canopies have been suggested for irrigation scheduling of cool- and warm-season turfgrasses. However, to date no automated remote sensing irrigation scheduling technology based on reflectance is commercially available.

CHAPTER 10: WATER CONSERVATION IN THE URBAN LANDSCAPE

- Managing water should be based on the premise that every drop wasted will affect not only our ability to maintain an acceptable quality of life but also the ability of our children's generation to do so.
- Many residential water users have a distorted idea of how much water they actually use and how they use it.
- Drought management plans that severely limit water use in the landscape or price water in a way that causes homeowners to reduce water consumption may produce water savings at the expense of the landscape, affecting the community's quality of life.
- Conservation should start with behavioral changes, followed by structural changes in the landscape and the entire residential or urban setting. Lifestyle infringement must be minimized for conservation efforts to be widely embraced by communities.
- The concept of sustainable landscape design has emerged as a way of raising consciousness and changing basic attitudes. In the purest sense, landscapes are sustainable only if they do not require any additional resources over what is naturally available.
- Using native plants or plants from a similar climate typically reduces the chance of plant failure, lowers maintenance costs, and helps establish a bioclimatic sense of place. The introduction of potential invasive species must be avoided.
- Landscapes differ in size, species composition, planting density, canopy structure, microenvironments, and soil types, causing water requirements to vary tremendously. Reduced water use in mixed-landscape areas can be achieved by varying the species composition (individual plant water use, size at maturity), density of plantings, and the total landscape area planted.
- Municipalities, water conservation agencies, and water purveyors often report water conservation occurring over time by homeowners who use published landscape guidelines. However, field research in several cases has demonstrated no water savings (conservation) associated with mixed landscapes over extended periods greater than 5 years.
- Published plant lists that rank the water requirements of trees, shrubs, and ground covers are rarely based on quantifiable water use.
- Fertilizers should be applied only to meet the basic nutritional requirements of plants and should not be applied at rates that encourage rapid and luxurious growth.
- Judicious pruning of trees and shrubs to maintain smaller canopies can reduce water requirements.

- Water savings expected to be gained through design and plant selection can be nullified by poor irrigation management. The water requirements of plant species shift between water use categories depending on how they are grown.
- Plants closer to the ground have significantly less aerodynamic resistance than do larger plants such as individual trees and are not prone to an "oasis effect."
- Trees should be planted in the landscape to create and enhance microenvironments. Energy savings from trees that provide cooling to residential structures are often outweighed by water costs.
- Select plants that can survive in acceptable condition under water shortages. Under extreme drought conditions, deficit irrigation may be imposed for prolonged periods of time. Not all plant species can survive under such conditions.
- Turfgrass species vary widely in drought tolerance. Warm-season grasses should be grown in water-limiting arid environments. Turfgrass should have a clear purpose in arid landscapes, such as a link to recreational use. Reducing turfgrass area has been strongly supported by water agencies. Cool-season grasses growing in arid climates should be replaced with warm-season grasses or other water-wise landscaping. More emphasis should be placed on reducing the amount of landscape that is irrigated.
- Recycled water is an irrigation resource in many communities. Recycled water contains soluble salts that can cause salt buildup in the soil, foliar damage, and plant death. The residential sector typically does not have the technical capability to manage recycled water in the urban landscape. However, large urban landscapes under professional management such as golf courses, parks, and schools should be encouraged to make the transition.
- Soil-based moisture sensors that assess the soil moisture in the effective root zone and weather stations that assess potential evapotranspiration can provide near-real-time data to irrigation controllers for adjusting water applications. This is a shift from setting irrigation clocks once or twice per year to allowing technology to adjust irrigations daily. Sprinkler distribution uniformities on residential turfgrass areas are typically very poor and must be improved to uniformities obtained on golf courses to achieve higher water use efficiencies.
- Residential landscapes should be metered separately from water delivered for indoor use. A tiered rate structure should be imposed that rewards individuals who, through design changes and proper management, reduce their outdoor water use.
- If homeowners use many of the resource management techniques outlined in this publication, 50% water reduction while still maintaining aesthetically pleasing landscapes is an achievable goal.

Measurement Conversion Table

U.S. Customary	Conversion factor for U.S. Customary to Metric	Conversion factor for Metric to U.S. Customary	Metric
Length			
inch (in)	2.54	0.394	centimeter (cm)
foot (ft)	0.3048	3.28	meter (m)
yard (yd)	0.914	1.09	meter (m)
mile (mi)	1.61	0.62	kilometer (km)
area			
acre (ac)	0.4047	2.47	hectare (ha)
square inch (in^2)	6.45	0.15	square centimeter (cm^2)
square foot (ft^2)	0.0929	10.764	square meter (m^2)
volume			
fluid ounce (fl oz)	29.57	0.034	milliliter (ml)
gallon (gal)	3.785	0.26	liter (l)
acre-inch (ac-in)	102.8	0.0097	cubic meter (m^3)
acre-foot (ac-ft)	1,233	0.000811	cubic meter (m^3)
cubic foot (ft^3)	28.317	0.353	liter (l)
cubic yard (yd^3)	0.765	1.307	cubic meter (m^3)
gallon per acre	9.36	0.106	liter per hectare (l/ha)
mass			
ounce (oz)	28.35	0.035	gram (g)
pound (lb)	0.454	2.205	kilogram (kg)
ton (T)	0.907	1.1	metric ton (t)
pressure			
pound per square inch	0.00689	145.0377	megapascal (MPa)
(psi)	6.89	0.145	kilopascal (kPa)
temperature			
Fahrenheit (°F)	°C = (°F – 32) ÷ 1.8	°F = (°C x 1.8) + 32	Celsius (°C)

Glossary

abiotic. Caused or produced by physical, climatic, or nonliving chemical aspects of an environment, as opposed to by the biological aspects.

absorption rate. Rate at which the soil will absorb water.

aeration, mechanical. See **cultivation, turf**.

aerify. See **cultivation, turf**.

amendment, physical. Any substance such as sand, calcined clay, peat, and sawdust, added to soil to alter physical conditions.

aquifer. An underground formation that contains sufficient saturated permeable material to yield significant quantities of water to wells and springs; a reservoir for underground water.

artificial turf. Synthetic surface simulating turf.

atmometer. Instrument that measures the rate at which water evaporates into the air.

bed knife. Stationary bottom blade of a reel mower against which the reel blades turn to produce a shearing cut. The bed knife is carried in the mower frame at a fixed distance from the reel axis and an adjustable fixed distance above the plane of travel.

bench setting. Height a mower's cutting plane (bed knife or rotating blade tip) is set above a hard, level surface.

biotic. Caused or produced by living organisms.

blend, seed. Combination of two or more cultivars of a single species.

broadcast sprigging. Vegetative turf establishment by broadcasting stolons, rhizomes, or tillers and covering with soil.

brushing. Practice of mowing a brush against the surface of a turf to lift nonvertical stolons and/or leaves before mowing to produce a uniform surface of erect leaves.

bunchgrass. A grass species that grows in clumps rather than spreading. See **bunch-type growth**.

bunch-type growth. Plant development by intravaginal tillering at or near the soil surface without the formation of rhizomes or stolons.

calcined clay. Clay minerals, such as montmorillonite and attapulgite, that have been fired at high temperatures to obtain absorbent, stable, granular particles; used as amendments in soil modification.

castings, earthworm (worm casts). Soil and plant remains excreted and deposited by earthworms in or on the turf surface or in their burrows.

catcher. Detachable enclosure on a mower used to collect clippings; also called basket, bag, or box.

centrifugal spreader. Applicator from which dry, particulate material is broadcast as onto a spinning disc or blade beneath the hopper.

chemical trimming. Using herbicides or chemical growth regulators to limit turfgrass growth around trees, borders, monuments, walks, etc.

cleavage plane sod. Zone of potential separation at the interface between the underlying soil and an upper soil layer adhering to transplanted sod. Such separation is most commonly a problem when soils of different texture are placed one over the other.

clippings. Leaves and stems cut off by mowing.

clonal planting. Vegetative establishment using plants of a single genotype placed at a spacing of 1 meter or more.

coefficient of uniformity. Percentage figure derived from the precipitation rates at various points of a sprinkler system; used in technical circles to determine the efficiency of a sprinkler system.

cold water insoluble nitrogen (WIN). Form of fertilizer nitrogen not soluble in cold water (25°C).

cold water soluble nitrogen (WSN). Form of fertilizer nitrogen soluble in cold water (25°C).

colorant. Dye, pigment, or paintlike material applied to turf to create a favorable green color when the grass is discolored or damaged.

combing. Using a comb with metal teeth or flexible tines, fastened immediately in front of a reel mower to lift stolons and procumbant shoots so that they can be cut by the mower.

consumption. Portion of water withdrawn for off-stream uses and not returned to a surface or groundwater source. In plants and animals the water is used metabolically.

controlled-release fertilizer. See **slow-release fertilizer**.

controllers. Apparatus for central automation of irrigation systems.
control valve. Turns water on and off to a sprinkler or a series of sprinklers.
cool-season turfgrass. Species best adapted to growth during cool, moist periods of the year; commonly having temperature optimums of 15° to 24°C; e.g., bentgrasses, bluegrasses, fescues, and ryegrasses.
coring. Method of turf cultivation in which soil cores are removed by hollow tines or spoons.
coverage. Refers to the way water is applied to an area. Coverage can be in relation to the throw of a head against the spacing of it or the overall job the head or system is doing in irrigating the turf.
creeping growth habit. Plant development by extravaginal stem growth at or near the soil surface with lateral spreading by rhizomes and/or stolons.
cultipacker seeder. Mechanical seeder designed to place turfgrass seeds in a prepared seedbed at a shallow soil depth followed by firming of the soil around the seed. It usually consists of a pull-type tractor rear-mounted unit having a seed box positioned between the larger, ridged, front roller and an offset, smaller, rear roller.
cultivation, turf. Working of the soil without destruction of the turf, e.g., coring, slicing, grooving, forking, shattering, spiking, or other means.
cup cutter. Hollow cylinder with a sharpened lower edge used to cut the hole for a cup in a green or to replace small spots of damaged turf.
cushion. See **resiliency**.
cutting height. Of a mower, the distance between the plane of travel (base of wheel, roller, or skid) and the parallel plane of cut.
density, shoot. See **shoot density**.
dethatch. Procedure of removing an excessive thatch accumulation either (a) mechanically as by vertical cutting or (b) biologically as by topdressing with soil.
detritus. Loose unconsolidated fragments of rock, minerals, and soil particles resulting from erosion.
distribution. The way sprinkler heads apply water to turf.
divot. Small piece of turf severed from the soil by a golf club or the twisting-turning action of a cleated shoe.
dormant seeding. Planting seed during late fall or early winter after temperatures become too low for seed germination to occur until the following spring.
dormant sodding. Transplanting sod during late fall or early winter after temperatures become too low for shoot growth and rapid rooting.
dormant turf. Turfs that have temporarily ceased shoot growth as a result of extended drought, heat, or cold stress.
dry spot. See **localized dry spot**.
effective cutting height. Height of the cutting plane above the soil surface at which the turf is mowed.
establishment, turf. Root and shoot growth following seed germination or vegetative planting needed to form a mature, stable turf.
eutrophication. A process that increases the amount of nutrients, especially nitrogen and phosphorus, in an aquatic ecosystem.
evaporation. Water evaporated as vapor from land, water, and vegetation surfaces.
evapotranspiration. Water vapor evaporated from surfaces plus that transpired by plants.
fertigation. Application of fertilizer through an irrigation system.
fertilizer burn. See **foliar burn**.
flail mower. Mower that cuts turf by impact of free-swinging blades rotating in a vertical cutting plane relative to the turf surface. See **impact mowing**.
flow. Movement of water expressed in gallons per minute (gpm).
foliar burn. Injury to shoot tissue caused by dehydration due to contact with high concentrations of chemicals, e.g., certain fertilizers and pesticides.
foot-head. Measurement of pressure based on the fact that a column of water 1 foot high has a 1 foot-head rating due to the weight of the water. One foot-head is equal to 0.433 pounds per square inch (psi).
footprinting, frost. Discolored areas of dead leaf tissue in the shape of foot impressions that develop after walking on live, frosted turfgrass leaves.
footprinting, wilt. Temporary foot impressions left in a turf when flaccid leaves of grass plants suffer incipient wilt and have insufficient turgor to spring back after treading has occurred.

forking. Method of turf cultivation in which a spading fork or similar solid tine device is used to make holes in the soil.
French drain. See **slit trench drain**.
frequency of clip. Distance of forward travel between successive cuts of mower blades.
friction loss. Amount of pressure loss due to friction in pipe, valves, or other components of a water system incurred with the movement of water in or through those components.
functional water use. Category of off-stream use of water, e.g., domestic, commercial, manufacturing, agriculture, steam electric generation, minerals industry.
genotype. Genetic makeup of an individual or group.
germplasm. Hereditary material that is transmitted to offspring.
grading. Establishing surface soil elevations and contours before planting.
grain, turf. Undesirable procumbently oriented growth of grass leaves, shoots, and stolons on greens: a rolling ball tends to be deflected from a true course in the direction of orientation.
gravity flow. Movement of water due to elevation differences. Water is often transferred from one place to another this way as no pumps are necessary.
grooving. Turf cultivation method in which vertical, rotating blades cut continuous slits through the turf and into the soil, with soil, thatch, and green plant material being displaced.
groundwater. Water located below the water table and contained in aquifers; usually does not extend below 2,000 to 3,000 feet.
head-to-head spacing. Locating of heads so that the throw of one head will reach the other head, giving 100% overlap.
hole punching. See **cultivation, turf**.
hot soil. Soil containing a high degree of chemicals that will cause rapid deterioration of metallic pipes and fittings.
hot water insoluble nitrogen (HWIN). Form of fertilizer nitrogen not soluble in hot water (100°C); used to determine the activity index of urea-forms. See **nitrogen activity index**.
hydraulic seeding. See **hydroseeding**.
hydroplanting. Planting vegetative propagules (e.g., stolons) in a water mixture that is pumped onto the plant bed. The water-propagule mixture may also contain fertilizer and a mulch.
hydroseeding. Planting seed in a water mixture that is pumped onto a seedbed. The water mixture may also contain fertilizer and a mulch.
impact mowing. Mowing in which the inertia of the grass blade resists the impact of a rapidly moving blade and is cut; this is characteristic of rotary and vertical mowers and in contrast to the shearing cut of reel and sickle bar mowers.
interseeding. Seeding between sod plugs, sod strips, rows of sprigs, or stolons.
irrigation, automatic. Water application system in which valves are automatically activated, either hydraulically or electrically, at times preset on a controller. System may or may not be integrated with an automatic sensing unit.
irrigation, manual. Water application using hand-set and hand-valved equipment.
irrigation, semiautomatic. Water application system in which valves respond directly to a manually operated remote-control switch.
irrigation, subsurface. Application of water below the soil surface by injection or by manipulation of the water table.
knitting. See **sod knitting**.
land rolling. See **roller, water ballast**.
lapping, mower (backlapping). Backward turning of the reel against the bed knife while a fluid-dispersed grinding compound is applied. Lapping hones the cutting faces and mates the reel and bed knife to a precise fit for quality mowing.
lateral shoot. Shoots originating from vegetative buds in the axils of leaves or from the nodes of stems, rhizomes, or stolons.
lawn. Closely mowed ground cover, usually grass.
lawn grass. See **turfgrass**.
layering, soil. Stratification within a soil profile, which may affect conductivity and retention of water, soil aeration, and rooting; can be due to construction design, topdressing with different-textured amendments, inadequate on-site mixing of soil amendments, or blowing and washing of sand or soil.

leaf mulcher. Machine that lifts leaves from a turf and shreds them small enough to fall down within the turfgrass canopy.
liquid fertilization. Method of fluid nutrient application in which dissolved fertilizer is applied as a solution.
localized dry spot. Dry spot of turf and soil surrounded by more moist conditions, which resists rewetting by normal irrigation or rainfall; is often associated with thatch, fungal activity, shallow soil over buried material, compacted soil, or elevated sites in terrain.
low-temperature discoloration. Loss of chlorophyll and associated green color that occurs in turfgrasses under low temperature stress.
maintenance, turf. See **turfgrass culture**.
mat. Thatch that has been intermixed with mineral matter that develops between the zone of green vegetation and the original soil surface; commonly associated with greens that have been topdressed.
matting. Dragging steel door matting over the turf surface to work in topdressing and smooth the surface; also used to break up and work in soil cores lifted out by coring or grooving.
mixture, seed. Combination of two or more species.
monostand. Turfgrass commonly composed of one cultivar.
mowing frequency. Number of mowings per unit of time, expressed as mowings per week; or the interval in days between one mowing and the next.
mowing height. See **cutting height**.
mowing pattern. The orientations of travel while mowing turf. Patterns may be regularly changed to distribute wear and compaction, to aid in grain control, and to create visually aesthetic striping effects.
mulch blower. Machine using forced air to distribute particles of mulch over newly seeded sites.
nitrogen activity index (AI). Applied to ureaformaldehyde compounds and mixtures containing such compounds; the AI is the percentage of cold water insoluble nitrogen that is soluble in hot water. AI = [(%WIN – %HWIN) × 100] ÷ %WIN
nursegrass. See **temporary grass**.
nursery, turfgrass. Area where turfgrasses are propagated for vegetative increase to provide a source of stolons, sprigs, or sod for vegetative planting.
off-site mixing. Mixing soil and amendments for soil modification at a place other than the planting site.
overseeding. Seeding into an existing turf. See also **winter overseeding**.
pegging sod. Use of pegs to hold sod in place on slopes and waterways until transplant rooting occurs.
planting bed. Soil area prepared for vegetative propagation or seed germination and establishment of turf.
playa. Shallow temporary lake overlying flat-floored basin. It fills during prolonged or excessive periods of rainfall and dries up during drought.
plugging. Vegetative propagation of turfgrasses by plugs or small pieces of sod to establish vegetatively propagated turfgrasses as well as to repair damaged areas.
poling. Using a long (bamboo) switch or pole to remove dew and exudations from turf by switching the pole in an arc while in contact with the turf surface; also used to break up clumps of clippings and earthworm casts.
polystand. Turfgrass community composed of two or more cultivars and/or species.
pop-up sprinkler. Sprinkler that raises the nozzle above the surface of the surrounding grass to avoid interference.
precipitation rate. Rate at which water is applied in a pattern of sprinkler heads; usually expressed in inches per hour.
pregerminated seed. Seed that is preconditioned before planting by placing in a moist, oxygenated environment at optimum temperatures to favor more rapid germination after seeding.
press rolling. Mechanical planting designed to push sprigs or stolons into the soil; followed by firming of the soil around the vegetative propagules.
pressure. Measure of the relative force of water expressed in pounds per square inch (psi) or foot-head.
pressure drop. Drop of pressure due to friction or restrictions when water is in motion or due to an elevation rise.
pseudo thatch. Upper surface layer above a thatch composed of relatively undecomposed leaf remnants and clippings.
puffiness. Spongelike condition of turf that results in an irregular surface.

rebuilding. Practices that result in complete change of a turf area.
recuperative potential. Ability of turfgrasses to recover from injury.
reel mower. Mower that cuts turf by means of a rotating reel of helical blades that pass across a stationary blade (bed knife) fixed to the mower frame; this action gives a shearing type of cut.
reestablishment, turf. Procedure involving (a) complete turf removal; (b) soil tillage; and (c) seeding or vegetative establishment of a new turf; does not encompass rebuilding.
release rate, fertilizer. Rate of nutrient release following fertilizer application. Water-soluble fertilizers are termed "fast-release," while insoluble or coated soluble fertilizers are termed "slow-release."
renovation, turf. Improvement usually involving weed control and replanting into existing live and/or dead vegetation; does not encompass reestablishment.
reseeding, turf. To seed again, usually soon after an initial seeding has failed to achieve satisfactory establishment.
residual response, fertilizer. Delayed or continued response to slow-release fertilizers, lasting longer than the usual response from water-soluble fertilizers.
resiliency. Capability of a turf to spring back when balls, shoes, or other objects strike the surface, thus providing a cushioning effect.
rhizosphere. Soil region in which increased microbiological activity results from the presence of plant roots; the root zone.
rippling. Wave or washboard pattern on surface of mowed grass, usually resulting from mower maladjustment, too fast a rate of mower travel, or too low a frequency of clip for the cutting height.
roller, water ballast. Hollow, cylindrical body, the weight of which can be varied by the amount of water added; used for leveling, smoothing, and firming soil.
root pruning, tree. Judicious cutting of tree roots to reduce their competition with an associated turf.
rotary mower. Powered mower that cuts turf by high-speed impact of a blade or blades rotating in a horizontal cutting plane.
rotary sprinkler. A sprinkler that covers a relatively large area with one or more nozzles that rise above the ground and rotate, throwing streams of spray over a circular area; driven by ball, cam, gear, or impact.
row sprigging. Planting of sprigs in rows or furrows.
salt glands. Found atop the leaf epidermis of some salt-tolerant plants and function to secrete salt from the plant.
scald, turf. Injury to shoots, which collapse and turn brown, when intense sunlight heats relatively shallow standing water to lethal temperatures.
scalping. Removal of an excessive quantity of green shoots at any one mowing, resulting in a stubbly, brown appearance caused by exposed stems, stolons, and dead leaves.
scarifying, turf. Breaking up and loosening the surface. See **vertical cutter**.
scorching. See **scald, turf**.
scum. Layer of algae on the soil surface of thin turf; drying can produce a somewhat impervious layer that impairs subsequent shoot emergence.
seed mat. Fabricated mat with seed (and possibly fertilizer) applied to one side; the mat serves as the vehicle to (a) apply seed (and fertilizer), (b) control erosion, and (c) provide a favorable microenvironment for seed germination and establishment.
semiarid turfgrass. Turfgrass species adapted to grow and persist in semiarid regions without irrigation, such as buffalograss, blue grama, and side-oats grama.
settling, soil. Lowering of the soil surface previously loosened by tillage or by excavation and refilling; occurs naturally in time and can be accelerated mechanically by tamping, rolling, cultipacking, or watering.
shattering. Turf cultivation method involving fragmentation of a rigid or brittle soil mass usually by a vibrating mechanical mole device.
shaving, turf. Cutting and removal of all verdure, thatch, and excess mat by means of a sod cutter, followed by turfgrass regrowth from underground lateral stems; used on bowling greens, especially bermudagrass.
shoot density. Number of shoots per unit area.
short-lived perennial. Turfgrasses normally expected to live only 2 to 4 years.

sickle-bar mower. Mower that cuts grass by means of horizontal, rapidly oscillating blades that shear the gathered grass against stationary blades.
slicing. Turf cultivation method in which vertically rotating, flat blades slice intermittently through the turf and the soil.
slip fitting. Fitting for plastic pipe into which the pipe fits and is glued with a solvent. There are various combinations of slip and threaded outlets on fittings for plastic pipe.
slit trench drain. Narrow trench (usually 5 to 10 cm wide) backfilled to the surface with a material such as sand, gravel, or crushed rock to facilitate surface or subsurface drainage.
slow-release fertilizer. Designates a rate of dissolution less than is obtained for completely water soluble fertilizers; may involve compounds that dissolve slowly, materials that must be decomposed by microbial activity, or soluble compounds coated with substances highly impervious to water.
sod. Plugs, squares, or strips of turfgrass with adhering soil to be used in vegetative planting.
sod cutter. A device to sever turf from the ground; the length and thickness of the sod being cut is adjustable.
sod cutting. See **sod harvesting**.
sodding. Planting turf by laying sod.
sod harvesting. Mechanical cutting of sod, for sale and/or transfer to a planting site, with a minimum of soil to facilitate ease of handling and rooting.
sod heating. Heat accumulation in tightly stacked sod; may reach lethal temperatures.
sod knitting. Sod rooting to the extent that newly transplanted sod is held firmly in place.
sod production. Culture of turf to a quality and maturity that allows harvesting and transplanting.
sod rooting. Growth of new roots into the underlying soil from nodes in the sod.
sod strength. Relative ability of sod to resist tearing during harvesting, handling, and transplanting; in research, the mechanical force (kg) required to tear apart a sod when subjected to a uniformly applied force.
sod transplanting. Transfer to and planting of sod on a new turf area.
soil heating. See **soil warming**.
soiling. See **topdressing**.
soil mix. Prepared mixture used as a growth medium for turfgrass.
soil modification. Alteration of soil characteristics by adding soil amendments; commonly used to improve physical conditions of turf soils.
soil probe. Soil sampling tool usually having a hollow cylinder with a cutting edge at the lower end.
soil screen. Screen used to remove clods, coarse fragments, and trash from the soil; may be stationary, oscillating, or, in the case of cylindrical screens, rotating.
soil shredder. Machine that crushes or pulverizes large soil aggregates and clods to facilitate uniform soil mixing and topdressing application.
soil warming. Artificial heating of turf from below the surface, usually by electrical means, to prevent soil freezing and maintain a green turf during winter.
solid sodding. See **sodding**.
spiking. Turf cultivation method in which solid tines or flat, pointed blades penetrate the turf and soil surface to a shallow depth.
spongy turf. See **puffiness**.
spoon, coring. Turf cultivation method involving curved, hollow, spoonlike tines that remove small soil cores and leave openings in the sod.
spot seeding. Seeding of small, usually barren or sparsely covered areas within established turf.
spot sodding. Repair of small areas of damaged turf using plugs or small pieces of sod.
sprig. Stolon, rhizome, tiller, or combination used to establish turf.
sprigging. Vegetative planting by placing sprigs in furrows or small holes.
spring greenup. Initial seasonal appearance of green shoots as spring temperature and moisture conditions become favorable, thus breaking winter dormancy.
sprinkler system. A system of pipes, valves, and sprinkler heads used to water ornamental plants and lawns.
spudding. Removal of individual weedy plants with a small spadelike tool that severs the root deep in the soil so that the weed can be lifted from the turf manually.

static pressure. Water pressure on a system when there is no water flowing through the system, thus incurring no friction losses

stolonize. Vegetative planting by broadcasting stolons over a prepared soil and covering by topdressing or press rolling.

stolon nursery. Area used for producing stolons for propagation.

strip sodding. Laying of sod strips spaced at intervals, usually across a slope. Turf establishment depends on spreading of the grass to form a complete cover; sometimes the area between the strips is interseeded.

subgrade. Soil elevation constructed at a sufficient depth below the final grade to allow for the desired thickness of topsoil, root-zone mix, or other material.

summer dormancy. Cessation of growth and subsequent death of leaves of perennial plants due to heat and/or moisture stress.

surface or stationary sprinkler. A fixed lawn sprinkler that does not pop up.

synthetic turf. See **artificial turf**.

syringing. Spraying turf with small amounts of water to (a) dissipate accumulated energy in the leaves by evaporating free surface water, (b) prevent or correct a leaf-water deficit, particularly wilt, and (c) remove dew, frost, and exudates from the turf surface.

temporary grass. Grass species not expected to persist in a turf and thus used as temporary cover.

texture. The composite leaf width, taper, and arrangement.

thatch. Loose, intermingled, organic layer of dead and living shoots, stems, and roots that develops between the zone of green vegetation and the soil surface.

thatch control. Preventing excessive thatch accumulation by cultural manipulation and/or reducing excess thatch by mechanical or biological means.

tip burn. Leaf-tip necrosis resulting from lethal internal water stress caused by desiccation, salt, or pesticide accumulation.

topdressing. A prepared soil mix added to the turf surface and worked in by brushing, matting, raking, and/or irrigating (a) to smooth a green surface, (b) to firm a turf by working soil in among stolons and thatch-forming materials, (c) to enhance thatch decomposition, and (d) to cover stolons or sprigs during vegetative planting; also the act of applying topdressing materials to turf.

topsoil planting. Modification of stolonizing that involves covering the area with soil containing viable rhizomes and/or stolons to establish a turf cover.

traffic. Movement of people or equipment across turf. Components are soil compaction, wear from friction, and shearing or tearing plant tissue.

transitional climatic zone. Suboptimal zone between the cool and warm climates where both warm- and cool-season grasses can be grown.

transpiration. The process whereby water is lost from leaves into the atmosphere as vapor, mainly through stomates in the leaf surface. A beneficial mechanism that results in cooling and pulls the water stream up the plant from the roots for nutrient transport.

trimming. Cutting edges and borders of turf to form clearly defined lines.

turf. Covering of mowed vegetation, usually a turfgrass, growing intimately with an upper soil stratum of intermingled roots and stems.

turfgrass. A species or cultivar of grass, usually of spreading habit, that is maintained as a mowed turf.

turfgrass color. Composite visual color of a turfgrass community perceived by the human eye.

turfgrass community. Aggregation of individual turfgrass plants that have mutual relationships with the environment as well as among the individual plants.

turfgrass culture. Composite cultural practices involved in growing turfgrasses for lawns, greens, sports facilities, and roadsides.

turfgrass management. Development of turf standards and goals that are achieved by planning and directing labor, capital, and equipment; the objective is to achieve those standards and goals by manipulating cultural practices.

turfgrass quality. Composite, subjective visual assessment of the degree to which a turf conforms to an agreed standard of uniformity, density, texture, growth habit, smoothness, and color.

turfgrass uniformity. Visual assessment of the degree to which a turfgrass community is free from variations in color, density, and texture across the surface.

ureaformaldehyde (UF). Synthetic slow-release nitrogen fertilizer known under the generic name ureaform, and consisting mainly of methylene urea polymers of different lengths and solubilities; formed by reacting urea and formaldehyde.
vadose. Water in the earth's crust above the water table.
valve. The part of an irrigation system that controls the flow of water.
valve in head. An automatic control valve that is part of a sprinkler.
vegetative propagation. Asexual propagation using pieces of vegetation, i.e., sprigs or sod pieces.
velocity. Speed of water in a pipe expressed in feet per second; not to be confused with pressure.
verdure. Layer of green living plant tissue remaining above the soil following mowing.
vertical cutter. Powered mechanical device having vertically rotating blades or tines that cut into the face of a turf below the cutting height to control thatch and/or grain. The tine type is also referred to as a power rake.
vertical mower. Powered mower that cuts turf by high-speed impact of blades moving in a vertical plane; the blades can be of varied shapes and fixed or free-swinging (flail).
warm-season turfgrass. Turfgrass species best adapted to growth during the warmer part of the year; usually dormant during cold weather or injured by it; commonly having temperature optimums of 27° to 35°C, e.g., bahiagrass, bermudagrass, St. Augustinegrass, seashore *paspalum* and zoysiagrass.
washboard effect. See **rippling**.
watering-in. Watering turf immediately after application of chemicals to dissolve and/or wash materials from the plant surface into the soil.
watering requirements. Requirements demanded by the turf, including infiltration rate and infiltration capacity.
water region. Water resources region as designated by the U.S. Water Resources Council. There are 21 regions, 18 in the conterminous United States and one each for Alaska, Hawaii, and the Caribbean.
water subregion. Subdivision of a region. There are 106 subregions used exclusively in the Second National Water Assessment.
water table. Top level of permanent groundwater zone.
wear. Collective direct injurious effects of traffic on a turf, as distinct from the indirect effects of traffic caused by soil compaction.
wet wilt. Wilting of turf in the presence of free soil water when evapotranspiration exceeds water uptake by roots.
whipping pole. Bamboo stalk or similar pole used in poling turf.
white discoloration. See **low-temperature discoloration**.
windburn, turf. Death and browning, most commonly occurring on the uppermost leaves of grasses, caused by atmospheric desiccation.
winter desiccation. Death of leaves or plants by drying during winter dormancy.
winter fertilization. A late-fall to winter application of fertilizer to turfgrasses at rates that maintain green color without adverse physiological effects; used in regions characterized by moderate winters for the species involved.
winter overseeding. Seeding cool-season turfgrasses over warm-season turfgrasses at or near the start of winter dormancy; used in mild climates to provide green, growing turf during winter when warm-season species are brown and dormant.
winter-protection cover. Barrier placed over a turf to prevent winter desiccation, to insulate against low-temperature stress, and to stimulate early spring greenup.
winterkill. Any injury to turfgrass plants that occurs during winter.
withdrawal. Water taken from a surface or groundwater source for offstream use.

Index

Tables, figures, and glossary entries are indicated with italic typeface, e.g., *70t, 38f, 153g*.